THE FIRST NATIONS
OF ONTARIO

Canadian Scholars' Series in Indigenous Studies supports student development and academic inquiry by highlighting leading scholarship on Indigenous peoples. With an aim to offer innovative pedagogical resources and emphasize Indigenous intellectual traditions, the volumes in this series provide diverse approaches to Indigenous knowledges, histories, and politics.

Titles in the Series

A Recognition of Being: Reconstructing Native Womanhood by Kim Anderson

Determinants of Indigenous Peoples' Health in Canada: Beyond the Social edited by Margo Greenwood, Sarah de Leeuw, Nicole Marie Lindsay, and Charlotte Reading

The First Nations of Ontario: Social and Historical Transitions by Edward J. Hedican

Iskwewak Kah' Ki Yaw Ni Wahkomakanak: Neither Indian Princesses nor Easy Squaws by Janice Acoose-Miswonigeesikokwe

Sivumut—Towards the Future Together: Inuit Women Educational Leaders in Nunavut and Nunavik edited by Fiona Walton and Darlene O'Leary

Strong Helpers' Teachings: The Value of Indigenous Knowledges in the Helping Professions by Cyndy Baskin

Walking in the Good Way / Ioterihwakwaríhshion Tsi Íhse: Aboriginal Social Work Education edited by Ingrid Thompson Cooper and Gail Stacey Moore

THE FIRST NATIONS OF ONTARIO

Social and Historical Transitions

Edward J. Hedican

CANADIAN
SCHOLARS

Toronto | Vancouver

The First Nations of Ontario: Social and Historical Transitions
Edward J. Hedican

First published in 2017 by
Canadian Scholars
425 Adelaide Street West, Suite 200
Toronto, Ontario
M5V 3C1

www.canadianscholars.ca

Library and Archives Canada Cataloguing in Publication

Hedican, Edward J., author
   The First Nations of Ontario : social and historical transitions / Edward J. Hedican.

Includes bibliographical references.
Issued in print and electronic formats.
ISBN 978-1-77338-012-4 (softcover).--ISBN 978-1-77338-013-1 (PDF).--ISBN 978-1-77338-014-8 (EPUB)

      1. Native peoples--Ontario--History. 2. Native peoples--Ontario--Social conditions.
3. Native peoples--Ontario--Economic conditions. 4. Native peoples--Ontario--Claims. I. Title.

E78.O5 H38 2017   971.3004'97   C2017-904476-1
                                             C2017-904477-X

Text design by Elisabeth Springate
Cover design by Gordon Robertson
Cover image: *Together*, painting by Shaun Hedican

Printed and bound in Canada by Webcom

MIX
Paper from
responsible sources
FSC® C004071

For my grandchildren Shauna, Taya, and Aaron

CONTENTS

FOREWORD

This book is a first. No published work before this has involved a comprehensive study of all of the First Nations of Ontario. It takes a long-term look at their cultures as they have developed throughout all 10,000 years of human history in the province, prior to and after first contact between those nations and the incomers. It is especially important that this book has come out, as Ontario has the highest Indigenous population of any province or territory, a little-known fact.

But this work should not be thought of as merely entailing the study of one province, as the definitions used and principles presented make it a useful textbook for an introductory course in Indigenous Studies, especially for, but not exclusive to, students in Ontario.

The author, Edward (Ed) J. Hedican, is an anthropologist who does not rely solely on information gathered by others for what is presented in this book. He has a long history of contact with some of the peoples he is writing about. He began engaging in fieldwork in the mid-1970s, when he lived with an Anishenaabe community in northern Ontario, some 300 kilometres north of Thunder Bay. It was all log cabins and paths on the reserve then, the people (and the anthropologist living among them) not having any cars, trucks, or electricity. They followed, for the most part, a traditional subsistence pattern of hunting, fishing, and gathering. Hedican's learning from this experience shows in this work. And his contact with the people has continued to this day. It wasn't just get a degree, publish a paper, and run. This continued contact shows through in the nature of the information presented.

Hedican has been writing and publishing books on this subject for over 30 years, including an up-to-date and important work (2013) on the Ipperwash Crisis that took place in southwestern Ontario during the mid-1990s, a series of events and legal cases that achieved a measure of closure only in 2016.

A key positive feature of this book is the continuing use of the voice of Indigenous people. You come to expect it, as you should, as the book proceeds. A significant case-in-point early in the book is that the section on the archaeology of early Ontario includes the views of Anishenaabe Kris Nahrgang, one of fewer than ten archaeologists of First Nations ancestry in Canada, the long-time elected chief of the Kawartha Nishnawbe First Nation, and a noted carver. Indigenous perspectives on archaeology are important for any book of this kind, as they have traditionally not been included. Throughout the book, we see Indigenous individuals as players in and interpreters of their history and issues, not just as part of the nameless, faceless collective that tended to populate earlier textbooks.

One point to note in this regard is the rarely mentioned but important Paypom Document (named after an elder) in which the people themselves recorded in writing 18 points concerning the negotiating of Treaty No. 3 (signed in 1873), which covers a massive amount of territory in northwestern Ontario. These points include the kinds of promises that did not find their way into the recorded language of the treaty (e.g., Métis rights and mining rights).

In Chapter Five, Hedican introduces and explains the complex weave of 46 treaties and land claims that exist in Ontario, a more complicated situation than found in most provinces and rarely collected together in one discussion. He well demonstrates the important point that all Indigenous issues have deep roots. An example in this chapter is his treatment of the issues involved with the Haldimand Tract, centred in the Brantford area, awarded to the Six Nations in 1784 as compensation for their losses fighting on the British side during the American Revolution. He carefully lays the foundation for understanding the 2006–14 conflict in Caledonia, part of the original tract, that flared up between members of the Six Nations and a developer, local citizens, and, inevitably, the provincial police. A similarly useful backgrounder is made of the Huron Tract Treaty of 1827, and the various ways in which awarded land was taken from the local Anishenaabe, leading up to the Ipperwash Conflict of 1995.

With these and other issues, Hedican directs the material in the chapter towards addressing the question of "What does it mean that treaties in Ontario should be regarded as 'living documents?'"

In Chapter Six, contemporary issues of major concern are addressed. One relates to the 2014 struggle between the Harper government and the Idle No More movement, which was largely focused on the federal government's Bill C-45. It was an omnibus bill, which is a collection of initiatives often fundamentally unrelated to each other. Such a bill is a political tactic wherein opposition is divided into different groups supporting and rejecting different sets of initiatives. In the case of Idle No More, the aspect of the bill opposed was that which involved deregulating waterways, which the people rightfully saw as challenging treaty rights concerning those waterways.

Another legal struggle addressed by Hedican in this chapter concerns Bill C-31, which relates to the Indian Act's rules concerning who is and is not considered a "status Indian." Prior to 1985, when the bill was passed, status Indian women would lose their status for marrying a man who was non-status, which, among other discriminatory features, kept these women from having the right to live on the reserve of their band. While Bill C-31 has enabled some people and their descendants to regain their status, it left a number of questions unanswered.

Hedican engages the story of Ontario Algonquin Anishenaabe Lynn Gehl, whose case was in the courts at the end of 2016. Her family lost their status under very questionable circumstances (to a large extent because Gehl does not know who her paternal grandfather was), and she has for decades been directing her energies into challenging that loss, as well as the means through which her family's status was lost.

Part of this book's uniqueness in treating issues rarely brought up in a comprehensive approach is demonstrated by the way in which the issues raised by the "Ring of Fire" communities are addressed. The term refers to the First Nations communities that are surrounded by rich mineral deposits, notably diamonds mined by De Beers in the territory of the Attawapiskat Cree. The issues concern impacts relating to the long-term problems of the lack of drinkable water, livable housing, and long-term employment. The argument put forward by the peoples involved is that the way they and the mineral resources have been treated is to their detriment, not to their advantage.

What truly makes this book an unparalleled work of reference necessary to student papers, teacher lecture notes, library consultation, government assessments, and First Nations legal challenges are the appendices. The first appendix comprises the First Nations of Ontario, alphabetically listed and briefly discussed. To the best of my knowledge, no comparable document exists.

This is followed by an indispensable annotated listing of Internet resources, something for which there is great need, as any teacher or student will tell you.

In conclusion, what this book provides is an excellent introduction to the complex history of the Indigenous peoples of Ontario, something that has been missing from the literature for too long. It highlights like no other work the key issues that have arisen in the province, and supplies resources useful to people who both want to learn and continue their learning.

John Steckley
December 2016

PREFACE

The purpose of this book is to discuss in a concise manner the social, economic, and cultural characteristics of the First Nations peoples of Ontario. As such, this volume aims to provide an accessible introductory text that represents as accurately as possible the complex and diverse socio-economic issues, histories, and **cultures** of the First Nations of Ontario, situated within the larger context of Indigenous issues in Canada. It also aims to provide, where possible, Indigenous perspectives on such topics as the **archaeology** of the Province of Ontario, neo-colonial trends, and contemporary relationships pertaining to the complexities of restorative justice. This book, then, is an attempt to draw together the various sources in **anthropology**, Aboriginal Studies, and ethno-history, among other disciplines, in a readable format that is accessible to the general public, students, government officials, and Aboriginal peoples themselves.

Human societies can be studied individually or in groups using various comparative methods of research. The field of **ethnography**, for example, is devoted to the descriptive recording of cultures based on such research techniques as **participant observation**, carried out through **fieldwork**. In addition, comparative studies can be conducted based on certain shared characteristics. In this regard, **ethnology** is a research technique devoted to the analysis, systematic interpretation, and comparison of cultural material with the intention of producing meaningful generalizations about human behaviour.

I have conducted first-hand research in the Aboriginal communities of Ontario since the mid-1970s. This research has involved living in a log cabin for almost two years in an **Anishenaabe** (Ojibwa) community situated in the boreal forest some 200 kilometres north of Thunder Bay (Hedican 1986, 2001). At this time, the First Nations people of this community did not have cars, trucks, or electricity; for the most part spoke their ancestral language; and continued to hunt and fish in the traditional subsistence pursuits that had been conducted for many millennia.

The purpose of this research was to study the local political leadership and the economic changes that were taking place during the construction of a tourist lodge in the Whitewater Lake area near the Ogoki River. I returned to this community for an extended period of time, comprising about 15 years, after the initial research to conduct comparative studies of community change as new educational, social, and economic initiatives took place.

My research in the general area of Aboriginal Studies continued for the ensuing decades, as I studied, for example, the relationship between applied anthropology and government policies towards First Nations people, economic development, and Aboriginal status and identity (Hedican 2008a). This kind of research provides a unique opportunity to make a significant impact on the manner in which Aboriginal issues are perceived, studied, and interpreted in Canada. In all, my research among First Nations people grew out of a passion to make Aboriginal issues more intelligible to students in the university classroom and to those in the wider Canadian society who find such issues difficult to understand. For over three decades, I have taught various courses at the university level on contemporary Aboriginal issues and the historical dimensions of Indigenous life in Canada. The purpose of these courses is to provide a much-needed increase in the knowledge concerning the life of Aboriginal people in Canada that students will take into their future endeavours. This impact can be enhanced immeasurably when researchers begin to take a more central role in supporting Aboriginal peoples in their struggles in the areas of land claims, community development, and advocacy roles, as well as other challenges. Of course, actually living with First Nations people in their own communities for an extended period of time is also an immense aid in understanding their local conditions.

I continued with these sorts of studies over the following decades, most recently completing a comprehensive history of the nature of government Aboriginal policy in Canada, focusing specifically on the **Ipperwash Inquiry** of 2007 and the tragic death of Dudley George during a protest in September 1995 (Hedican 2008b, 2013). During a protest at Ipperwash Provincial Park, members of the Stony and Kettle Point Bands were fired upon by officers of the Ontario Provincial Police. Dudley George was shot by OPP officer Kenneth Deane and died shortly after midnight the next day.

Probably few people have bothered to read the transcripts of the Ipperwash Inquiry conducted by the Honourable Sidney B. Linden (2007), yet this inquiry points to the institutional racism that First Nations people have been subjected to in Ontario and in Canada generally. There is therefore a definite need to continue discussions and research into Aboriginal land claims in this country and the manner in which the Indigenous population is dealt with under existing provincial and federal government policies and practices.

There have been many such protests in the province of Ontario, going back to at least the occupation of Kenora's Anishenabe Park by the Ojibwa Warrior Society in the mid-1970s. Media attention has focused on the Teme-Augama (Temagami) First Nation logging blockage and the controversial Supreme Court decision of

1991. More recently, the Caledonia and Grand River land dispute continues to garner news coverage, as well as the Grassy Narrows mercury poisoning and forest management protest in northern Ontario, along with the Akwesasne border confrontation of 2009 (Hedican 2012a).

In other words, these seemingly intractable Aboriginal issues need to be discussed in a public forum of debate and serious investigation, in a climate of tolerance and respect. It is in this sense that this volume is presented, with the hope that the history, cultural traditions, and contemporary social issues of Ontario's First Nations peoples will continue to be a matter of value, concern, and debate among Canadians.

The Scope of the Book

The purpose of the present book is two-fold. The first of these purposes is to provide a readable account of the social and economic history of the First Nations of Ontario for a general audience, from the earliest prehistoric records to modern-day current events. In this attempt, material is drawn together from available sources of information derived from the fields of anthropology, ethno-history, linguistics, and archaeology, as well as associated material from other related disciplines.

Attempting to translate what are at times complicated issues and debates from the scholarly literature is somewhat of a formidable task, but I have made every effort to decipher what is known in the academic literature in a relatively jargon-free manner. When terms in anthropology or archaeology are used, these are explained in what one could call "every-day language" to the extent possible. A glossary of terms is included in the book in an attempt to facilitate an understanding of academic concepts.

Chapter One discusses various general issues concerning First Nations of Canada, as well as providing information on concepts used throughout the book. Chapter Two focuses on the prehistory of Ontario from the early Paleolithic period after the melting of the Wisconsin Ice Age, during which large game animals such as **mastodons** and mammoths were hunted. Then the so-called Archaic period is discussed, during which Aboriginal peoples expanded their population base, adapted to new resources such as fishing, and created innovative new technologies such as the use of copper for tool-making.

Chapter Three discusses the Algonquian hunters of the boreal forest of northern Ontario by describing their lifestyle and history of involvement in the fur trade. Chapter Four includes a discussion of the Haudenosaunee farmers of southern

Ontario, their trading partners to the north, and the eventual movement of Joseph Brant and the Six Nations into the Grand River area after the American Revolution.

Ontario treaties and land claims are the subject of Chapter Five. A detailed history of the many treaties involved and their various characteristics, locations, and attributes is provided. Chapter Six focuses on current events such as the Idle No More movement, as well as resource development issues pertaining especially to the Ring of Fire mineral discoveries in northern Ontario. The Afterword discusses the challenges that the First Nations of Ontario currently face and those that are expected in the near future.

The second purpose of this volume is to provide a readily available resource of information on the First Nations of Ontario. In Appendix A, for example, information is provided on every First Nation in Ontario, both those recognized by the federal department of **Indigenous and Northern Affairs Canada (INAC)**, as well as those seeking official status. Each of the First Nation profiles includes up-to-date information on population size, including the number of people resident on their reserve; location; number of reserves; affiliated organizations; and current issues. Each First Nation website is also researched, when these are available, for a summary of current events, such as land claims, cultural activities, and other concerns.

Appendix B includes an extensive listing of various Internet and web-related sources about First Nations, grouped under relevant headings for easy reference. These include, for example, information and links to Aboriginal organizations, government departments and agencies, academic associations, and research and reference sources. Throughout the book, notable First Nations personalities are profiled in separate textboxes, including individuals such as Tom Longboat, Jay Silverheels, Norval Morrisseau, and Daphne Odjig. After reviewing these profiles, there can be no doubt of the significant cultural, social, and athletic contributions that First Nations people have made to the enhancement of Ontario.

And finally, a note on terminology. The literature on First Nations can be quite puzzling because of the the different names and designations that have been used in the past and are currently in use. In order to standardize certain terminology for the First Nations people of Ontario, the following designations will be used in the subsequent text:

1. *Anishenaabe* (pl. Anishenaabeg) for Anishenabe, Ojibwa, Chippewa, etc.;
2. *Haudenosaunee* for the Iroquois Six Nations (however, note that each of these Nations has its own name; see Table 1.1 and Figure 1.1 in the following chapter for the names of specific languages);
3. *Wendat* for Huron, but not for other related Nations such as Petun.

Also note that the names of specific historical designations have not been altered, such as the "Ojibwa Warrior Society" of Kenora, Ontario. The same principle has been applied for the specific usages that the individual First Nations apply to themselves, as, for example, those that are found in the websites listed in Appendix A.

1 INTRODUCING FIRST NATIONS AND THEIR CHARACTERISTICS

Ontario has the largest Aboriginal population in Canada, making up just over 20 percent of the country's overall total of approximately 1.4 million (Hedican 2013: 261–62; Statistics Canada 2008). This Aboriginal population is composed of primarily First Nations peoples (60% of the overall total), who number about 700,000. The First Nations population is further divided by those defined as having "Indian" status under the Indian Act (81%) and those First Nations people who do not have official status (19%).

Other Aboriginal people identified in the Canadian census records are the Métis (33%), Inuit (4%), and those who have indicated multiple identities (3%). For the purposes of our discussion in this book, the focus is on First Nations people with official status, commonly referred to as "registered Indians." However, the reader is encouraged to consult as subsidiary reading the various publications on Ontario's Métis, Inuit, and non-status First Nations population for a more complete picture of the province's Aboriginal population.

Terms for Aboriginal Peoples

There is a diversity of names or terms for Aboriginal peoples in Canada depending upon the particular legal, social, linguistic, or cultural context in which these are used. In the Canadian Constitution Act of 1982 (Section 35), for example, it is stated that "In this act, 'aboriginal peoples of Canada' include the Indian, Inuit, and Metis peoples of Canada." In this regard, the term **Aboriginal** has a broad connotation that is similar to the *Oxford English Dictionary* definition, in which *Aboriginal* means "indigenous, existing in a land at the dawn of history, or before the arrival of colonists."

In the final report of the Royal Commission on Aboriginal Peoples (RCAP) of 1996, the term **Aboriginal nation** is used to refer to a "sizeable body of Aboriginal people with a shared sense of national identity that constitutes the prominent population in a certain territory or collection of territories." The term **Indian** may be regarded by some people as largely obsolete these days, or even as having a pejorative connotation, yet it does have an important legal context within Canada's Indian Act. "Indian," as specified in the Indian Act, Section 2(1), "means a person who pursuant to this Act is registered as an Indian or is entitled to be registered as an Indian."

Powwow dancers Elizabeth Eshkibok-Trudeau and her son Waaweyeseh ("Whirlwind"), Wikwemikong First Nation, Manitoulin Island.

Source: Photo used by permission of Elizabeth Eshkibok-Trudeau.

Therefore, according to the Indian Act (1985), there are Aboriginal persons who have a special legal status in Canada, which also implies certain rights and obligations (on the government's part) that those without this status do not possess. There are therefore certain Aboriginal people in Canada who are entitled to special status because they are regarded as **registered Indians**, upon whom special rights are conferred. At the national political level, the **Assembly of First Nations** represents the status Indian population in Canada as a broad umbrella group with provincial affiliates comprising approximately 630 communities (see www.afn.ca).

The term **non-status Indians** is a reference to those Aboriginal people who are not recognized under the Indian Act because they have either lost their status or have been unable to prove that they are entitled to Indian status. Under new legislation of 1985, Aboriginal people who had previously lost their status could apply to have their status reinstated. The primary reason for a loss of status was an Indian woman marrying a non-status man, which stripped her of her status, as well as prevented their dependent children from claiming status. Notice in this regard that Indian status has very little to do with one's cultural heritage or biological make-up—European women could just as easily acquire Indian status as their Aboriginal counterparts.

Bill C-31: Redefining Legal Status

Under the provisions of **Bill C-31** of 1985, the Indian Act was amended so that neither Indian women nor men would lose their legal status as a result of marriage to non-status persons. Bill C-31 also allowed for the reinstatement of Indian status under application for those who had lost their status. Over the five-year period from 1985–90, more than 750,000 applications for reinstatement were received by the Department of Indian Affairs (now Indigenous and Northern Affairs Canada; [INAC]), affecting about 135,000 individuals (see www.aadnc-aandc.gc.ca).

By 2001, just over 105,000 persons had been added to the status Indian population through the Bill C-31 registration process since its inception in 1985, which increased the total status Indian population by nearly 17 percent. The success rate, therefore, for applicants seeking a reinstatement of their status was a mere 14 percent. Since INAC controlled the application process and selected (in secret) those applicants who would gain status and rejected those deemed unsuccessful, the review process was highly controversial, especially in light of the fact that the federal government had a vested interest in keeping the status Indian population at low levels because of administrative and other cost factors (Hedican 2008a: 227–29).

Some terms fall into disuse with time or become superseded by other terms as fashions and legal designations change. A term such as **Native** was widely used in decades past as a cover term for all Aboriginal people but is not as popular today, although *Native American* is still a widely used term in the United States. Names for various Aboriginal and government ministries tend also to reflect this changing usage.

Aboriginal Organizations

The Native Council of Canada was the name for an organization representing non-status and Métis people, established in 1971; however it changed its name to the **Congress of Aboriginal Peoples** in 1994 (see www.abo-peoples.org). Other organizations that represent Aboriginal people in Ontario include the **Métis Nation Council**, founded in 1983 (metisnation.ca), and the **National Association of Friendship Centres**, dedicated to the improvement of the quality of life of Aboriginal peoples in urban environments (nafc.ca).

During the 1970s, the provincial government in Ontario established the Indian Community Branch within the Ministry of Community and Social Services. This ministry was primarily established to provide services to Aboriginal people who lived outside the administrative structure of the federal Department of Indian Affairs. In later years, this name was changed to the Native Community Branch, then the Ontario Secretariat for Aboriginal Affairs.

By June 2007, the name had been changed again to the Ministry of Aboriginal Affairs, which represents the approximately 300,000 First Nations, Métis, and Inuit Ontarians (see www.ontario.ca/ministry-aboriginal-affairs). The Ipperwash Inquiry (Linden 2007) had suggested that a provincial "Ministry of Aboriginal Affairs" be created, although it was less clear how such a proposed ministry would be coordinated with other government agencies at the provincial and federal levels. It appears Ontario merely changed the name of its existing ministry, rather than creating an entirely new department.

The Meaning of Reserves

Reserve is another term that is frequently encountered in the literature. In the context of the Indian Act, reserves are geographical areas specifically set aside for the habitation of status Indians and are administered by the federal government through the Department of Aboriginal Affairs and its minister. In other words, a *reserve* refers to land set aside by the Crown for the use and benefit of a band. Reserves were usually allocated at the time various treaties were signed, but some were added later, and a band may occupy several reserves. However, today, many Aboriginal people use the term **First Nation community**, which is becoming a preferred term, while the term *reserve* is falling out of favour.

During the 1970s, the term **First Nation** began to come into more popular usage as *Indian* and *band* began to be replaced. It should be noted, however, that the term *First Nation* should not be regarded as synonymous with *Aboriginal people* because the latter includes both Métis and Inuit, as in Section 35 of the Constitution Act (1982), while the former does not imply such broad coverage. It should also be noted that the term **band**, under Section 2(1) of the Indian Act, simply means a body of Indians (i.e., First Nations people with status) for whom the government has set aside lands for their common benefit.

In Canada, there are approximately 2,700 reserves associated with 617 bands recognized by INAC as of 2016. These numbers fluctuate somewhat, as bands may combine or divide depending upon particular circumstances, economic needs, and changes in government policy. At present, only about half of Canada's First Nation population lives on reserves, and there has been a steady decline in the on-reserve population because of the lack of employment in many reserve communities and the attraction of the perceived benefits in the larger urban centres.

Most of the reserves in Canada are relatively small, numbering about 500 people, and are often situated in rural or remote areas, a factor that negatively impacts on economic development programs, employment opportunities, transportation costs, and labour mobility. The largest reserve in Canada is the Blood reserve in Alberta, at 900 square kilometres with a population of about 10,000 people. The Six Nations band, near Brantford, Ontario, as a whole has the largest population, with about 22,000 members; however, about half of the band's members live off the reserve. The next largest is the Akwesane Mohawk First Nation community, comprising about 12,000 people.

Other Terms

There are various other terms that should be noted. **Treaty Indians**, for example, are descendants of Aboriginal peoples who had previously signed treaties with the British Crown or, later, with the Canadian government. Generally speaking, most of Canada's treaties were signed during the 1800s, at which time band members were enumerated and reserves selected and set aside. In other cases, such as that of the Haudenosaunee who never signed a treaty with the Canadian government, reserves were nonetheless set aside and are included under the Indian Act.

The Inuit of the Canadian North are also an Aboriginal people specified under the Constitution Act (1982), yet they occupy an ambiguous position in the administration of Aboriginal affairs because they never signed treaties with the British or Canadian governments. Although the Inuit are clearly not "Indians" in the legal sense, they were nonetheless included as such in a Supreme Court decision of 1939 so that they would receive the same benefits as other First Nations people under the Indian Act. In 1999, a vast tract of land comprising 300,000 square kilometres, now called Nunavut or "Our Land," was set aside for the approximately 25,000 people of Inuit ancestry in the Baffin Island area.

As far as the specific names or terminology for various Aboriginal peoples are concerned, there is often interesting linguistic and cultural background underlying such terms. The name *Assiniboine* refers to a Siouan-speaking people living in southeast Saskatchewan, North Dakota, and Montana. Their name, however, is not of Siouan derivation at all, but is actually an Algonquian term meaning "people who cook with stones." The etymology is derived from the Anishenaabe (or Ojibwa) words *ahsin*, meaning "stone," and *eboine*, "to eat or cook." Other terms are of obvious European derivation, such as the *Montagnais* ("mountain people") who live on the north shore of the St. Lawrence River.

Another example is the *Saulteaux* (or *Soto*) who inhabit southern Manitoba and a few other areas of western Canada. Apparently, when fur traders travelled farther west, they noted a linguistic similarity with the Aboriginal people they were familiar with in the Sault Ste. Marie area of northwestern Ontario, and so called them "people of the Sault" even though they were not linguistically different from the other Anishenaabe of Ontario.

Similarly, the people known as *Bungi* in the Western provinces have their named derived from the Anishenaabe word for begging, or literally "give me a little." Many other such examples could be cited, lending further apparent confusion to a plethora of names, terms, and other linguistic designations.

Wider Cultural and Linguistic Considerations

The preceding discussion amply illustrates that using such a term as *Indian*, as used in the Indian Act, or even one such as *Canadian Aboriginal people* implies a degree of social, linguistic, and cultural uniformity that is hardly warranted. One of the unfortunate consequences of the use of one term to designate all Aboriginal people in Canada has been a tendency to develop what could be called "cookie-cutter" government policies towards the Indigenous population. If they all have the same name, one could mistakenly presume that all of them might be treated the same, despite an apparent diversity of cultural traditions, languages, and social communities.

When the first explorers and missionaries arrived in what is now known as Canada, there were many different languages spoken by the Aboriginal populations in this land. Nearly 60 different Aboriginal languages spoken by the First Nations people of Canada are recorded in the 2006 Census (Statistics Canada 2008). These various languages appear to linguists quite diverse, as different as English might be from Chinese, suggesting multiple origins and migration patterns. In addition, across Canada, there are at least six different language families.

First Nations–language use is currently decreasing in some areas, but holding steady in others. The 2006 Census (Statistics Canada 2008) indicates that the Aboriginal language spoken by the greatest number of First Nations peoples in Canada is Cree, spoken predominantly in northern Quebec, Ontario, and western Canadian areas, with about 87,200 speakers fluent enough to carry on a conversation in this language.

This is followed by 30,200 people who speak Ojibwa (Anishenaabe), spoken mainly in Ontario and a few Western provinces; 12,400 who speak Ojib-Cree, which is a combination of the two languages common in northern Ontario; and 11,080 who speak Montagnais-Naskapi, spoken in southeast Quebec and the Labrador Peninsula. In Nunavut, nine out of ten Inuit continue to speak their Inuktitut language. First Nations people living on reserves have higher fluency rates in an Aboriginal language (at 51%) than those who live away from reserves (12%).

Spread over the eastern part of North America live the **Algonquian** (or **Algonkian**) speakers, who eventually spread into the Plains area when horses became available through trade in the 1700s. In northern Ontario, Manitoba, and Quebec live the Anishenaabe (Ojibwa) and Cree. The Mi'kamq and Malecite live in the eastern Maritime provinces, while the Blackfoot, Piegan, and Blood inhabit southern Alberta (Darnell 2000; Pentland and Wolfart 1982). In the Northwest Territories and northern British Columbia live speakers of the **Dene** (or Athapaskan) language family. Prominent members of this language family include the Chipewyan, Tutchone, Kutchin, and Dogrib. The Eskimo-Aleut language family is represented in northern Canada by the Inuit, composed of such peoples as the Caribou Inuit, Netsilik (called "people of the seal"), and the Iglulik who all speak the same Inuktitut language. British Columbia has a complex mix of First Nations and language families.

The Six Nations are members of the Iroquoian language family, comprising the Mohawk, Oneida, Cayuga, Onondaga, Seneca, and Tuscarora (McCarthy 2008; Lounsbury 1978). The Iroquois, who call themselves the Haudenosaunee or "People of the Longhouse," migrated into southern Ontario in 1784 when they received a large parcel of land, called the Haldimand Tract, as compensation for supporting the British during the American Revolution. The Wendat (also called Huron), Petun (sometimes referred to as the "Tobacco Indians"), Neutral, and Erie which together make up the Huron Confederacy originally lived in an area south of Lake Huron, down to the north shores of Lakes Erie and Ontario. After their defeat by the Haudenosaunee, members of these various First Nations moved to reserves near Quebec City and other locations in the northern United States (Trigger 1987; Tooker 1963, 1964).

At a later date, the Mississauga, an Algonquian-speaking people who were originally from the Sault Ste. Marie area of northern Ontario and allies of the Haudenosaunee, moved onto the Brantford reserve in an area called New Credit. It is important to note, though, that the conventional names commonly used to refer to the Haudenosaunee, such as Mohawk and Seneca, are not necessarily the names that the First Nations people use for themselves. Table 1.1 presents a list of the First Nations of Ontario in terms of the Aboriginal names that First Nations peoples use for themselves, as well as the conventional ones often used as terms of reference. Figure 1.1 illustrates a typology of Ontario First Nations languages in terms of similarity groupings.

Table 1.1: Languages of the First Nations in Ontario

Algonquian (Algonkian)	Algonquin (Algonkin)
Language Family	Anishenaabe (Ojibwa, Chippewa, Saulteaux, Mississauga)
	Delaware (Lenapi, Munsee)
	Odawa (Ottawa)
	Nehiyawak (Cree)
Iroquoian	Huron-Wendat
Language Family	Haudenosaunee (Iroquois)
	Gayogho:no (Cayuga)
	Kanien'kehaka (Mohawk)
	Khionontateronon (Petun)
	Onodagagehono (Onondaga)
	Onodowaga (Seneca)
	Onyata'a:ka (Oneida)
	Ska-ru-ren (Tuscarora)

Source: Canadian Museum of Civilization, "Gateway to Aboriginal Heritage, Culture Areas Index," www.civilization.ca.

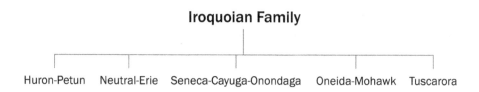

Iroquoian Family

Huron-Petun   Neutral-Erie   Seneca-Cayuga-Onondaga   Oneida-Mohawk   Tuscarora

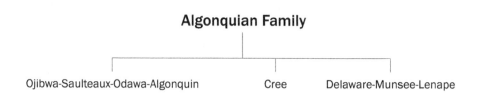

Algonquian Family

Ojibwa-Saulteaux-Odawa-Algonquin   Cree   Delaware-Munsee-Lenape

Figure 1.1: Typology of Ontario First Nations Languages

Sources: Rhodes and Todd 1981; Goddard 1978; Lounsbury 1978.

As with language, traditional social and cultural patterns also vary considerably among Canadian First Nations. Hunting and gathering societies were prominent in the northern subarctic regions of Ontario. Such societies were usually composed of family units numbering in total about 25 to 30 persons, bonded by kinship and marriage, for example. When treaties were signed, these family hunting units were often combined with other similar entities in the geographical vicinity to form government-administered bands.

The bands of today do not necessarily have the sorts of social cohesion that the designation might imply, although later marriage ties among the various families tended to produce a degree of integration not known in the historical past. Leadership among band members today is usually based on elections as stipulated in the Indian Act; however, in the past, leadership tended to be based on a less formal basis, with support given to leaders who demonstrated hunting skills and generosity.

Kinship and Descent

There are many ways by which people in different societies choose who they are related to, and who they are not. For example, some societies trace their descent through only their father's relatives (**patrilineal descent**), while others may trace relatives through only their mother's side (**matrilineal descent**). The ancestors of the First Nations of Ontario primarily traced their relatives through both their father's and mother's sides of their family.

As such, kinship among Algonquian hunters and gatherers, such as the Anishenaabe and Cree who inhabit most of the northern areas of Ontario, was usually based on a principle of **bilateral descent**, meaning that descent was traced through both sides of one's family. Upon marriage, the married couple often moved near the husband's relatives, referred to as **patrilocal residence**. Some theorists believe that a bilateral kinship network has the advantage of providing many more relatives for social and economic support in times of need than a principle by which descent is traced only on one side of a family (Hedican 1990a).

In the southern areas of Ontario, the Wendat and members of the Haudenosaunee Confederacy made a living by growing crops, such as corn, beans, and squash. Hunting and fishing was conducted to supplement their diet on a seasonal basis, but these activities were not a primary basis for their diet as the people in these areas relied on the growing of crops. The settlements of the Haudenosaunee and Wendat were considerably larger than their Algonquian neighbours to the north, comprising at times 1,000 or more persons, and were occupied on a relatively permanent basis.

Kinship among the Iroquois-speaking peoples is based on the principle of matrilineal descent, meaning relatives are determined by links to mothers, grandmothers, and so on. Upon marriage, men moved into the village of their wives, a pattern called **matrilocal residence**. Such family groups that result from following a matrilineal principle are called matrilineages. These lineages are subsequently also combined into larger units, called clans. Members of the same **clan** occupied the same longhouse, headed by an elderly matron, and were not allowed to marry among themselves (Wallace 1978).

Kinship in Other Areas of Canada

In contrast to the First Nations of Ontario, on the northwest coast of Canada the Indigenous people lived primarily by fishing and hunting large sea mammals. Their houses were constructed of large cedar timbers and housed families related by bonds of kinship. Village size varied from several houses to over 30, with the population ranging up to perhaps 700 in total. Like the Haudenosaunee, Pacific Coast First Nations also followed a **unilineal** (tracing descent through one line only) kinship principle, with matrilineages in the north coastal regions and patrilineages predominant among peoples in the southern coast (Hedican 2012b: 188–92).

Social and political relationships were much more highly structured than among other First Nations of Canada. The political systems on the northwest coast were based on a hierarchical class system, called a **chiefdom**, in which certain kinship groups wielded more power than others in a pyramid fashion. In a ritualized system of exchange, called the **potlatch**, material utilitarian goods, food, and valued objects were given away as a means of validating a person's claims to high status positions within the society (Boas 1897).

Contemporary Characteristics

In terms of overall population numbers, the Aboriginal population of Canada (which includes First Nations, Métis, and Inuit people) passed the 1 million mark (1,1172,790) during the census period of 2006. This population represents a substantial increase of 45 percent over the 1996–2006 period, which is nearly six times faster than the 8 percent growth rate for the non-Aboriginal population of Canada over this same decade. Canada also has a relatively high proportion of Aboriginal people, at 4 percent of the total Canadian population, which has increased from 2.8 percent in 1996. This ranks Canada second, behind only New Zealand, where the Maori account for 15 percent of the population. Indigenous people make up just 2 percent of the total population of both Australia and the United States.

Population Characteristics

The Aboriginal population as a whole is composed of predominantly First Nations people (60%) with those classed as having "status" under the Indian Act at 81 percent and "non-status" at 19 percent. The Métis population is next largest at 33 percent of the total Aboriginal population, while the Inuit make up 4 percent. Three percent of Aboriginal persons identified on the Census indicated affiliation with more than one Aboriginal group.

The predominant demographic trend is towards a greater urbanized Aboriginal population in Canada, as 54 percent now live in urban areas, compared to 50 percent in the 1996 Census. The largest urban Aboriginal population in Canada lives in Winnipeg, Manitoba (68,380 persons), while other cities such as Edmonton, Toronto, and Vancouver also have substantial Aboriginal populations. Eighty percent of Canada's Aboriginal population lives in either Ontario (21%) or the four Western provinces.

A striking feature of the 2006 Census is that the Aboriginal population is far younger, with a median age of 27 years, than the Canadian population as a whole, whose median age is 40 years. In fact, 48 percent of the Aboriginal population in Canada is 24 years of age or younger, compared with 31 percent for the non-Aboriginal population. Among Aboriginal people, 51 percent of families include children less than 15 years of age, compared with just 38 percent for Canadian families as a whole. This statistic alone will no doubt mean that in the future, there will continue to be a strong demand for child and youth services, such as schooling and daycare, among Aboriginal people, while in the wider Canadian population a declining youth share will orient services away from schools, possibly leading to closures and mergers.

Economic Characteristics

As far as the economic statistics are concerned, the unemployment rate among Aboriginal people (12.3 percent of the workforce) is nearly double that of the wider Canadian population (6.6 percent in 2006). The unemployment rate among Inuit is particularly severe, as 18.2 percent of workers are unemployed, a figure which is nearly three times the national average. Income levels for Aboriginal workers are also considerably lower than for other Canadian workers. Aboriginal workers earn about $27,838 annually, an average of approximately $8,500 less than the wider Canadian worker population ($36,301). These figures combine both part-time and full-time incomes.

Lower levels of income among Aboriginal workers can probably be accounted for by several factors, such as the lesser availability of employment in Aboriginal communities and lower rates of pay for those jobs that are available. Other important factors stem from the fact that many Aboriginal communities are situated in rural and remote areas, leading to higher transportation costs for goods imported into the community and lower economic competitiveness for locally produced goods that need to be shipped outside to southern markets.

Educational and training level could be another factor in workforce expertise, as 14 percent more Aboriginal persons are without a diploma or university degree, compared with the national Canadian average. If income levels in a population can be positively correlated with the skill level of the workforce, as conventional wisdom would appear to indicate, then lower incomes among Aboriginal workers could be at least partly accounted for by their lower levels of educational achievement.

Demographic Patterns

Taken as a whole, by way of summary, the 2006 Census (Statistics Canada 2008) indicates that the Aboriginal population of Canada is steadily shifting away from their home communities in rural areas towards larger urban centres. This trend is probably a reflection of the lower levels of employment, social services, and educational opportunities at home compared to those available in the larger cities. However, the statistics also suggest that Aboriginal migrants to cities probably arrive with less training and fewer educational skills than their urban counterparts possess.

This rural-to-urban migration could, in the short term at least, exacerbate an already dire economic situation for Aboriginal people who now suffer from an unemployment rate that is twice that of the overall Canadian work-force. In turn, with regard to Canada's policies towards Aboriginal people, it is increasingly evident, on the basis of the latest available statistics, that current government practices and programs have done little to ameliorate the disheartening socio-economic conditions among Canada's Indigenous population.

In the next chapter, we turn to a discussion of Ontario's ancient past in an attempt to understand how the ancestors of today's First Nations people in Ontario successfully adapted to the many ecological changes that occurred over the many centuries following the last ice age in the province.

Suggested Readings

Belanger, Y.D. 2010. *Ways of Knowing: An Introduction to Native Studies in Canada.* Toronto: Nelson Education.

Dickason, O.P., and W. Newbigging. 2010. *A Concise History of Canada's First Nations.* 2nd ed. Don Mills, ON: Oxford University Press.

Hedican, E.J. 2008. *Applied Anthropology in Canada: Understanding Aboriginal Issues.* 2nd ed. Toronto: University of Toronto Press.

Hedican, E.J. 2013. *Ipperwash: The Tragic Failure of Canada's Aboriginal Policy.* Toronto: University of Toronto Press.

Muckle, R.J. 2012. *Indigenous Peoples of North America: A Concise Anthropological Overview.* Toronto: University of Toronto Press.

Steckley, J.I., and B.D. Cummins. 2008. *Full Circle: Canada's First Nations.* 2nd ed. Toronto: Pearson Prentice Hall.

Review Questions

1. Compare and contrast several terms for First Nations people in Canada.
2. How do First Nations people differ in terms of their kinship systems?
3. How would you describe the demographic conditions of First Nations people in Canada?

2 FIRST NATIONS IN ONTARIO'S ANCIENT PAST

Conducting research into the past of peoples without written records is a precarious matter. Assessments must at times be made on the basis of a body of scant evidence. The evidence is usually not much more than the unintentional physical remains left behind from past human activities, which have survived as discarded or lost remnants of people's lives. These items often include broken clay potsherds and objects manufactured from stone, shells, or metal.

Objects consisting of household goods, tools, and personal adornments have survived because they were made from durable materials, but many other aspects of previous lives have not survived because of their perishable, organic nature. All that may remain of people's ancient dwellings would include not much more than the stains left in the soil from posts that supported a building, remnants of hearths and fire pits, or the bone refuse from the animals that were eaten by the members of a prehistoric community.

An Aboriginal Perspective on Ontario Archaeology

Kris Nahrgang (2013) is an elected chief in his community and has been on council for 23 years. He is also an archaeologist, one of fewer than ten archaeologists of First Nation ancestry in all of Canada. From his perspective, Nahrgang regrets that most of the Indigenous history in this country has been gathered by others. The result is that knowledge about the pasts of First Nations has not been written by Indigenous people themselves.

When the people of Ontario's First Nations do not have a say in what is written or understood about them, they, in turn, do not have much control over their history or the manner in which it is interpreted. As Nahrgang indicates, "there are larger societal implications of what [archaeologists] do." As such, archaeologists need to realize "that for First Nations [archaeologists'] work is not only colonial but also an intrusion and a catalyst for conflict. Once archaeologists understand this then maybe we can start to work together" (2013: 203).

Box 2.1: Norval Morrisseau

NORVAL MORRISSEAU (1932–2007): SAND POINT FIRST NATION

- Founded the Woodland School of Canadian art
- Art depicted the legends of the Anishenaabe people and their spiritual life
- Numerous exhibitions at major Canadian art galleries
- Member of the Order of Canada (1978)

Still image of Norval Morrisseau, from the film *The Paradox of Norval Morrisseau.*

Source: *The Paradox of Norval Morrisseau* ©1974 National Film Board of Canada. All rights reserved. Used by permission.

In an attempt to protect First Nations history and heritage in Ontario, an organization called the Founding First Nations Circle was formed. This group is composed of the Wendat, Six Nations, and members of various Algonquian Nations. Members of the Circle agreed to certain rules, such as refraining from engaging in conflicts over artifacts, history, bones, or ancestral resting places. Their purpose is to deal strictly with archaeological issues and to form a representative organization that could provide a basis for consultation with First Nations of the province.

From an Aboriginal perspective, the people of First Nations ancestry wish to be consulted over legislation and the archeological process that is carried out. They would also like to be involved in creating a working relationship with each other and with archaeologists so that Aboriginal heritage and history in Ontario is no longer destroyed in the name of development or research. As Nahrgang says, "it is simply a matter of respect for those who lived on the lands before others arrived. It is long overdue" (2013: 211).

Origin Stories

Creation stories of Algonquian-speaking peoples, such as the Anishenaabe and the Cree, begin when the world was covered with water. Stories generally include a hero, such as Nanabozho, who seeks the assistance of his animal relatives in recreating the Earth.

The Anishenaabe origin story begins with Nanabozho camped on the bank of a river, when the waters began to rise slowly and steadily, forcing him to retreat. Before the water covered what remained of the mountain that he stood on, Nanabozho caught two logs to form a crude raft. As far as he could see in every direction, there were animals of every species, many out of their element, their eyes wide and rolling in terror. He called to the birds and animals swimming nearby: "Would you fetch some soil, so I can try to restore the Earth?" It was not the strong or the gifted, as might be expected, who retrieved the soil. Rather, it was the least of their kin, the muskrat, who dove and brought back the small bit of soil. Nanabozho breathed into a small pawfull of soil, and a miracle took place … he created his island and his world.[1]

The Thunderbird
The Ojibway (Anishenaabe) believed thunder to be a great, massive bird called a thunderbird, whose eyes shoot out lightning and thunder. The first

thunder in early spring was something good to hear, for the Ojibway welcomed their protector again from its home in the south, where it had been all the winter. Offerings of tobacco were placed on the ground, on water, or put into the stove to burn, or sacred pipes were smoked by the elders as tribute to the thunderbird in the early spring.

It is known among the Ojibway that the thunderbirds had a huge nest on the mountains of the Earth and large blankets of clouds were always seen to cover the nest. Although the thunderbird was never seen to come and go from its nest, it was known to be there. Lightning and thunder were heard only at these places. At Lake Nipigon in olden times, there was a mountain across the old Sand Point Indian Reserve where the thunderbirds had a nest made of stones that was always seen by the Ojibway. No one ever went to find out what was really up there, but the people did not need to find out, for the Ojibway knew it was the thunderbird and considered that place sacred. About 30 years before the coming of the white man into the area of Lake Nipigon, the blanket of clouds seen at the mountain began to lift and moved away forever, and the Ojibway saw a huge nest. Later that summer, the thunderbirds destroyed every trace of the place and pretty nearly levelled half the mountain in order to leave no evidence (Morriseau 1965: 4).

Principles of Archaeology

Meticulous attempts are made during an investigation to determine the relationships of objects as a means of uncovering past lifestyles. The principle of **stratigraphy**, which is a study of layers of soil within a site, is used to determine the "living floor" when a particular location was inhabited. Objects found at the same level, or stratigraphic horizon, are assumed to be associated with one another during the same time period. The age of other objects may also be determined using the method of **radiocarbon dating** if the material is composed of an organic substance, such as bone or charcoal, that was alive during the last 50,000 years.

A study of the early inhabitants of northern Ontario poses particular challenges because of the mobility of the hunter-gatherer populations who have left only the sparsest evidence of their existence. Limited soil depth is also a problem, because many centuries or even millennia of habitation may occur in deposits compacted into only a few centimetres of earth.

This problem of limited soil depth means that separating out different levels of occupation becomes a difficult task. Furthermore, soils in northern Ontario are often quite acidic because of the decomposition of spruce and pine needles, which could lead to the rapid destruction of artifacts made from organic materials. An inhospitable or inaccessible terrain in the north is another problem as prehistoric investigations in the area could be inhibited by swamps, large lakes and rivers, forest fires, or other such difficulties.

In southern Ontario, the soil depth tends to be greater and conditions more favourable for the preservation of organic material. In addition, the First Nations populations of this region tended to live in sedentary settlements, so refuse of various kinds had a tendency to build up over relatively long periods of time. On the other hand, with a much larger population than in the north of the province, movements from one area to another and less homogeneous **settlement patterns** pose a level of societal complexity that is perhaps not found in the north, or at least not to the same degree because of differences in subsistence patterns and overall population size.

Ice Age Dynamics

The Wisconsin glaciation period lasted for 60,000 years, ending about 11,000 years ago (Sutton 2011: 9-12; Scuderi 2002). The **Laurentide** ice sheet, the major one of this glaciation period, emanated from the Hudson Bay area and pushed out in all directions. The movement of the ice formation acted as a giant bulldozer, plowing earth from the surface of the Precambrian Shield and depositing it in long heaps or ridges of soil and debris called **moraines**.

At the height of the Wisconsin glaciation about 16,000 years ago, the ice sheet was about a kilometre thick in places and covered most of northern North America. The region south of the ice sheet was generally cooler and wetter than today, with extensive grasslands similar to the tundra area of contemporary northern Canada. This large accumulation of ice also had a dramatic effect on the water levels of the oceans, lowering them by at least 100 metres. Thus, when the last glaciation period was at its maximum extent, there were large areas of the world's land mass that were much more exposed than in modern times, especially along the wide, relatively shallow continental shelf. This 100-metre drop in sea level would have also created a very wide connection between Asia and the northwest corner of North America, allowing an interchange of plants, animals, and people between the two continents.

The Upper Great Lakes Region

At the height of the Wisconsin glaciation period, a continental glacier covered virtually all of the Great Lakes region. The enormous weight of the ice sheet depressed the land, and the area was essentially devoid of life. As the climate became warmer, the glaciers retreated and life returned to the area.

Plant life was the first to populate the Upper Great Lakes, and then the animal life returned, followed by human beings. Lying north of Lakes Superior and Huron was a vast glacial lake called **Lake Ojibwa-Barlow**, which was virtually trapped between the height of land in northern Ontario and the retreating ice sheet. North of Lake Superior, the ice sheet lasted until at least 6,500 years ago, preventing plants and animals from populating the area.

As the ice retreated northward, black and white spruce trees were among the early pioneers to populate the vacated area. Balsam and various species of pine trees also took root. These were followed by such deciduous species as birch and aspens, with maple also finding a suitable environment in the well-drained moraines. Various animals such as mammoths and mastodons also moved northward, along with caribou, deer, and a species of giant beaver that lived in the area after the mastodons left. There is also evidence that whales lived in the Lake Huron basin, as there was a direct channel through the St. Lawrence to the Atlantic Ocean.

The Chippewa-Stanley Stage

During the **Chippewa-Stanley stage**, the ice front had regressed to about present-day Cochrane, Ontario, with glacial Lake Ojibwa-Barlow still not drained out of northern Ontario. Water levels of modern Lake Huron were as much as 135 metres lower than present day, so that a separate name, Lake Stanley, was given to the water occupying the Huron basin. Similarly, water in the Michigan basin was over 100 metres below the level of modern

Lake Michigan, designated as Lake Chippewa-Stanley for this period. Lake Chippewa, in the Michigan basin, drained to Lake Stanley, in the Huron basin, through a long river that passed through where the Straits of Mackinac exist today.

Lake Stanley then drained through the North Bay outlet into the Ottawa River. Lake Superior also had water levels as much as 100 metres lower than present and may have partly drained into Lake Ojibwa-Barlow to the north, and partly into the present location of St. Mary's River at Sault Ste. Marie. Eventually, about 5,000 years ago, further melting of ice in northern Ontario allowed Lake Ojibwa-Barlow to drain northward into the Hudson Bay basin, which left an extensive aquatic environment.

The Lake Nipissing Stage

The period of the Chippewa-Stanley low water levels of the Great Lakes was subsequently followed by the **Lake Nipissing stage** (5,000–4,500 years ago), during which a further change in the Great Lakes drainage pattern occurred. The land around the North Bay outlet into the Ottawa River had been compressed by the tremendous weight of the continental ice sheet for a very long period of time. With the melting of the ice, the land began to rebound, as much as 135 metres, estimated to recover about a metre every 30 years.

This up-warping of land caused the North Bay outlet to rise extensively, greatly reducing the outflow of Great Lake water. In turn, water levels rose dramatically in the Great Lakes, such that the rising water levels caused a merging of Lakes Huron, Superior, and Michigan into one great lake for the first time.

Rising water levels also caused water to now flow not out of the North Bay outlet as in previous periods but out of the southern portion of Lake Huron, into Lake St. Clair, and over present-day Niagara Falls. From here, water travelled to the Atlantic Ocean through Lakes Erie and Ontario, along the St. Lawrence River. Deciduous forests began to dominate the region south of the Great Lakes, with spruce and pine again populating the areas to the north of Lakes Huron and Superior. The climate also became much drier and hotter than at any time in the previous 20,000 years (Sutton 2011; Wright 1972, 1981, 1995; Quimby 1960).

Stone Quarries and Workshops

In the Thunder Bay District of northern Ontario, the Brohm archaeological site has yielded evidence of human occupation from about 9,000 to 8,000 years ago (Quimby 1960: 36–37). Many of the **projectile points** were made of **taconite**, which was available locally and shows the distinctive **ripple or parallel flaking**. Other tools made at this site include scrapers, various blades made from chipped stone, and chopping tools, as well as spear points. This site suggests that hunters lived along the ancient shoreline of Lake Superior during the early part of the Chippewa-Stanley stage of the Upper Great Lakes. Today, this beach area is about 75 metres above the present shoreline (Hamilton 2013; Dawson 1983; Wright 1963; MacNeish 1952).

The Brohm site, however, does not appear to represent the start of continuous occupation in this area of northern Ontario, but a location of temporary use, probably because of the availability of taconite for tool-making. It would appear that when the ice melted, hunters began to scour the receding glacial till, seeking favourable material for tool-making. Much farther to the southeast of the Thunder Bay District, on the northern part of Lake Huron, other ancient sites have been discovered, in which the most prominent material was **quartzite** for tool manufacturing. These sites are littered with numerous waste flakes, cores from which stone tools have been made, and other unfinished blades, scrapers, and spear points that were probably broken and then discarded during the manufacturing process (Dawson 1983: 4–7).

The Cummins site is in the Kaministikwia River valley, about 90 kilometres to the northeast of the Brohm site, and shows evidence of an extensive taconite workshop and habitation site in the Thunder Bay District (Steinbring 1976; MacNeish 1952). In both locations, it is apparent that the people were living on the original beach of Lake Superior. Radiocarbon dates derived from accumulated humus that covered the artifacts left behind suggest that humans occupied this area of Lake Superior as early as 9,530 **Before Present (BP)** (Zoltai 1965: 268).

Near the town of Sheguiandah, Ontario, on the eastern end of Manitoulin Island, is an archaeological site that shows evidence of quarrying activity, a habitation area, and a possible workshop for manufacturing tools. A radiocarbon date of 9,175 BP was derived from material retrieved from the site, suggesting that a reasonable date for the earliest occupation of the Sheguiandah site was sometime between about 9,500 and 8,000 BP. There is also evidence that this site was occupied for a long period of time, at least up to the Lake Nipissing stage of the Upper Great Lakes (5,000 to 3,500 BP). However, occupation of this site is abruptly terminated at the end of this period, suggesting that the rising water levels of the Lake Nipissing stage caused it to be vacated (Lee 1954, 1956, 1957).

Another quarry and prehistoric workshop was discovered just 20 kilometres east of Sheguiandah, near the village of Killarney at the George Lake site. White quartzite was the preferred material for making tools such as various blades, leather perforators, scrapers, and projectile points. These objects were discovered on an ancient fossil beach about 100 metres above the present level of Lake Huron; some even show evidence of being subjected to wave action as they appeared water-worn.

Clovis point, 11,000 Before Present (BP)

Source: Galt Museum and Archives.

The Old Copper Culture

Members of the **Old Copper Culture** were the first fabricators of metal in either North or South America, and possibly even in the entire world (Hamilton 2013: 88–89; Levine 2007; Pleger 2000; Hedican and McGlade 1982, 1993). Their culture survived for a very long period of time, from about 7,000 BP to about 3,000 BP. It was situated in a climatic period of increasingly warmer temperatures, culminating in the **altithermal period** (7,000 to 4,500 BP). This period was considerably drier and hotter than today and probably had the mildest year-round temperatures in the last 11,000 years. Temperatures then cooled down somewhat to that which we experience today (Jenning 1989: 150).

The people of the Old Copper Culture lived in the Upper Great Lakes region, primarily around Lake Superior and the western shore of Lake Michigan where native copper was found in relative abundance. They were fabricators of copper tools and personal ornaments, but the Old Copper people were engaged in extensive mining as well. Along the Ontario shore of Lake Superior there are many mines, as well as numerous prehistoric mining pits on Isle Royale and the Keweenaw Peninsula in the Upper Peninsula of Michigan (Hamilton 2013; Pleger 2000; Jury 1965, 1973; Griffin 1961; Popham and Emerson 1954).

In all probability, native copper was first found on the shores of the Great Lakes as nodules left behind in the till of the receding glaciers. It would have been discovered that this rock could not be chipped or fractured into a useable tool, as is the case with flint or quartzite. Instead, taking a beach boulder, one could pound on the copper nodule until it flattened out and thereby shape the copper into a spear point, axe, knife, or other useful object. In other words, the mindset in the case of utilizing copper was entirely different from that which had previously been conceptualized by the Aboriginal hunters.

Making Copper Tools

Another important metallurgical discovery made by the members of the Old Copper Culture was the process of **annealing**. Initially the nodule of copper was shaped into the desired shape by cold hammering, but copper in this state is too brittle and soft for most useful purposes. Annealing involves the repeated heating and cooling of a copper tool, which has the effect of compressing the copper molecules and thereby strengthening the tool. Edges could then be sharpened by grinding. As such, annealing is the first important step in metallurgical science.

After the surface nodules began to disappear, mining of copper took place. Old mining pits around Lake Superior have been discovered at numerous locations, showing evidence of wooden levers for prying copper from rock, hammer stones for pounding on rock veins, and charcoal from fires used to heat the rock surface that contained copper ore. Several of the old mining pits were dug to a depth of at least ten metres.

The method of extracting the copper ore from a rock surface was first to build a fire as close as possible to the copper vein. Second, the heated copper vein was doused with cold water, which served to fracture the surrounding rock. Thirdly, the ore was loosened by pounding with boulders, then pried loose with wooden levers from the surrounding rock matrix. Smelting and casting of copper was not practised at this time. There was often no need for these processes as native copper is often found in an almost pure state and does not require removal of impurities. The copper could then be transported back to the hunters' camps, where it could be subsequently fashioned into various weapons and tools.

Mining Copper Ore in Ancient Times

The scale of the mining operations at several places was truly impressive. At the Minong mine on Isle Royale, more than 10,000 ancient mine pits have been discovered within a single square kilometre (Pleger 2000: 169–90; Holmes 1901). As one early observer noted, "excavations are connected underground, drains being cut in the rock to carry off the water. A drain of sixty feet long presented some interesting features—having been covered for its entire length by timbers felled and laid across" (Gillman 1873: 173). Certainly, Isle Royale must have been richly endowed with native copper.

We should not also overlook the fact that Isle Royale is a considerable distance out into Lake Superior. Travel to and from the Lake Superior shore to Isle Royale is at least a ten-kilometre journey at the shortest distance to the mainland. It is hard to imagine such a trip being accomplished with conventional birch bark canoes, especially ones laden with a load of copper ore and the miners themselves, over waters that are often perilous and unpredictable even for modern watercraft.

Trade and Settlement Patterns

Trade in copper tools from the Great Lakes area went on for many thousands of years. Copper artifacts from the Lake Superior region have high silver content compared to copper from other regions. Such a high silver content, about 25 percent in some cases, is a distinctive characteristic that allowed scientists to conclude that copper tools found in the Gulf of Mexico area originated in the Upper Great Lakes region. In turn, sea shells that no doubt originated in the southern United States have been found in the Great Lakes region.

Such trade in copper tools probably involved hand-to-hand transactions over an extensive geographical area. From the Great Lakes, copper tools could have found their way down the Mississippi River system to the Gulf coast, with other valuable items returning northward along the same route. Even more extensive trading networks involved other areas as well. The Rocky Mountains were the source of obsidian, a prized material of black volcanic glass that was often made into ceremonial knives, as well as grizzly bear teeth. Sheets of mica came from the middle Atlantic coastal region, and lead (or galena) was brought into the Upper Great Lakes region from Missouri and northwestern Illinois (Quimby 1960: 75–77).

There is evidence that various locations in Ontario and the surrounding Great Lakes area involved periodic barter journeys to a number of central places such that a trade in copper goods was connected with a network of exchange linking together various copper-producing areas. For example, a cache of copper artifacts was discovered on an ancient trail leading to the waters of Georgian Bay and in two river valleys (the Thames and Ausable) that flow westward to Lake St. Clair and Lake Huron. These caches include projectile points of both the socketed and tanged variety (Jury 1965, 1973).

It is this uneven spacing and concentration of copper sources around the Great Lakes basin that is no doubt an important factor leading to inter-tribal trade. As Wright (1967) explains, "The Western Great Lakes region is particularly interesting in that it contains both ecological diversity in the form of several biotic communities, and a concentration of resources like Lake Superior copper and chert in small areas" (185). It has also been noted that "the scattered occurrences of Old Copper implements in some of the cultures of the Great Lakes area is, in many instances, the result of trade, but a few cultures, particularly those having a number of traits in common with the complex may have been historically related. The finds of Old

Copper implements in Ontario are evidence for an extension of the complex in that area" (Wittry and Ritzenthaler 1957: 324–25; see also Hamilton 2013: 88–89).

Copper was traded by way of the Ottawa and St. Lawrence Rivers (Rickard 1934). At Morrison's Island on the Ottawa River, considerable working of copper took place in a habitation site apparently far removed from the actual mine sites, which was then traded with other centres along the river system (Kennedy 1967). Altogether, over 270 copper artifacts were discovered at the Morrison's Island site; one can only speculate about the possible extent of networks of exchange that must have existed in prehistoric times when such a quantity of copper tools are involved. Possibly, copper-producing areas were linked by exchange networks ranging over great distances. For example, 70 kilometres north of Peterborough, at Lake Farquhar, nearly 100 copper artifacts were discovered in 1952. At Reflection Lake, near Lake Nipigon in northwestern Ontario, a cache of 47 copper tools was uncovered during an excavation of foundations for tourist cabins, while about the same time, more than 1,000 copper tools were found on Alumette Island on the Ottawa River (Hedican and McGlade 1982: 20).

Laurel Culture

The term *Laurel Culture* does not refer to the intrusion of a separate population movement into northern Ontario, but to the appearance of a distinctive style of pottery at about 2,500 BP. This period represents an occupation of northern Ontario with direct linear descendants of the people who occupied this area in earlier periods. Ultimately, members of the Laurel Culture are the predecessors of the First Nation Ojibwa and Cree who occupy northern Ontario today (Reid and Rajnovich 1991; Dawson 1983: 15–19; Wright 1972: 56–63, 1981: 89–91).

The source of this style of pottery is uncertain, but probably the idea was borrowed from peoples living in the more southern areas of Ontario. The pottery is the product of skilled crafting, suggesting an intimate knowledge of ceramic technology. The adoption of pottery in the northern areas of the province suggests that there were cultural contacts between the Indigenous peoples around the Great Lakes and in southern Ontario at this time. Laurel Culture pottery also bears resemblances with the ceramics produced along the Border Lakes region, west of Lake Superior, and across eastern Manitoba, northern Minnesota, and Michigan, hinting at wider social contacts that transversed these regions.

Besides pottery, burial mounds are another feature that distinguishes the Laurel Culture. Such mounds are particularly prominent in the Rainy River area near the Manitoba border. In fact, these mounds are the largest prehistoric structures in all of Ontario, containing as many as a hundred burials. Most of the mounds are over 20 metres in diameter and 2 metres in height, although one mound was over 40 metres across and attained a height of 8 metres. Burials inside the mounds consist of bundles of bones, suggesting that the bodies were allowed to decompose on scaffolds for a period before interment in the mounds.

Eventually, the Laurel style of pottery gives way to a new ceramic innovation referred to as Blackduck pottery. This style was produced extensively across northern regions, such as in northern Minnesota, west to the Red River in Manitoba, and east to the Michipicoten River on the north shore of Lake Superior in Ontario. Thus, it is assumed that Blackduck evolved out of an earlier Laurel Culture base. Radiocarbon dates for Blackduck sites in Manitoba, Ontario, and Minnesota range from about 620 to 1560. In fact, a number of Blackduck sites in Ontario have also included European trade goods. While there is not complete agreement by scholars, convincing arguments are made based on historical and linguistic evidence that the Blackduck culture provided the socio-cultural background from which the contemporary Ojibwa First Nation eventually emerged in Ontario (Wright 1965).

Pictographs

Pictographs are rock paintings (as opposed to *petroglyphs*, which are rock carvings) of animals, people, and various symbols that appear to be associated with the Laurel and later Blackduck cultural periods that have been produced in the Ontario Shield country (Dewdney and Kidd 1962). Many of the pictographs depict what could be termed a "naturalistic" representation, such as a moose or men in a canoe, while others are of supernatural or mythological origin, such as thunderbirds or the *Maymaygwaysiwuk*. According to Norval Morrisseau, the Maymaygwaysiwuk "had with them a stone boat, with stone paddles. ... At one time they were chased in order to know who they were. The Maymaygwaysiwuk would head for the shore line of cliffs, and the stone boat would go right into the opening as if through a door, which would be shut when the Ojibways got to the place." The Ojibways were then advised to "put on the rock a sacred sign" (1965: 26). There are also many abstract or unidentified symbols of twisted lines, circles, and zig-zag lines connecting figures. The dates that the various paintings were produced for the most part can only be guessed, although there are rare instances in which historical incidents are depicted, such as at the Agawa Bay site on the northeast shore of Lake Superior, which probably illustrates Chingwauk's historical voyage with five canoes across Lake Superior.

There is also no certainty about how the paintings were made. The paint, probably made from a combination of crushed red ochre, sea gull eggs, and grease as a binder, seems to have merged into the granite rock. Such paint appears extremely durable; in fact, someone attempted to deface a painting using household paint at the Agawa Bay site by writing "1937" across a painting of a night panther, but the defacer's paint has weathered into oblivion while the red ochre still shows clearly through underneath. This durability of the pictographs is one of their remarkable qualities, as noted by researchers Dewdney and Kidd (1962: 11): "again and again I have found [a pictograph] so bonded to the rock that it defied my efforts to remove it. Compared with commercial pigments used in this century, the Indian paint stands up far better."

While there are hundreds of pictographs located in Ontario, there are also many more in northern Minnesota, Quebec, Manitoba, and Saskatchewan. This would suggest that the paintings may have been the product of the members of several cultures, such as the Ojibwa and Cree, or travelling artists from one culture who were specialists in cultural lore and mythology.

The Location of Rock Paintings

Many of the pictographs were painted on granite rock faces with overhanging ledges, often along canoe routes or well-known waterways. However, there is no typical location for a rock painting since some are located in out-of-the-way places or on the shore of small lakes. Some were painted on rocks that today are higher than a person can reach, suggesting that water levels might have been high during past times, or maybe the paintings were done in the winter when ice at the water's edge could have provided a platform that supported the artist. In some places, the pictographs are at water level where the action of ice and waves have kept the rock surface clean, but it is remarkable that such erosive agents seem to have had little effect on the paintings themselves.

The Depiction of Spiritual Beliefs

There is also an apparent relationship between the Great Lakes pictographs on the **Canadian Shield** and birch-bark inscriptions produced by the Ojibwa living south and west of Lake Superior (Dewdney 1975). The birch-bark inscriptions fall into two broad categories. In one group are small sheets on which are inscribed characters that serve as reminders for incantations that were used to increase a person's prowess in war, hunting, or love. A second kind of scroll is much larger, up to two metres in length, which could be considered as a combined textbook and prayerbook, such as the directions for the initiation ritual of the **Midewiwin** (Grand Medicine Society).

Ruth Landes' study of the Midewiwin also makes reference to an association with Ojibwa religion and pictographs. As she notes, "the specific bearing of any pictograph in a mystic song or other notation was the secret of the **shaman** who wrote it. He must teach this explicitly to another before the notation was usable. More esoteric and expressive of the writer's secret intentions or knowledge was a sequence or combination of pictographs" (1968: 172–73).

Dewdney also learned from contemporary Ojibwa people that "specially gifted Ojibwa shamans, I was told, had the power to enter the rock and exchange tobacco for an extremely potent 'rock medicine'" (Dewdney and Kidd 1962: 14). This would account for the practice of leaving gifts of tobacco in the water as First Nations people pass certain rocks, as they say, "for good luck."

Famed Ojibwa artist Norval Morrisseau draws a connection between painting and spiritual beliefs. For example, he notes that "Ojibway Indians of Lake Nipigon had what is known as the Midaywewin Society. … According to Ojibwa custom, bear skulls are sacred [and are] carefully decorated and painted. Before paint, red matter or earth colors replaced the paint we use today. According to a medicine dream, the sacred bear is white in color, has red feet with yellow spots and two horns" (1965: 40).

Presumably the pictographs were painted on the granite cliffs for a reason, which could be that the artists wished to send a message, either to the other members of their society or to the spirit world that surrounded them. In any case, the pictographs represent an important dimension of a complex cultural world of the Algonquian peoples as they relate to the environmental and social settings in which they lived.

Early Southern Ontario

As the climate of southern Ontario became increasingly warm with time, the tundra environment gave way to the growth of coniferous pine and spruce forest, followed eventually by deciduous hardwoods. Thus, game animals hunted changed from the barren-ground caribou of the tundra to the deer and moose populations of the later forests. Population densities would have been particularly low at this time, numbering probably not much more than 1 person for every 200 or 300 square kilometres.

A warming climate in southern Ontario between 8,000 and 5,000 BP established a hardwood forest ecology that spread northwards to the southern parts of the Canadian Shield. Local populations tended to cease their more transitory patterns of hunting migratory animals and became more settled in particular areas. Gathering of nuts and fruits became an important element in the diet, along with freshwater fish, in addition to deer hunting. This is suggestive of the emergence of a more generalized foraging strategy (Kuehn 1998).

The many artifacts from habitation sites in southern Ontario indicate that population densities were becoming increasingly large compared to previous periods. Seasonal patterns of resource utilization are indicated from sites on the Ottawa River. These locations were base camps from which groups hunted in the interior in the winter, returning each summer to fish along the river (Hurley and Kenyon 1970: 112–13). It was this sort of resource use that allowed for maximum utilization of the plants and animals of an area. Population densities would have increased in a corresponding manner with the greater availability of food, possibly as high as 1 person for every 25 square kilometres (Lovis 2008).

New Cultural Patterns

By about 3,500 BP, new cultural patterns had begun to emerge, characterized by the appearance of pottery, and somewhat later, the use of bows and arrows replacing the earlier spears for hunting. Cultural affinities are difficult to determine from the archaeological record, yet by the agreement of most scientists the prehistory of southern Ontario has been primarily associated with Iroquoian-speaking peoples (Wright 1999: 607–702). Thus, there would appear to have been a more or less continuous habitation of southern Ontario by the same genetically derived population from its earliest phases of occupation to the time when the people of this region first encountered Europeans.

Two populations appeared to have co-existed in southern Ontario during the pottery-making Woodland period, termed *Point Peninsula* and *Saugeen*. While distinct from one another, the members of both populations are related to the later Iroquoian-speaking peoples. Using genetic and cranial evidence, for example, it has been clearly stated that "the prevailing view among Iroquoianists of **in situ** biological and cultural developments in the Woodland period of southern Ontario prehistory is unequivocally supported by the evidence of discontinuous cranial morphology" (Molto 1983: 234).

Woodland Period Cultures

The Point Peninsula Culture

The Point Peninsula culture (2,700 BP to 1,000 BP) was composed of small groups of hunters who continued a way of life that had been carried on for many centuries before the introduction of pottery. The term **Woodland period** refers to the appearance of a single item of technology—pottery—and is therefore a somewhat arbitrary designation for what is otherwise a continuous occupation of southern Ontario by its earlier inhabitants.

The primary geographical location for Point Peninsula peoples involved a territory roughly bounded by an area east of Georgian Bay, north of Lake Ontario, and extending to the Ottawa River. They tended to occupy a number of village sites and small hunting camps on a seasonal basis, which were used by successive generations of people. The methods used by Point Peninsula people to decorate their pottery evolved into a distinctive style in which the wet clay was impressed with a series of toothed or notched instruments, by which they produced a wide range of artistic designs. It is through their unique pottery designs that Point Peninsula settlements have been identified.

Burial practices were other distinctive aspects of the Point Peninsula culture of the Woodland period. These new ideas were apparently adopted from the Hopewell culture of the Ohio area, via New York state, and involved the construction of earthen burial mounds. The most impressive of these new burial practices is the "Serpent Mound" at Rice Lake, southeast of Peterborough, which measures about 70 metres in length.

These burials are evidence of new religious beliefs entering the area as well as communal work efforts. Artifacts found in the mounds suggest extensive trade connections and the importation of exotic goods from widely separated areas of eastern North America. However, by about 1,600 BP, the ritualistic treatment of the dead appears to have diminished significantly for unknown reasons (Wright 1972: 44–51).

The Saugeen Culture

The Saugeen culture (starting about 2,700 BP) was situated over a large area extending south of the Bruce Peninsula to Lake Erie and west of the territory occupied by the Point Peninsula culture north of Lake Ontario. The Saugeen culture does not appear to differ significantly from the Point Peninsula culture, although pottery styles developed their own distinctive patterns between the two groups of people. One significant difference, however, between the two populations is that the Saugeen people do not appear to have constructed burial mounds, preferring instead to bury their dead in small cemeteries. Grave goods such as deposits of red ochre, copper artifacts, and marine shell implements, were quite similar to those found in the burial mounds of Point Peninsula people.

The settlements of Saugeen people were generally found at the mouths of rivers or along rapids emptying into Lake Huron and Lake Erie. The debris left behind in their villages and camp sites shows evidence of a diet favouring large fish such as sturgeon and drum. These fish tend to spawn in the rivers during the spring and early summer, suggesting that Saugeen campsites were occupied at the same time. It is probable that the Saugeen people gathered at such river sites when fish were abundant, which would allow individual families to gather together into larger communities in a seasonal round of subsistence activities. With the coming of winter, these villages would have been abandoned as individual families returned to their winter hunting grounds.

For unknown reasons, the Saugeen people appeared to have abandoned their territory. There is evidence that a new influx of people, referred to as the Princess Point culture, began to push into southern Ontario from an area along the north shore of Lake Erie, eventually displacing the Saugeen culture. It is possible that the Saugeen people moved eastward because of this new population influx, eventually merging with their Point Peninsula neighbours, who lived north of Lake Ontario.

The Princess Point Culture

The Princess Point culture (1,500 BP–1,000 BP) is a significant development in southern Ontario prehistory because it is with this population that corn agriculture begins in the region. The pottery styles of the Princess Point people bear no resemblance to that produced by the earlier Saugeen culture. The people of the Princess Point culture appear to be a separate migration into southern Ontario entering via the Niagara Peninsula, the Windsor area, or both of these regions.

The Princess Point people do not appear to have extended into the territory formerly occupied by the Saugeen culture, preferring to stay located in a somewhat narrow area north of Lake Erie to the southern tip of Lake Huron and to the eastern shore of Lake Ontario. Available evidence indicates that for the 500-year period between 1,500 BP and 1,000 BP, the northern reaches of southern Ontario were abandoned altogether.

Corn (Maize) Horticulture

The adoption of corn or maize **horticulture** in southern Ontario represents a significant social and economic development. It is probable that in the early years, a diet of corn continued to be supplemented by hunting, fishing, and gathering. As time went on and crop production became more predictable, people would have increasingly relied on their agricultural produce, with hunting and fishing becoming less important (Rose 2008). An increased reliance on crops also meant that migratory hunting practices would have been abandoned in favour of more sedentary, permanent village locations (Chilton 2005: 138–60). Local populations would have also become enlarged in accordance with increases in agricultural production. Matrilineal **kinship systems** could have emerged during these transitions, as well from perhaps bilateral ways of reckoning relatives. The development of clans and lineages is also a likely process as well, such that separate long houses would have been built so that the members of particular kinship units would have their own dwellings to occupy.

Pickering and Glen Meyer Cultures

The Princess Point people began to expand their territory north of Lake Erie about 1,000 BP, and, since they entered a new phase of development, are thereafter called the Glen Meyer culture. Similarly, the Point Peninsula culture is also given a new designation about this time as they are referred to as the Pickering people. These names are derived from the sites of contemporary villages where significant remains of these cultures were first discovered.

For nearly four centuries, from about 1,100 BP to about 700 BP, the Pickering and Glen Meyer populations developed in parallel fashion, approaching the cultural characteristics of the historic Haudenosaunee patterns that became known to the early European explorers and missionaries. These patterns include, most prominently, an increasingly greater reliance on corn agriculture as a source of food, only occasionally supplemented by hunting and gathering (Rose 2008).

Traditional snowshoe maker, c. 1900

Source: Frank and Frances Carpenter Collection, Library of Congress.

Villages and Ossuaries

Village sites also became progressively larger, comprising up to ten hectares or more in extent, usually situated in easily defensible positions such as hill-tops and frequently surrounded by palisades constructed of vertical poles. Villages were often located in somewhat isolated areas, such as on the edge of swamps, especially removed from navigable waterways, which could create a greater susceptibility to attack.

The dead were buried in pits, called ossuaries, after a period in which the deceased was placed on a scaffold. At various periods of time, large cere-monies were conducted, called the Feast of the Dead, sometimes containing over 500 bodies as is the case with the Fairy **Ossuary** situated on the out-skirts of Toronto at the Robb site (Trigger 1987: 147).

There appears to be little in the way of cultural differences between the Pickering and Glen Meyer peoples aside from differing pottery styles, suggesting trade and other possible social relationships between the two populations, although evidence for this cultural communication is very limited. However, between about 1,100 and 700 BP, a major conflict of unknown origin appears to have developed between the Glen Meyer and Pickering populations, resulting in a pattern of chronic warfare engulfing the two groups.

The Late Woodland Period

This period of warfare apparently lasted for about four centuries. About 700 BP, a portion of the Pickering population began to expand to the southwest of their territory and subsequently conquered the Glen Meyer people. Some of the Glen Meyer people were dispersed, escaping into southeastern Michigan and adjacent Ohio where Glen Meyer sites abruptly appear around 700 BP.

Other Glen Meyer people also probably were absorbed into Pickering villages, because for the next century, there emerged a somewhat common cultural base across southern Ontario. A military conquest of this size would appear to suggest that the Pickering peoples had organized into a confederacy of their various villages, since such an organization would have facilitated the articulation of such a large-scale invasion.

By about the year 1400, four separate **tribes**, which later constituted the Ontario Iroquois, began to emerge out of this common cultural base in what is referred to as the Late Woodland period. These tribes of Iroquoian speakers began as two separate streams based on dialectical differences representing the Huron-Petun group, probably a product of Pickering cultural development, and the Neutral-Erie peoples from the former Glen Meyer population, along with cultural elements borrowed from Pickering colonists.

One group, the Wendat (Huron), developed in an independent fashion in the region south of the Bruce Peninsula between Lake Simcoe and Georgian Bay. South of the Wendat, the Petun and Neutral cultures evolved in southeastern Ontario in the valleys and on the rivers emptying along the north shore of Lake Ontario. The Erie, on the other hand, migrated into southwestern New York, east of the territory occupied by the Five Nation Haudenosaunee (see Martin 2008).

The Ontario Iroquois had their first direct European contacts in 1615 when the Recollect missionaries encountered the Wendat. Soon after, in 1625, the Jesuits also began missionary activities among the Wendat and to a lesser extent among the Petun. Samuel de Champlain's first view of Lake Huron occurred in 1615 while travelling in the Lake Nipissing region. The French and Wendat-Petun peoples maintained a close relationship based primarily on the fur trade until 1649, when the latter were defeated and scattered by the Haudenosaunee League of Five Nations.

Conclusion

The Aboriginal occupation of Ontario extends back at least 10,000 years, beginning soon after the retreat of the Wisconsin ice sheets. In time, with the increasingly warm and dry climate of the altithermal period, forests of pine and spruce in the north and deciduous tree cover in the south became the prominent ecological pattern of Ontario.

Cultural innovations corresponded with increased population densities, such as the emergence of the innovative Old Copper Culture around Lake Superior, probably associated with Algonquian-speaking peoples of the boreal forest. Subsistence patterns changed from sole preoccupation with hunting of large game animals to a more generalized foraging strategy incorporating fish, smaller animals, nuts, and fruit in the diet.

Pottery was also a significant technological innovation, along with the development of the bow and arrow that replaced the spears of earlier periods. By about 1,500 BP, Haudenosaunee peoples in Ontario began to grow their own crops of corn, combining this activity with localized hunting and gathering.

Within 500 years, beans, squash, and tobacco were also grown, which provided quantities of food sufficient for the large palisaded villages of long houses and elaborate clan systems that the first Europeans encountered in the early 17th century. However, Algonquian hunters north of Lake Superior had already encountered European fur traders by the end of the 1600s. These merchants were becoming established along the coasts of Hudson Bay and James Bay in Ontario's northern periphery and began to draw First Nations people into a commercial alliance that would last for the better part of four centuries.

Suggested Readings

Boyd, M., and C. Surette. 2010. "Northernmost Precontact Maize in North America." *American Antiquity* 75 (1): 117–33.

Dawson, K.C.A. 1983. *Prehistory of Northern Ontario.* Thunder Bay: Historical Museum Society.

Munson, M.K., and S.M. Jamieson. 2013. *Before Ontario: The Archaeology of a Province.* Montreal: McGill-Queen's University Press.

Sutton, M.Q. 2011. *A Prehistory of North America.* Upper Saddle River, NJ: Prentice Hall.

Wright, J.V. 1972. *Ontario Prehistory: An Eleven-thousand-year Archaeological Outline.* Ottawa: National Museums of Canada.

Wright, J.V. 1999. *A History of the Native People of Canada,* Vol. II: *1,000 BC–AD 500.* Ottawa: Canadian Museum of Civilization, Archaeological Survey of Canada, Mercury Series Paper 152.

Review Questions

1. What were several important cultural and technological innovations that the First Nations made in their history in Ontario?
2. How did growing corn change the lifestyle of First Nations people?
3. What important adaptations did First Nations people make to cope with the last ice age?

Note

1. Basil Johnson, from www.historymuseum.ca/cmc/exhibitions/aborig/fp/fpz2f30e.shtml.

3 ALGONQUIAN HUNTERS OF THE BOREAL FOREST

This chapter reviews the interrelationships between First Nations cultures and environmental settings in Ontario utilizing the **culture area** concept as a theoretical frame of reference. It traces historical developments that have resulted from adaptations in **subsistence economies**, which have primarily involved hunting, gathering, and fur trapping among Algonquian peoples in the northern boreal forest/subarctic areas of the province. Certain social dynamics are also analyzed, such as relationships between marriage and kinship patterns, as these are reflected in local First Nations economies.

Culture Areas of Ontario

As far as the culture area concept is concerned, Ontario consists primarily of a northern **Subarctic** zone inhabited for the most part by members of Algonquian First Nations, and an **Eastern Woodland** ecological area that was the home of Iroquoian-speaking peoples with some Algonquian groups living in the northern part of this zone, such as the Odawa (Ottawa) and a branch of the Anishenaabe (Ojibwa) called the Mississauga. The northern Subarctic zone will be covered in this chapter, and Chapter Four will cover the Eastern Woodland zone.

The Subarctic Region

The Subarctic is a vast area of Canada, stretching in a wide arc across the northern portions of Newfoundland, Quebec, Ontario, and Manitoba, into the Northwest Territories. This zone is basically divided between Algonquian First Nations living in the east and Dene (Athapascan) peoples in the west. It consists of a wide belt of boreal forest and swampy areas, populated most notably by spruce and pine trees, tundra in the extreme northern portions of this region, and many lakes and rivers. Extremes of temperature predominate, with long, cold winters and short, relatively warm summers. Transition periods between these extremes suggest more of a two-season year with freeze-up and spring thaw the major characteristics of the yearly climatic cycle.

In northern Ontario, the prominent geographical pattern is domination by the Canadian Shield. North of Lake Superior, the land rises up to a ridge called the "height of land," which is situated just north of Lake Nipigon and extends to the Quebec border. From this point, all rivers flow south into Lake Superior and eventually into the St. Lawrence River system and the Atlantic Ocean. North of the height of land, the territory is characterized by sloping, low-lying terrain with many swamps, lakes, rivers, and muskegs. North of the height of land, waters flow into the Hudson Bay Lowlands and from there into Hudson and James Bays.

The major large mammals are moose, caribou, and deer. Caribou herds migrate across the barren grounds in the north, while small herds are found in forested regions. The moose for the most part is a solitary animal; however, they do congregate in small clusters during the breeding season in early winter. Deer are generally found in only the more southerly regions of the Subarctic, near the more moderately temperate Great Lakes area.

Smaller mammals, such as the beaver, otter, and muskrat, were at one time found in great abundance because of the favourable swampy, aquatic habitats. Heavy trapping for centuries has reduced their numbers appreciably in most areas. Fish, especially trout, pike, pickerel, and sturgeon, were also an essential part of the northern diet, along with seasonally available waterfowl (Rogers and Smith 1981).

The Northern Fur Trade

The fur trade dominated the history of northern Canada for well over 300 years (Innis 1970). Not only did the fur trade have important economic consequences for the history of Canada, it also conditioned contacts between Europeans and the First Nation inhabitants of this country. The early fur trade took place along the coastal regions of eastern Canada, soon after the initial voyages of Jacques Cartier, beginning in 1534. It was noted by Cartier that First Nations people, probably the Micmac, approached his ships in the Gulf of St. Lawrence in two fleets of canoes, making "frequent signs to us to come ashore, holding up to us some furs on sticks" (Biggar 1924: 49).

It did not take long before French traders made contact with First Nations trappers, such as the Montagnais and Algonquians, who lived along the St. Lawrence valley, and the Wendat, who acted as middlemen in the trade of furs from the Georgian Bay region. With the threat from the Haudenosaunee of New York state disrupting the flow of furs to Quebec City along the St. Lawrence, the Ottawa River became a main thoroughfare for canoes venturing into the lower reaches of Lake Superior and the Canadian Shield country.

European trade goods were actively sought in exchange for beaver pelts, especially goods that replaced those of Native manufacture, such as copper pots for clay ones, steel traps for those constructed of twine and wood, or muskets for bows and arrows. As described by one fur trader, "They have abandoned all their own utensils, whether because of the trouble they had as well to make as to use them, or because of the facility of obtaining from us, in exchange for skins which cost them almost nothing, the things which seemed to them invaluable, not so much for their novelty as for the convenience they derived therefrom" (quoted in Innis 1970: 18).

Further exploration into the northeast of Ontario pushed the fur trade into Lake Nipissing, Georgian Bay, and along the north shore of Lake Superior. Fur-trading posts were established along important transportation routes, such as Sault Ste. Marie (1668), Fort Kaministikwia (1679) at present-day Thunder Bay, Nipigon (also in 1679) at Lake Superior's most northerly point, and Nipigon House (1792) on the north shore of Lake Nipigon.

Meanwhile, while the fur trade was pushing northwards from Lake Superior, the English Hudson's Bay Company (HBC) was expanding its enterprises along the major rivers entering into James and Hudson Bays, such as Moose Factory (1677) on the southernmost point of James Bay, Fort Albany (1677) on the Albany River, and Fort Severn (1759) on the Severn River. Further interior expansion of trading posts followed to counteract competition from Quebec, such as Osnaburgh House (1786) on the Albany River near Lake St. Joseph, and Rat Portage (1832) near present-day Kenora.

Effects on First Nations Societies

The most dramatic effect of the fur trade on First Nations societies was to draw them inexorably into an increasingly complicated web of world capitalism. The fur trade set in motion a process of trade and exploration that would profoundly influence the early economic and political growth of Canada, but it also had far reaching consequences for the Aboriginal populations. Over increasingly larger and larger geographical areas, the members of First

Miscocomon (the Red Knife), chief of the Anishenaabe (Ojibwa), c. 1861

Source: Mississauga Library System, identifier MC0056, First Nations Gallery. Used by permission.

Nations societies began to abandon their subsistence-based hunting way of life for one based on trapping furs for exchange purposes. It is important to indicate, however, that First Nations peoples were far from hapless victims in the commercial expansion of the Canadian north. Aboriginal people took from the fur trade items of European manufacture that increased their proficiency in an essentially traditional way of life. In other words, European goods tended to replace items of Aboriginal manufacture but did not fundamentally alter the social and economic foundations of First Nations societies.

Ethno-historical research, such as Ray and Freeman's (1978) study *Give Us Good Measure*, aptly indicates that not only were the members of First Nations proficient trappers but they were also adept at driving a hard bargain with the fur traders themselves. They were able to achieve greater value for their furs by visiting different fur trading companies and effectively bargaining one supplier of trade goods against another.

Reciprocity, not Domination

It could be suggested with ample evidence that Aboriginal peoples benefited more by selling their furs than the Europeans did by marketing them in Europe. It has been noted by Harold Innis, perhaps Canada's greatest economic historian, that "No monopoly or organization could withstand the demands of the Indian civilization of North America for European goods" (1970: 16). However, as indicated in one historical study of northern Ontario, "the traders were more dependent on the Indians for goods and services than the Indians were on them." It was also noted by trader Duncan Cameron that the fur traders were seen by Aboriginal peoples "as poor, pitiful creatures who could supply neither themselves nor the Indians" (quoted in Bishop 1974: 229).

The picture often conveyed in Canadian history books is one of an essentially amiable Aboriginal population compliant to the newcomers' mercantile interests and eager for the benefits of European commerce. This interpretation, while no doubt accurate in its broad outline, nonetheless conceals the fact that the granting of the vast territory of Rupert's Land by the British Crown to HBC was done without the consent of First Nations societies, who were the land's proper owners, and the grant was one for which no treaties were signed or negotiated (see Rogers and Smith 1994).

There are also other unfortunate aspects of the fur trade that are not commonly mentioned in Canadian history texts. Jennifer Brown's (1980)

Strangers in Blood, for example, is a study of fur-trade company families. It was a common practice for fur traders to take Aboriginal women as wives, but when a fur trader retired back to Europe, he sometimes abandoned his "country wife" and children to the mercies of their own natal families. There were also attacks on fur-trading posts, such as occurred at Henley House on the Albany River.

Expansion into Ontario's Interior

In order to counteract the growing influence of traders moving into Ontario's north from the St. Lawrence and Lake Superior, the Hudson's Bay Company proposed to travel inland and establish trading posts in the interior. Henley House, built in 1743, was the first of the inland posts, strategically situated on the east-flowing Albany River at the mouth of the Henley River (Bishop 1974: 237; Innis 1970: 139, 142). At this time, the Albany River was the major supply route for HBC into the interior. The advantage of HBC's expansion into the interior of Ontario was that First Nations trappers no longer had to make the long and arduous journey to trading posts on James Bay and Hudson Bay. Supplies and other trading goods could now be available closer to their trapping grounds.

In 1755, Henley House was attacked and burned, and four of the post's employees were killed. The reasons for the attack are not well understood. Some blamed the attack on French-Canadian fur traders who were trying to provoke animosity between the First Nations trappers and HBC. It has also been suggested that two Aboriginal women were being held at the post against their will. In any event, Joseph Isbister, who was head of the Fort Albany post, captured and hanged three of the First Nations men regarded as responsible for the attack. Isbister was subsequently fired from HBC service for this action (Bishop 1974: 315–16).

Henley House was quickly rebuilt on the same site after this incident. However, in 1759, the post was attacked again by a group of French-Canadians and First Nations people, although this time most of the HBC employees managed to escape back to Fort Albany. A third Henley House was built in 1768 on an island eight miles downriver from the first location. The post continued operation until 1850; however, by 1880, no vestiges of this post remained. Thus, while relationships between European traders and Aboriginal trappers were generally understood to be peaceful on the whole, there were periods of intense conflict, resulting from both difficulties in interpersonal relationships and competition between English and French traders.

Fur Trade Conflicts

Conflicts also emerged between members of different First Nations themselves. It is indicated, for example, that "at Osnaburgh House in 1787 an Ojibwa family was murdered by a Cree from Fort Severn. Such incidents are common in the Archival records dating to this period. However, skirmishes between Indians in the interior never existed on the tribal level; warfare involved families and extended kinship groups at most. Conflicts arose when two groups found themselves to be in the same area competing over local fur resources, or when drunk on trade rum at the posts" (Bishop 1974: 325–26).

As indicated in this comment, then, another significant source of conflict between First Nations trappers and European traders was related to the vast quantities of liquor that became a major trade item. After First Nations trappers had secured all the muskets, blankets, copper pots, beads, and other trade goods that they needed, the incentive to trap more furs tended to decline. In order to stimulate a declining fur-trade market, HBC embarked on a major policy change under which liquor became a major item of trade (Ray 1974: 85–91).

The Liquor Trade

Liquor had the advantage of being relatively inexpensive for the Company to purchase, more easily transported than many other trade goods, and a basis for increasing profits with little effort. "The consumption [of rum and brandy]," Ray notes, "increased steadily through time and was especially high during periods of intense competition" (1974: 85). The volume of liquor consumption underwent a dramatic rise between 1720 and 1753, at which time it reached a peak and was relatively constant, until after 1771, when consumption began to rise again.

The general per capita increases in alcohol consumption throughout the fur-trade period were compounded by the addictive nature of this substance. The fur traders' reports indicate that much of the trappers' free time was spent drinking at the local trading posts (Ray 1974: 142). Alcohol was also given away to trappers in lavish gift giving. In 1775, trader Samuel Hearne complained that "the Indians would not trade their Furs because I had no brandy" (quoted in Ray 1974: 143). It was Hearne's opinion that alcohol had assumed a central role in the fur trade and that a sizable quantity of quality trade goods was no longer a sufficient incentive in attracting Indigenous trappers to interior posts.

The adverse effects of the liquor trade on First Nations populations were becoming particularly evident. Trader John Long, while travelling along the north shore of Lake Superior in August of 1791, stayed at the village of Pays Plat. Long recounts, "I traded for their skins and furs, and gave them some rum, with which they had a frolic, which lasted for three days and nights; on this occasion five men were killed, and one woman dreadfully burnt. When the fumes of the liquor had evaporated, they began, as usual, to reflect on the folly of their conduct" (Long 1791 [1974]: 104).

By the 1820s, it was evident to HBC officials that the liquor trade had destructive consequences, and a concerted effort was made to reduce the use of alcohol as a trade item. Governor George Simpson, in 1822, informed the Company directors that

> We have taken steps as well to wean the Indians from their insatiable thirst for Spirituous Liquors by passing a resolution that no more than half the quantity usually allowed be given as presents and that the trade in Furs for that article (which was very limited) be altogether discontinued. (quoted in Ray 1974: 198)

As early as 1826, the temperance policy introduced by Simpson was beginning to take effect in the northerly forested regions. Thus, after a brief transition period, the Company was actively pursuing a policy of totally banning alcohol as an item of trade. However, it was not until the 1860s that HBC discontinued the trade in alcohol and the practice of gifting it altogether.

Changes in Northern Population Movements

First Nations people of northern Ontario moved about on a seasonal basis in search of fish and game supplies. The fur trade provided new economic opportunities that resulted in different migratory patterns. In general, the opening of new trading posts on James Bay and Hudson Bay drew Aboriginal populations northward as one group after another began to shift about, seeking new economic advantages as trappers and middlemen in the fur trade.

At the time of European contact, around 1620 in northern Ontario, the Ojibwa occupied a traditional territory about the east side of Lake Superior, extending down to the Wendat territory on Georgian Bay, centring on Sault Ste. Marie. However, several authors maintain that the Ojibwa were also situated in the boreal forest at this time (see Morrison and Greenberg 1982; Bishop 1974; and Rogers 1963 for different opinions on this issue). The Cree were situated on the north shore of Lake Superior, beyond Lake Nipigon and extending perhaps as far as the Albany River. North of this area, Ontario appears to have been largely uninhabited, except for occasional hunting and fishing forays.

With the advent of the fur trade, and especially the establishment of fur-trading posts on James Bay and Hudson Bay, the Cree were drawn north, especially along the Albany River. After an initial period of trapping and trading at coastal ports, the Cree began to find it economically advantageous to act as middlemen with the First Nations people southwest of Hudson Bay. As a consequence, the Cree language became the **lingua franca** of fur-trade communication.

The James Bay Cree

The Cree are a populous northern First Nation who inhabit a large swath of territory extending from the shores of Hudson Bay and James Bay through-out Quebec and Ontario. There are also many Cree living in the Northwest Territories and the northern parts of Manitoba, Saskatchewan, and Alberta, where they travelled during the fur-trade era.

In term of linguistic relationships, the Cree are more closely related to the Montagnais, who live north of the St. Lawrence River in southeast Quebec, and the Naskapi (Innu), who inhabit the southeastern third of the Labrador Peninsula. This suggests that the Cree originally lived in the southwestern third of the Labrador Peninsula before migrating west-ward across northern Quebec and Ontario. In Ontario, the Cree occupy a territory that encompasses the low-lying region on the west coast of James Bay, roughly from the Moose River northward to the Severn River on Hudson Bay.

The territory occupied by the Cree is characterized by several large riv-ers, such as the Moose, Albany, Attawapiskat, and Severn, which drain the muskeg country of northern Ontario. Spruce, tamarack, and willow trees are most common to this region. Narrow coastal strips of tundra are also found along Hudson Bay and the northeastern extreme of James Bay, on which caribou are hunted.

Generally, this area does not have the populations of large mammals, such as moose and deer, that are found in the more southerly areas of the Canadian Shield. As a result, the Cree have tended to live near the coastal regions where large numbers of geese and ducks are found. This swampy country is home to many aquatic mammals, principally beaver, otter, marten, and muskrat. Polar bears are sometimes found foraging along the coast, and the estuaries of the rivers occasionally attract seal and belugas. Although these sea mammals are not normally used for food by the Cree, they are sometimes used for their oil and their meat fed to dogs.

Early Historical Records

Early historical records and maps refer to the Cree as the *Kilistinos* or *Christinaux*, and place their territory north of Lake Superior to James Bay (Bishop 1974: 333–34). They have also referred to themselves as the "Swampy Cree" (*omaske.ko.*w). It is suggested in the *Jesuit Relations* of 1658 that the Cree, who are identified as the *Alimbegouek*, lived around Lake Nipigon, just north of Lake Superior.

Thirty years later, in 1688, the French fur trader Jacques de Noyon encountered Cree as far west as Rainy Lake, near the present Manitoba border. Sometime later, Henry Kelsey, another trader, indicated in his journal that the Cree inhabited a territory in a forested region between the lower Nelson River and the lower Saskatchewan River (Ray 1974: 12). However, according to Charles Bishop (1981: 159), "There is no strong evidence that the Cree occupied the sea coast until after the Hudson's Bay Company posts were established in the late seventeenth century."

The first Hudson's Bay Company trading post in Ontario was founded at Moose Factory on the southwest shore of James Bay in 1677. Soon after, trading posts were also established at Fort Albany (1677) and Fort Severn (1759). In the early 18th century, the HBC built an outpost at Winisk and, following 1733, constructed smaller posts on James Bay between Fort Albany and Winisk. About this same time, other fur trading companies, such as the

Revillon Frères, began to enter the James Bay area, initiating a period of competitive fur buying that tended to benefit the First Nations trappers.

The Cree began to trade at York Factory for guns and ammunition only a decade after the establishment of the Hudson's Bay Company in 1670. The Cree then began to take over the role of middlemen in the fur trade, which was becoming increasingly oriented towards the Hudson Bay region, away

A Native spokesman's use of a wampum in addressing the British

Source: Mississauga Library System, identifier: MC0705. Used by permission.

from the southern St. Lawrence River system, which was controlled by the French out of Quebec City.

As Ray (1974: 13) explains, the Cree's "early historic occupation … placed them in a strategically advantageous position to control the trade of the largest and probably most densely populated river system that drained into Hudson Bay." In addition, their early acquisition of European firearms, at a time when other First Nations groups were still equipping themselves with bows, arrows, and spears, permitted the Cree to exploit their locational advantage. With the use of firearms, the Cree were able to exert a military advantage over their neighbours, such as the Dakota Sioux to the south, the Blackfoot to the southwest, and the Chipewyan to the north.

The Cree's advantageous position as the First Nation closest in proximity to English trading posts on James Bay and Hudson Bay encouraged them to relinquish trapping for furs directly and engaging in other, more profitable activities. The Cree, for example, travelled to more remote groups with trade goods, which they would then exchange for furs, charging many more furs per trade item than could be demanded if the transaction was conducted at the trading post itself.

These furs that were acquired farther inland, in turn, were then traded to the English, and the Cree profited again from the transactions with the English. The Cree also participated in the freighting of trade goods and furs to and from HBC trading posts. In 1684, the French reported that as many as 300 canoes embarked on the journey to Hudson Bay to trade, and many of these were manned by Cree.

Missionaries on James Bay

Between 1686 and 1693, Jesuit missionaries had begun to live in what became Fort Albany. Christian missionaries from the Church of England were stationed at York Factory by 1823. A Wesleyan missionary was active in converting Cree at Moose Factory, before Roman Catholic oblates began missionizing there in 1847. The oblates gradually extended their influence northward to Fort Albany, apparently reporting little success. However, at Attawapiskat and Winisk practically the entire population was converted to the Catholic faith. It is reported that the missionizing success at Attawapiskat and Winisk was a factor in many Aboriginal families becoming established closer to the James Bay coast (Niezen 1994: 463–91; Brown and Brightman 1988; Honigmann 1981: 218).

At Attiwapiskat, the oblate missionaries spoke Cree fluently, while the manager of the Hudson's Bay Company needed an interpreter for communication with his customers. The oblates also exercised an educational role in the Attiwapiskat community, operating a day school and offering advice on personal problems. On occasion, they even provided medical assistance, issuing pharmaceuticals that had been deposited with them by the Indian Affairs agent.

In later years, the church radio was used on occasion to send messages to the Indian agent at Moose Factory in the event of a serious medical case. It was reported by resident fieldworker John Honigmann (1981) that the relationship between missionaries and the Aboriginal residents occasionally "showed strain," although the priests were able "to maintain a dominant moral role and to be a strong force for social control in the community" (225).

A history of the Anglican Diocese of Moosonee was written to commemorate its centennial anniversary in 1972 (Petersen 1974). Bishop Anderson journeyed to Moose Factory in 1852, making the six-week trip by canoe from Red River. In the summer of 1882, whooping cough broke out at Moose Factory and Albany, which killed 44 at Albany. Unfortunately, there is little mention of the Aboriginal converts in this history, as it is mainly an account of the various missionaries and their personal lives.

Narrative and Oral Traditions

Oral traditions are an important part of First Nations societies. Survival techniques are passed from person to person, and then from generation to generation, in the form of narratives that encompass a wide variety of learning skills. In this sense, oral and narrative traditions encompass the store of a society's repository of cultural worldview, moral training, and lessons for coping with difficult situations.

Such knowledge often is invested and stored in certain elders, who are regarded as "memory keepers" or the "living memory" of a society. In *âtalôhkâna nêsta tipâcimôwina: Cree Legends and Narratives*, Ellis (1995) explains that among the Cree of western James Bay—that is, among the people of Kashechewan (formerly Albany Post), Moosonee, and Moose Factory where the oral traditions were recorded—the different types of narratives "illustrate a life-style and, in the case of traditional legends, a conceptual universe of considerable intrinsic interest and one which differs substantially from that of the typical non-Indian reader" (xiii). In other words, narrative and oral traditions, while having some general interest unto themselves as "stories," nonetheless have greater value in the context of surviving cultural memory. This also means that the translation of such narratives into a language that has different worldviews from that of the Cree poses particular difficulties. This is especially true in the translation of oral texts into the literary traditions of another society.

This problem of translating First Nation narratives into literary contexts is the subject of *Talking on the Page: Editing Aboriginal Oral Texts* (Murray and Rice 1999). Basil Johnston, one of the contributors to this volume, is a member of the Cape Croker First Nation and a person who has devoted his life to preserving and communicating Anishenaabe heritage. He explains that "it is precisely because language has been separated from literature in Native language programs for teachers and students that language studies have by and large failed" (1999: 43). Johnston further suggests that language, and the narrative and oral traditions that are the subject of discourse, should be considered not "as an element unrelated to literature but as an integral constituent of it" (ibid). This view is further echoed in John Steckley's (2007) *Words of the Huron*, in which he raises the problem of "the connection of language to an understanding of the culture of a people" especially when "no native speakers exist to act as knowable informants" (xiv).

In *Our Story: Aboriginal Voices on Canada's Past*, various well-known First Nation authors such as Tomson Highway, Tantoo Cardinal, and Thomas King express their views on the issue of translating oral traditions into different cultural understandings. As the editor of this volume observes, "the traditional narrative of the history of Aboriginal peoples confirms that we read their story through our systems of understanding" (Griffiths 2004: 2). As an illustration, Tomson Highway, in an essay entitled "Hearts and Flowers," relates the story of Daniel Daylight in the context of federal withholding of the vote from Aboriginal peoples until 1960. Highway explains that he chose to write on the subject of Canada's Native people winning the right to vote in federal elections because this was the date "whereby we, as a people, were able to decide our own fates." He also explains that "a people are not truly considered full-status human beings until their intelligence is recognized as being that of human beings" (2004: 180).

In a classic work, *Cree Narrative*, Preston (2002) delves further into "expressing the personal meanings of events," as the subtitle to the volume indicates. Preston explains that "the sense of controlled human competence in a contingent world is fundamental to the ethos of Cree culture, and is expressed both in action and in narration" (2002: 237). However, Preston also points to the "substantial difference between Cree and Western cultures," which makes the translation and comprehension of narrative traditions a tenuous matter, fraught with many difficulties. When a Cree elder, for example, discusses the Mistabeo concept, this involves intuitions and perceptions that are essentially spiritual and related to concepts of power that are intimately related to the person himself, and therefore are largely beyond the comprehension of a person who is not a member of the Cree First Nation.

The Cree's Adaptive Success

Historically speaking, the Cree have been a very successful and adaptable First Nation society. From the beginnings of the fur trade, the Cree showed that they could invent new entrepreneurial roles as middlemen, acquiring an economic advantage in the process. While other Aboriginal groups dwindled in size throughout colonial history or became extinct altogether because of disease or loss of territory, the Cree tended to prosper. It is true that the Cree did suffer from population decline because of episodic diseases during the initial contact period, but since then they have recovered substantially and, in the process, expanded far beyond their original territory.

According to the 2006 Census (Statistics Canada 2008), for example, Cree is the Aboriginal language with the largest number of speakers in Canada. According to the Census, a total of 87,285 individuals reported that they could carry on a conversation in Cree, while the next most commonly spoken language (Ojibwa), with 30,255 individual speakers, has only a third as many speakers as Cree.

In terms of literacy in their Aboriginal language, many Cree are able to use the syllabic writing system developed by Wesleyan missionary James Evans at Norway House in 1840. Before 1900, almost all Cree adults understood the syllabic system; however, most available reading materials were church-related, such as hymn books, bibles, and prayer-books. This has meant that the Cree were technically "literate," but "literacy" did not come to characterize the culture outside of church texts (Salisbury 1986: 128–30, 162).

In addition to responding to changing environmental and economic conditions, the Cree have also demonstrated a skillful adaptation to multiple environmental settings, including the subarctic forests, the eastern woodlands, and the central plains. It can therefore be said with some accuracy that, "in many ways the Cree are the most important North American Indian group in Canada. [No other First Nations people] can lay claim to the central historic position, to the geographical extensiveness, or to the contemporary significance of the myriad Cree-speaking bands spread across Canada" (Fisher 1973: 126).

Another important factor accounting for the Cree's adaptive success is no doubt the relatively remote geographical locations of their settlements. In the many areas where the Cree live, they are the dominant population, unlike most other areas of Canada where Europeans have become the majority, reducing First Nations people into virtual numerical obscurity in some cases. The Cree's numerical advantage in the northern boreal forest region has acted also as a buffer to the impacts of European influences and contagious diseases.

This advantage of numerical supremacy has meant that the Cree have retained the ability to maintain a relatively autonomous lifestyle, which has been reflected in the continuing use of the Cree language and traditional cultural practices. All of these factors lend the Cree a sense of accomplishment, pride, and success in the modern world, which is perhaps a stark contrast to the demoralization felt in some other Aboriginal communities.

In sum, the Cree have found ways to adapt their culture to the changing ecological, economic, and social conditions brought by the coming of the Europeans and the fur trade. The material culture of the Europeans did not effectively alter Cree culture because these new items simply replaced existing ones, such as canvas canoes for ones made of birch bark, rifles for bows and arrows, or copper pots for clay ones. In the process, the essential ideology of Cree culture has remained largely intact into modern times.

Cree adaptive success has also been attributed to a "common-sense" view of the world. As Tanner (2005) explains, "Common sense and ordinary language divides [Cree] experience into discrete units. The common-sense viewpoint works within a framework of many discrete contexts, each defined by the specific and habitual tasks in which members of the group often engage. Thus, ... the observations of the Cree hunter include many which when put together make immediate sense, in terms of a particular and limited task he has in mind" (208). The Cree approach to life is a practical one based on task-oriented and context-bound relationships to the world.

Cree Social Organization

Social organization is another important aspect of cultural adaptation. In the case of the Cree, adaptation is facilitated by a flexible kinship system that allows for a wide basis of support in the form of food sharing and other cooperative efforts. For the Cree of Attawapiskat in the James Bay region of northern Ontario, households frequently consisted of two nuclear families, each headed by brothers or men who had married sisters (Honigmann 1953, 1981). Cross-cousin marriage (marriage between two people whose related parents were of opposite sex, for example, one's mother's brother) would appear to have taken place in the past, based on kinship terms that group siblings and parallel cousins together, but at present, this marriage practice is not common. There is little evidence that patrilineal clans were once a form of social organization among the Cree, as was the case with their Anishenaabe (Ojibwa) neighbours to the south.

The smallest unit of social organization was the **nuclear family** consisting of a husband, a wife, and their children. Occasionally, if the surrounding resources were sufficient enough, a man might have had several wives (**polygynous family**), the second wife often being a sister of the first, although this arrangement was not common. A household might consist of a lodge occupied by 10 to 14 relatives, but added extensions of this arrangement were possible.

The Cree Hunting Group

Local bands consisted of several related families, which constituted the hunting group in the winter and spring seasons. Several local or regional hunting bands gathered together during the summer for several months, usually along the shore of a larger lake, where fishing sustained the larger population. Membership in these local and regional bands was a flexible arrangement, dependent upon the supply of fish and game, leaders' abilities, or other environmental and social conditions. These various bands did not appear to have set territorial boundaries, and members were free to join other such groups in which they had kinsmen.

The kinship system also reflected a flexible and adaptable social system. The kinship system, which traced bilateral descent, allowed for a maximum possible affiliation of kinsmen. Marriage with cross-cousins, who were not considered kinsmen, was a preferred pattern, although marriage with any unrelated person was permitted. Parallel cousins, on the other hand, were considered in the same class as brothers and sisters (i.e., siblings) and marriage with these individuals was prohibited. Overall, the structuring of marriage maintained kinship relationships between neighbouring families and bands, providing a web of cooperation and support when needed (Smith 1981: 259–60).

"Cree society," Feit (1995) remarks, "is organized around principles of community, responsible autonomy, and reciprocity" (191). The central resources upon which Cree life is based, such as the land and wildlife, are not considered to be owned by individuals because the land continues, while people are born and pass on. The land and wildlife are God's creation, and so the Cree attempt to preserve these resources so that they can be passed on to future generations.

Reciprocity and Social Ties

Resources are also shared with other members of the Cree community in such a way that the social sphere is based on a system of reciprocal obligations. Such obligations for sharing, in turn, serve to minimize the shortages that could occur within families, and help to preserve the survival of the entire community. Half the food produced in the bush is circulated in gift exchanges with friends and kinsmen back at the home settlement. Those giving such gifts also receive gifts of food, supplies, or equipment in return, thus cementing community ties within the Cree settlements.

Cree communities can therefore be characterized as networks of social and reciprocal responsibilities. Individuals are joined in a system of giving privileges that link them with other hunters, which then ensures that each hunter has a place to hunt each year. As far as the community as a whole is concerned, this system of shared responsibilities and obligations spreads the hunters out across the land in such a way that no area in Cree territory is either under-utilized or over-exploited. In turn, the flexible system allows community members to respond to fluctuations in game populations so that each family has enough to eat and survive.

The Anishenaabe

The Anishenaabe began to move out of their territory at Sault Ste. Marie around 1615, and by 1775 had occupied a region well north of the Albany

River. In response, the Cree moved farther north in Ontario, to the Fort Severn area, west to Moose Factory, and west into the northern parts of Manitoba and Saskatchewan. Among the Anishenaabe and Cree groups in the interior of northern Ontario, there now occurs a linguistic mixing extending for perhaps 200 kilometres, such that a mutually intelligible language area exists, which is commonly referred to as "Oji-Cree" (Bishop 1974: 305–21; Rogers 1963).

Population shifts in northern Ontario also corresponded to significant changes in First Nations social organization. During the period of early contact with Europeans (1640–80), there is strong evidence in the available records, especially those kept by the Hudson's Bay Company, to indicate that the Anishenaabe lived in semi-permanent villages based on patrilineal clan groups, situated along the east end of Lake Superior and near the north shore of Georgian Bay.

As one noted authority on the subject has indicated, the Anishenaabe in early contact times were "divided into autonomous territorial patrilineal totemic groups" (Hickerson 1962a: 88). These villages were often based on

Aboriginal women mending a birch-bark canoe at the North-West Angle, Lake of the Woods, Ontario, 1872

Source: Library and Archives Canada, PA-074670.

the sites of clan-possessed fisheries, which allowed for settled village life for extended periods during the year. The various villages were also linked through ties of kinship and marriage.

The Anishenaabe Move Northwest

With the expansion of the fur trade westward along the north shore of Lake Superior during the 1680s, the Anishenaabe and other Algonquian-speaking groups were eager to retain their lucrative middlemen positions with First Nations to the west. Eventually, to the north of Lake Superior, the Anishenaabe began to replace the Cree, who were themselves moving westward. Both First Nations sought to occupy territory in the Canadian Shield of northern Ontario that was rich in fur-bearing animals and was still relatively unexploited.

For the Anishenaabe, the basis of their social organization continued to revolve around clans and lineages, and the economic basis of their subsistence patterns centred on hunting big game, especially moose and caribou, and fur trapping. Hunters trading with the HBC during this period were identified according to the animal names of different tribes, such as Eagle, Crane, Sturgeon, Moose, and Pelican, which were the clan designations that provided the identifying symbols for group membership (Rogers and Taylor 1981: 232–33; Bishop 1974: 266–777).

Anishenaabe Social Organization in Transition

As the Anishenaabe population began to diversify after 1680, the large clan units started to fragment into smaller groups. By the 1730s, the clan fragments themselves were dissolving into smaller, more localized groups in which kinship ties were starting to be based on bilateral ties, as descent was traced through both the father's and mother's sides of families, although a pronounced patrilateral emphasis continued (Hedican 1990a).

By the 1850s, and continuing for the next century until about 1945, the stable basis of Anishenaabe social organization was centred on groups of brothers and their wives, children, and aging parents on the father's side (termed a **co-residential group**). After marriage, men tended to remain in the territory that they grew up in (patrilocal residence) because it was more economically efficient for trappers to remain in environmental settings that they knew best and could most effectively exploit. With the signing of treaties and the establishment of permanent reserves, semi-permanent villages began to emerge after 1945. During this period, the large trapping families based on **patrilateral** kinship ties began to break down into smaller, nuclear family units.

It is evident from this historical discussion, therefore, that northern Anishenaabe social organization has undergone several fundamental changes from original patrilineal clans, to clan segments, to relatively large bilateral extended families (co-residential groups), and then finally to nuclear families. These changes were in large part adaptive responses to new economic opportunities afforded by the fur trade and to the ecological conditions of the Canadian Shield in which these economic opportunities were situated.

Recent Social and Economic History

Social and demographic patterns of the Cree and Anishenaabe of northern Ontario were largely related to the patterns of hunting, gathering, and trapping economies. In a study of the Pekangekum community near the Manitoba border in the 1950s, it was indicated that the average co-residential group numbered about 22 persons: "The normal daily tasks of living are carried out within this grouping, and for the most part this co-residential unit makes up the total group within which constant social interaction takes place. Geographically and to a large extent socially isolated for eight months of the year, these trapping communities form the total society for persons in the groups" (Dunning 1959: 84).

Similarly, for the Round (Weagamow) Lake community, the "Ojibwa still obtain large quantities of their food from the land, and some clothing and equipment, but each year move farther away from a purely subsistence economy" (Rogers 1962: E3). By the 1970s, there were much more drastic changes occurring in the Anishenaabe economy due to the influx of outside goods and a generally more sedentary community setting. As described for the Osnaburgh House community, "a community identity remains and there are many features that distinguish it as 'Indian' and 'Ojibwa,' although these are not necessarily aboriginal" (Bishop 1974: 350).

An ethnographic study conducted in a later decade, in the Fort Hope (Eabomatoong) community on the Albany River, describes an emerging way of life in the far reaches of northern Ontario in which the traditional economy is diminishing, yet the wage labour economy has not taken hold to any large extent. However, a "sense of community is extremely important to the band ... an overwhelming majority indicated that they would much rather live in the villages than in a city or town. They said that their own communities were easier to live in, provided them with a better social life, made them feel secure, and let them make friends more easily and raise children better" (Driben and Trudeau 1983: 46).

On the CNR Rail Line

Farther south, in an Anishenaabe community near the Canadian National Railway (CNR) line just north of Lake Nipigon, Aboriginal people had the opportunity to build a local economy based on the tourist industry, which combined traditional bush skills with earning much-needed income from the cash economy. Income from social assistance programs in the community of Collins was relatively low, compared with some other neighbouring villages, because of earned income derived from employment on the CNR, guiding for tourists, sale of handicrafts, and fur trapping, among other activities. The Anishenaabeg (the plural form of Anishenaabe) of Collins were still living in log cabins at the time of fieldwork in the mid-1970s, yet the people were relatively successful in combining traditional and Euro-Canadian economic aspects (Hedican 1986, 1990b).

In the late 1990s, the Fort William First Nation, living just outside Thunder Bay on the northern shore of Lake Superior, experienced much greater integration into the modern industrial economy because of the availability of more extensive wage labour opportunities from occupations in pulp and paper mills, grain elevators, and railway work. However, all of northwestern Ontario has been subjected to the vulnerabilities of a boom-and-bust cycle typical of economies based on extractive industries. As indicated in one study of the area, "the most deeply affected [by economic boom-and-bust cycles] are Native communities where unemployment may run as high as 90 percent, and the social pathologies associated with deplorable economic conditions are taking a heavy toll" (Dunk 2007: 58).

The Southeastern Anishenaabe

The Anishenaabe began to expand out of a homeland that is difficult to determine with any accuracy within a century or so of European contact. Available cultural and linguistic data suggests that this territory was roughly bounded by an area extending from the east shore of Georgian Bay, westwards along the north shore of Lake Huron, and a relatively short distance along the northeast shore of Lake Superior (Rogers 1978).

In this area lived a number of First Nations who are assumed to have spoken a common dialect, although there were probably regional variations, which became known by a number of appellations, such as Chippewa, Ochipwa, Mississauga, and Saulteaux. In time, a branch of these various groups began to migrate along the north shore of Lake Superior, following the fur trade and becoming known as the "Northern Ojibwa" (Bishop 1974). Other groups moved into southern Ontario and became known by the rubric of "Southeastern Ojibwa" (Schmalz 1991).

The Anishenaabe were first encountered by the French in the early part of the 17th century. The Jesuits reported in 1647–48, just before the Wendat-Haudenosaunee conflict, that in the vicinity north of the Wendat lived an Algonquian tribe who frequented the "Northern Sea" (presumably Hudson Bay), trading their furs. It was also noted by the Jesuits that "all of these tribes are nomads, and have no fixed residence, except at certain seasons of the year, when fish are plentiful, and this compels them to remain on the spot" (quoted in Rogers 1978: 760). The Jesuits would no doubt have found such a tribe in socio-economic contrast to the Wendat, who hunted only on rare occasions, who lived by growing corn, and who lived in sedentary villages.

The Haudenosaunee Presence in Southern Ontario

After the Wendat were dispersed in 1650, the Haudenosaunee (Iroquois) remained a significant presence in southern Ontario. The Anishenaabe maintained their home territory around Sault Ste. Marie during the 1670s. A process of political and social unification started to take place, as many clan-based units, such as the Amikwa, Marameg, and Nikikouek who were identified in the *Jesuit Relations*, began to lose their individual group identity. Until the last decade of the 17th century, the Southwestern Anishenaabe remained only on the Canadian Shield, occupying a region just north of Lake Huron. By the 1690s, however, the Haudenosaunee threat appears to have diminished, and the Anishenaabe began moving into southern Ontario.

There were still Haudenosaunee residing in this area, and conflicts were reported such as one that occurred in 1702 at the mouth of the Humber River, in which a Haudenosaunee village was destroyed. By 1707, the Ojibwa had pushed all the way south to the Niagara region, now unopposed by the Haudenosaunee. A branch of the Ansihenaabe, the Mississauga, made peace with the Seneca and became their allies by transferring their trade to the English, away from the French. With their alliance with the Haudenosaunee, the Mississauga became entrenched as a regional power in southern Ontario.

The Initial Land Purchases

In 1764, the British made their initial purchase of land in Ontario. Called the Treaty of Fort Niagara, it was signed by Sir William Johnson for the Crown and 24 Nations from the Six Nations, Seneca, Wyandot of Detroit, Menominee, Algonquin, Nipissing, Anishenaabe, and Mississaugas, among others. The treaty transferred possession of a narrow, four-mile strip of land along the Niagara River's western shore. As Indigenous lawyer John Borrows (1997) explains in his article "Wampum at Niagara," the Niagara Treaty was a pivotal point as it shifted the trend from earlier peace and friendship treaties towards later land cession treaties.

Chippewa women gathering wild rice

Source: Mississauga Library System, identifier: MC0702, First Nations Gallery. Used by
    permission.

By 1830, most of the land in southern Ontario had been ceded to the British, and the Anishenaabe were forced to reside on relatively small reserves. As they became confined to less and less territory, hunting became less available, causing a change in their food-getting strategy. Fishing therefore became a more dominant subsistence activity, along with the growing of corn for some groups. Salmon and other large fish were speared in large quantities along the north shore of Lake Ontario. Fish were dried and smoked over large fires to help preserve them for future use.

During the period 1830–1930, farming became a more pronounced economic activity among the Southeastern Anishenaabe, as their former hunting territories became less available and a more settled lifestyle was taking precedence. Corn, wheat, oats, and peas were grown, and livestock was raised. A combination of fishing and small-scale hunting continued to augment this agricultural activity, along with fur trapping. In time, though, enthusiasm for this new way of life began to diminish.

After 1930, increasing urbanization began to take place in southern Ontario among the Anishenaabe First Nations. Many Aboriginal peoples started to vacate their reserves for new employment opportunities in nearby cities. Others were able to remain on their home reserves and commute to their jobs if necessary. Today, they are employed in a number of roles, such as educators, nurses, social counsellors, and administrators. On-reserve economic activities are provided by local stores, building and construction businesses, handicraft manufacturing, and the tourist industry.

Today, there are approximately 40 Anishenaabe First Nation reserves in southern Ontario. There are relatively large reserves between Lake St. Clair and the southern portion of Lake Huron near Sarnia, such as Walpole Island, Kettle Point, and Stony Point. More numerous reserves are found around Lake Simcoe (Alnwick, Rama, Scugog, and Rice Lake), on the Bruce Peninsula (Saugeen and Cape Croker), on Manitoulin Island (Wikwemikong, West Bay, and Sheshegwaning), and around Georgian Bay up to Sault Ste. Marie (Dokis, Nipissing, Mattagami, and Spanish River).

Traditional Religious Beliefs and Rituals

At the time of European contact, Anishenaabe villages were semi-permanent places of residence, based on clan membership, with relatively large local populations. The most highly organized form of Anishenaabe religious life revolved around the Grand Medicine Society, or the Midewiwin (Hickerson 1962b; Hallowell 1936; Hoffman 1881). The Society was organized around various degrees or grades that one could progress through and was devoted to healing the sick using various rituals, chants, and ceremonies.

Less-organized religious activities pertained to shamanic divination of disease in a person, dreams about the success of hunting animals, and charms that could attract lovers. Among various Algonquian peoples, ceremonies about bears were often prominent (Hallowell 1934). In northern Ontario, it has been reported that "fear of witchcraft leads on occasion to strained if not hostile interpersonal relations inhibiting group co-operation and interaction outside the effective range of kinship" (Rogers 1962: D2). The concept of power (*manito.hke*) was also a fundamental aspect of religious beliefs. Power was seen to have both good and evil aspects. The "evil" use of power, for example, was seen to be responsible for most sickness, accidents, or even death.

Power was acquired primarily through the vision quest by both men and women. Dreams were also an important source of power and were interpreted in various ways, especially as a portent of impending harm coming to individuals. Spirits could also present themselves in dreams, and animal spirits would transport a person to a distant location where game could be plentiful.

The Shaking Tent Ceremony

As far as religious rituals are concerned, the most prominent of these in northern areas is the so-called shaking tent ceremony, or *kossa.pancikan* rite (Rogers 1962: D11-12; Hallowell 1942). The shaking tent is a cylindrical structure constructed of poles driven into the ground, tied together with horizontal hoops of wood, and covered with hides or bark. There is an opening at the top of this structure, about a metre wide, into which various spirits are thought to descend. A specialist in this ceremony crawls into a small opening, covered with a hide flap, at the base of the tent.

The performance takes place only in the evening or late at night. After the specialist enters the tent, a period of quiet prayers takes place, with a crowd of onlookers gathered around the vicinity of the structure. Before long, the structure begins to vibrate or shake, at times violently, and various voices are heard, thought to be those of spirits entering the tent. Those gathered outside are allowed to kneel down close to the entrance and ask the performer questions, often about lost objects or loved ones who have passed away. The principal spirit to enter the tent is thought to be the Great Turtle, *Mikinak*. Mikinak talks to the audience in a nasal voice, which at times makes people laugh because of its comical tone.

Mikinak is the most popular spirit to address the audience because he always has a witty answer ready, is good natured, and loves to joke around with the people gathered around the tent. Since Mikinak is present at every shaking tent ceremony, people develop a familiarity with this spirit, which is not the case with other entities in the tent. Mikinak also likes to smoke tobacco in the tent and has a peculiar habit of emitting a long, uninterrupted whistle. He is believed to have travelled great distances to partake in the ceremony, and takes long journeys to distant parts of the country seeking the information that is requested by members of the audience (Hallowell 1942).

Nanabozho, the Sleeping Giant

Among all Anishenaabe people, there was strong belief in their culture hero, Nanabozho, who is believed to have created human beings by first fashioning them out of clay, placing the small statues in fire, and then breathing life into them (Smith 1987: 9–11). Nanabozho also created the Earth in its present form after a great flood. Floating around on a raft of sticks and logs, Nanabozho sent the lowly muskrat down to the depths of the water. The muskrat emerged, tightly clutching a small amount of soil in its claws, which Nanabozho then magically expanded, fashioning a new world. Nanabozho is the superhero of the Ojibwa, and today is thought to be resting as the "Sleeping Giant" across the harbour from Thunder Bay, on the north shore of Lake Superior (Hedican 2001: 111–23).

Missionaries and Residential Schools

The Anishenaabe communicated with the spirit world through their dreams and various religious ceremonies. At the time of the first contacts with Europeans, the "early missionaries in the Great Lakes region found the Ojibwa religion strong and resistant to change. The first few Christian converts [were composed of] deserted women, the sick old men, the diseased children, the blind, and the sexually maladjusted" (Schmalz 1991: 10). As long as Anishenaabe society remained strong, there was no need for

Christian beliefs because the traditional ones had always served the people well. However, with time and the increase in the European population in Ontario, the Anishenaabe began to experience a loss of their traditional lands, and their food supply diminished.

The widespread culture shock experienced by First Nations people because of European colonialism engendered a sense of powerlessness in the face of an overwhelming force. It was at this point in time that missionaries began to convince Anishinaabeg people to abandon their traditional ceremonies and beliefs, which the missionaries called pagan and primitive. The guardian spirits of the Anishinaabeg no longer seemed able to protect the people from the onslaught of destructive outside forces, and traditional leaders seemed incapable of providing spiritual guidance. The Midewiwin lost adherents and played less of a role in the normal functioning of Anishenaabe culture as time went on.

The European population of southern Ontario increased dramatically with the influx of white settlers. The district around York (Toronto) increased from a population of only 224 white inhabitants in 1799 to 19,706 by 1845. The deer and wild animal populations began to go into rapid decline as so many fields were cleared for farm agriculture, making it impossible for the Anishinaabeg to subsist by hunting. Commercial fishing also contributed to the destruction of the Anishinaabeg's livelihood, as fishing had traditionally been one of the most important sources of First Nations subsistence. Some Aboriginal people in a half-starved state resorted to begging for food in nearby towns.

First Nations Missionaries

It was under these desperate circumstances that missionary societies became active in "converting" the Anishenaabe people. These religious organizations also effectively used Aboriginal peoples themselves to aid in the conversion process (see Graham 1975; Grant 1984). Some of the most influential were those working for the Methodists, such as Kahkewaquonaby (Rev. Peter Jones), Kahgegagahbowh (Rev. George Copway), and Rev. John Sunday, all of the Mississauga First Nation. Peter Jones's father was of Welsh descent, but his mother was the daughter of Wahbanosay, a chief of the Mississauga (Chute 1998; Smith 1987). For the Methodists, these converted First Nations people who could speak their own Aboriginal language were an immeasurable help in the conversion process. It is nevertheless important to note that while the term *conversion* has a wide usage, as Neylan (2003) indicates, "'converting' to Christianity has multiple meanings. ... The idea that Euro-Canadian missionaries converted First Nations to Christianity without Native participation in the process is as preposterous as it sounds. Missionary work involved complex relations of religious cultures" (27).

Peter Jones, with the aid of other Methodist missionaries, began to establish schools and churches among the Ojibwa in 1824. Jones established a school for Ojibwa at Davisville on the Six Nations Reserve (Schmalz 1991: 151–52; Smith 1987: 52–53, 2013). Thomas Davis was a cousin of Joseph Brant, and the area around his farm was called Davisville.

At this time, ties were being formed between the Mississauga and Mohawk Christians. Peter Jones and the Davisville Christians were particularly critical of the effects of alcohol on First Nations people. In particular, Jones detested drunkenness for the "evil it had done to my poor countrymen, many thousands of whom have had their days shortened by it, and been hurried to destruction" (Smith 1987: 53). The village of Brantford was called "Sodom and Gomorrah" by the Methodists, because it was seen as spreading the vice by selling liquor to Aboriginal people.

It was more than an abhorrence of alcohol that united the Mississauga and Mohawk Christians. They all believed that First Nations people needed to adjust to white society. As Chief Davis said in a speech, "I have told our people that they must set a good example for their children, and learn them to read, pray, and work, for it is a great sin to bring up their children in idleness" (Smith 1987: 53). The Davisville farm was successful in attracting converts. While a new school was being built, about 100 Mississauga adults pitched their tents nearby, hoping that their children would receive an education there.

The Mission School on the Credit (1826)

A new mission school was also established on the mouth of the Credit River in 1826, led by Kezigkoenene (David Sawyer), son of the chief of the Credit River band. Sawyer and Jones became the first ordained Methodist ministers of First Nations descent in Canada. In time, they both travelled to other First Nations communities around Ontario, holding positions as teachers, interpreters, writers, and preachers. Kahgegagahbowh (George Copway) was another Anishenaabe who had received an excellent education in the 1820s. He was a graduate of a Methodist mission school at Rice Lake and had as a teacher Reverend James Evans, who was the inventor of the Cree syllabic writing system.

Copway had spent the winter of 1834 at the Kewawenon Mission, situated on the south shore of Lake Superior, and the winters of 1835 and 1836 at La Pointe, Wisconsin. He is also known as the first Aboriginal person in Canada to publish a book, called *The Life, History and Travels of Kah-ge-ga-gab-bowh*, in 1847. In addition, both Jones and Copway made successful speaking tours of Europe. By any standards, George Copway, Peter Jones, and the other First Nations Methodist missionaries were considered highly literate at a time when the average pioneer child might have attended only Sunday school.

The Industrial Residential School (1849)

The missionary schools made an attempt to teach Aboriginal children agricultural and European domestic skills. In turn, a curriculum based on such principles was also seen as encouraging sedentary habits and self-sufficiency among the First Nations population of Ontario. The Alnwich School, for example, was established as an experimental project and later became a model for the industrial residential school system. The Muncey Institute opened in 1849, with an initial capacity to accommodate 100 girls and 100 boys in 2 schools. The British government was quick to see the advantages of these schools for all Aboriginal groups. It was thought that if Aboriginal people could be transformed into self-sufficient farmers, the burdensome expenses incurred by the Indian Department could be eliminated.

Yet, as early as 1857, the objective of establishing farming communities for Aboriginal peoples throughout southern Ontario was not considered entirely successful. Many Anishenaabe failed to become prosperous agriculturalists after almost 30 years of experimentation. A major problem had nothing to do with the Aboriginal people themselves. Even under optimal conditions, farming in southern Ontario at this time was a precarious venture. Market prices for produce fluctuated in an unpredictable manner, as did the vagaries of weather conditions such as rainfall amounts, frost, and insect infestations.

Periods of Transition

The Subarctic region of northern Ontario is roughly situated on the Canadian Shield, extending from Sault Ste. Marie on the southeast shore of Lake Superior north to the James Bay and Hudson Bay coastlines. Large game animals such as moose and deer were common in the days before large-scale logging and deforestation took place. Fish and geese were also abundant, and thus were staples in the diet of First Nations people.

Beginning in the 1670s, the fur trade drew large numbers of Ojibwa and Cree hunters and trappers away from the territory north of Lake Superior. Before long, many areas of northern Ontario, which were at one time almost uninhabited, were occupied by First Nations people and fur traders in a thriving economic enterprise, which lasted for more than two centuries. Today, the First Nations people of northern Ontario live in many relatively small communities, which have been designated as reserves according to treaties signed after the 1850s.

While the Cree and Ojibwa hunters were moving north to take advantage of the material benefits of the fur trade, another branch of the Ojibwa, variously referred to as the Southeastern Ojibwa or Mississauga, moved into the area that had been vacated during the Wendat–Haudenosaunee conflict of 1650. Some of this population became allies of the Haudenosaunee and moved onto the Six Nations reserve in a community called New Credit.

Missionary activity was also a particularly prominent aspect of the Southwestern Ojibwa adaptation to southern Ontario. Agriculture was also practised for a time in the mid-1800s but this endeavour did not appear to have a lasting economic effect on the Aboriginal population of the area. Thus, the historical experience of the Anishenaabe of southwestern Ontario differed substantially from their northern counterparts and their fur-trade activities.

Colonialism from an Indigenous Perspective

The term **colonialism** can be defined as a policy whereby a dominant nation seeks to establish long-term socio-political and economic domination over another people. Usually, this is accomplished by the installation of an administrative structure using members of the dominant society to facilitate such control (see, for example, Devens' [1992] study of Great Lakes missions in *Countering Colonization*). Colonialism is also a term that is often associated with the concept of imperialism, which can be seen as "the domination of another land and people through economic and political control established by violent or coercive force" (Cannon and Sunseri 2011: 276).

There can be little doubt that the Indigenous populations of this country have been subjected to the colonial pressures of domination and control throughout Canadian history. The Indian Act, formulated in 1876, is the foremost piece of legislation affecting First Nations in Canada. The Act isolates First Nations people on reserves, subjects them to various means of control, and tends to marginalize them from the mainstream of Canadian society.

Various authors have referred to the Indian Act as a sexist, even racist, piece of legislation in its orientation. It has been noted, for example, that the Act was "administered in the interest of benign rule but its implementation created isolation, control, and enforced poverty. It has become the most vicious mechanism of social control that exists in Canada today" (Frideres and Gadacz 2008: 37). There are numerous incidents in Canadian history to support this point of view. In 1884, for example, the Canadian government enacted the anti-potlatch law, which forbade the First Nations of British Columbia from participating in an important Indigenous cultural tradition. This legislation was not repealed until 1951, meaning it was enforced for a period of almost 70 years. In 1885, Canadian armed forces defeated the Métis people of the Canadian Prairies in the Northwest Rebellion and other Aboriginal peoples, mainly Cree, at the Battle of Batoche in Saskatchewan. The leader of the Métis people, Louis Riel, was subsequently hanged for treason in Regina, although today he is regarded by many as a Canadian folk hero for his role in forming the provisional government of the Métis Nation at Red River in 1870 and for his role as a founder of the province of Manitoba.

Later, in 1927, legislation was used to prohibit the formation of Aboriginal political organizations beyond the local level. Aboriginal people with status did not even have the right to vote in provincial elections until the 1950s, and they were barred from voting federally until 1960. It is clearly difficult to promote any rights whatsoever without the ability to vote and exercise one's prerogative to choose representatives who could speak for your rights in various provincial and federal legislatures. In other words, denying

Aboriginal people the right to vote kept them isolated from the dominant Canadian political processes and thereby denied them representation that could further their rights as citizens of this country.

Indigenous authors have been particularly critical of the Indian Act as a mechanism by which control is exerted over First Nations. Taiaiake Alfred and Jeff Corntassel (2011) assert that in Canada, "Indigenousness is an identity constructed, shaped and lived in the politicized context of contemporary colonialism" (139). Other Indigenous authors, such as Marie Battiste and Sakej Young Blood Henderson, point to the "Eurocentric" attitudes of those in the dominant society as a main source of oppression of First Nations. "Eurocentrism," they note, "postulates the superiority of Europeans over non-Europeans. It is built on a set of assumptions and beliefs that educated and usually unprejudiced Europeans and North Americans accept as true, as supported by 'the facts,' or as 'reality'" (Battiste and Young Blood Henderson 2011: 11).

Similarly, in her study *Fighting Colonialism*, Schwarz (2013) suggests that popular images of Native North Americans play an important role in the colonial process because these images portray and promote negative

Big Trout Lake school children, 1930

Source: Canada, Department of Indian Affairs and Northern Development/Library and Archives C-068924.

stereotypes of the Indigenous population. As she indicates, "images meant to depict Native Americans have traditionally stood as signs or fetishes for such contradictory concepts as primitiveness, nature, spirituality, unbridled sexuality, violence, nobility, or heathenness, depending on the particular time and agenda of the presenters and the code or codes understood by the various audience members" (1). Thus, control over the manner in which Native Americans are characterized and defined is an important aspect of power over Indigenous individuals and communities. As well, such negative stereotypes can be understood as an important aspect of colonialism, because it justifies the paternalistic attitudes that have historically informed and articulated the interaction between Indigenous peoples and Euro-Americans. Portrayals of Aboriginal peoples in the wider society, one could conclude, have therefore historically allowed for the exercise of symbolic power over the oppressed members of a society.

"Decolonizing antiracism," to employ a term used by Bonita Lawrence and Enakshi Dua, involves "challenging the ongoing colonization of Aboriginal peoples" (Lawrence and Dua 2011: 19). From their perspective, it is important to recognize that Canada should be regarded as a colonialist state and as a "settler society." "Settler states," in their view, "are founded on, and maintained through, policies of direct extermination, displacement and assimilation" (Lawrence and Dua 2011: 20). It is evident, therefore, that from an Indigenous perspective, people of First Nations ancestry perceive Canadian history quite differently than the history presented in books written by members of the dominant society and taught in the schools of the nation.

This chapter has discussed the lifestyle and history of the Algonquian hunters of northern Ontario. In the following chapter, we will explore the second main culture area of Ontario—the Eastern Woodland ecological area, which was primarily the home of Iroquoian-speaking peoples.

Suggested Readings

Bishop, C.A. 1974. *The Northern Ojibwa and the Fur Trade*. Toronto: Holt, Rinehart and Winston.

Brown, J.S.H. 1980. *Strangers in Blood: Fur Trade Company Families in Indian Country*. Vancouver: University of British Columbia Press.

Cannon, M.J., and L. Sunseri, eds. 2011. *Racism, Colonialism, and Indigeneity in Canada.* Don Mills, ON: Oxford University Press.

Hedican, E.J. 1986. *The Ogoki River Guides: Emergent Leadership among the Northern Ojibwa.* Waterloo, ON: Wilfrid Laurier University Press.

Hedican, E.J. 2001. *Up in Nipigon Country: Anthropology as a Personal Experience.* Halifax: Fernwood Books.

Schmalz, P.S. 1991. *The Ojibwa of Southern Ontario.* Toronto: University of Toronto Press.

Review Questions

1. How does the culture area concept help us to understand the adaptation of First Nations people to different ecological conditions?
2. What important effects did the fur trade have on the economy and social organization of Algonquians living in northern Ontario?
3. Describe the role of missionaries in changing the culture of First Nations people.
4. How would you use the concept of colonialism to describe the impact of European settlers on the lives of First Nations people in Ontario?

4 THE WENDAT AND HAUDENOSAUNEE OF THE EASTERN WOODLANDS

When the Wendat and Haudenosaunee adopted growing corn as a food source about 1,500 years ago, it constituted more than just a change in their subsistence economy. When corn horticulture was first introduced, it was probably only a part-time activity that supplemented an already established food-getting economy of hunting, fishing, and gathering. Over time, with an additional available food source, population increases would probably also take place in those areas where corn, and later beans and squash, were cultivated.

Corn might also have been regarded as a preferable food source over hunting and fishing because of its reliability over the vagaries, inconsistencies, and unpredictability of animal movements. With an increased reliance on horticulture, and the population expansions that resulted, First Nations people would no doubt have become more sedentary. There was also an increased need to protect their new-found sources of food. Villages inhabited on a year-round basis would then inevitably replace migratory patterns.

Internal changes in social organization also developed, with emergent new concepts such as the idea of a Mother Earth that provided food for her children. People began to reckon their kinship relationships through their mother's side of the family, resulting in matrilineal descent systems, as opposed to prior systems relating relatives bilaterally or through the father's line of descent. Marriage patterns would change as well, with men now moving to their wives' villages, in recognition of women's prominent role in food production.

The Haudenosaunee Creation Story

The Sky-World

The creation of the Earth for Haudenosaunee people begins with a woman who falls from the Sky-World. In some versions of the creation story, she then proceeds to give birth to twins, one of whom is good and the other evil; in other versions, she gives birth to a daughter, who eventually becomes the mother of the twins. The woman who falls from Sky-World also gives to the Haudenosaunee the "three sisters," corn, beans, and squash, the basis of sustenance for the people. The Haudenosaunee account of creation serves to explain the complementarity of good and evil, the social ideal of balance and harmony, and the dual character of spiritual power that is responsible for both the malevolent and the beneficial aspects of life (Labelle 2013: 1; Hertzberg 1966).

In the beginning, there was no world as we know it, no people or land, but only a great ocean. Far above this ocean was a Sky-World inhabited by god-like creatures, who were like the Haudenosaunee people themselves. In this world lived a man and his wife, who was expecting a child. In the middle of Sky-World grew a great tree, which had enormous roots, and it had grown there forever. This was a sacred tree that stood at the very centre of the universe. Any of the beings who lived in Sky-World were not supposed to harm or disfigure this great tree in any way, but the pregnant woman decided that she wanted some bark from this tree, possibly as a means of making some medicine.

The woman pestered her husband to get some of the great tree's bark for her. This was against his better judgment, but he eventually relented and began to dig a hole among the roots of the tree. The husband was not aware that the ground of Sky-World was rather thin, and before long, he broke a hole through it. When he told his wife of this discovery, she became curious and looking through the exposed area saw the ocean far below. The wife then proceeded to stick her head through this hole, and for whatever reason—she slipped or was pushed by her husband—the woman fell through towards the ocean below.

The Ocean World

Although this ocean world did not contain animals or people, great flocks of birds flew about. When these birds saw the woman falling towards the ocean, they spread their wings, interlocking with one another, forming a great feathery raft that supported the woman. The birds had trouble supporting her so they called out for help to a giant sea turtle from the ocean, who agreed to support the woman on his back. This turtle then began to float about the huge ocean while supporting the woman.

As time went on, the woman eventually gave birth to a daughter. The back of the turtle was a great area. With the help of a muskrat, some soil was dug up from the ocean floor which ultimately expanded as the Earth grew. The woman and her daughter planted some roots that she had managed to grab while falling through the Sky-World floor. These roots grew into plants that sustained the woman and her daughter. After the woman's daughter grew, she happened to meet a man, who was said to be associated with the gods above, but no one knew for sure. At the sight of this man, the woman's daughter fainted. As she laid on the ground, the man took out two arrows from his quiver, one sharp and one blunt, and laid each one across her body.

When at last the daughter recovered from her fainting spell, she realized that she was going to have a child. She did not know it at the time, but this child was actually going to be twins. Before long, the twins began to argue and fight with each other. The main point of contention between the two was that the right-handed twin wanted to be born in the normal way, but the other, the left-handed twin, wanted to be born in another direction, from which he saw a light.

The Antipathy of Twins

The quarreling continued between the twins. Eventually, the left-handed twin saw light through his mother's mouth but was unable to be born that way, so he tried to be born through his mother's armpit, which caused her death. However, just before she died, the right-handed twin was born in the normal way of children. When the two twins then met in the outside word, they began to argue over who had killed their mother. The grandmother tried to stop the fighting. First the twins buried their mother and from her grave grew all sorts of plants that people use, such as corn, beans, and squash. From the mother's heart grew the sacred tobacco, which the Haudenosaunee use in their ceremonies even today.

The left-handed twin continued to pick fights with his right-handed brother. The right-handed twin did everything as he should in life, as he always told the truth and tried to do everything as he should. The left-handed twin always lied and did everything backwards. One could never count on this twin because he was so devious. As the two brothers grew up, they began to represent the two forces that characterized people. The Haudenosaunee called this dual nature the straight mind and the crooked mind, the upright man and the devious man.

The twins grew up to be men, and they continued to contest one another. They did so with gambling, but neither won. Next they battled one another at lacrosse, but neither won at this game either. The brothers then decided to hold a duel. Each selected his weapons, with the left-handed twin choosing only a mere stick, while the other chose a deer antler. In the end, the right-handed twin won the duel. He then cast his brother's body off the end of the Earth, to some place below the world, where the left-handed twin still lives today.

After the duel, the right-handed brother returned home to his grandmother, but surprisingly she called this brother a murderer. He grew angry and tried to explain that the left-handed brother had killed their mother by not being born in the proper manner. Eventually the right-handed twin, called the Master of Life, returned to Sky-World. The left-handed twin lives in the world below with the humans who were the product of his creation. While he enjoys the scent of rising tobacco smoke, the left-handed brother also finds contentment in the troubles of people, such as warfare and other hardships that humans are forced to endure.

The Eastern Woodlands

As a culture area, the Eastern Woodlands covers an extensive area of North America including the Atlantic coastal region, westward to the Great Plains and north to the Great Lakes and St. Lawrence River system, up to the northern Subarctic. In its original state, this area was characterized by large stands of hardwood forests, relatively mild winters, and warm summers.

In southern Ontario and adjacent areas of New York state, the Wendat (Huron) and Haudenosaunee (Iroquois Six Nations) lived a horticultural way of life, growing primarily corn (maize), beans, and squash. Supplemental crops included sunflowers and tobacco. Hunting and fishing, in season, provided protein to the local diet. Forest products provided sources of medicine, wild rice, berries, nuts, and various leafy vegetables that augmented the corn, meat, and fish diet. Bark was used to make canoes and cover longhouses. The Haudenosaunee also manufactured pottery in a variety of distinctive styles and lived a sedentary life in their relatively large villages defended by high palisades of vertical poles.

As a form of food production, corn horticulture slowly diffused northward from the highlands of Mexico, where it began about 4,500 years ago. In a series of hand-to-hand contacts, spreading from society to society, knowledge of the growing of corn travelled through the Mississippi River system, arriving, eventually, in southern Ontario by about 1,500 BP (Wright 1999: 607–702). Eventually, corn was cultivated as far north as the Bruce Peninsula, Lake Simcoe, Georgian Bay, and Lake Huron.

The Wendat of Southern Ontario

This Eastern Woodland region of southern Ontario was inhabited by the Wendat Confederation of First Nations (Huron). This area is the maximum extent that horticulture can be reasonably practised within the limitations of the northern growing season of frost-free days. Petun (*Tionnontate*, or Tobacco Nation) villages were located immediately southwest of the Wendat and appeared to be differentiated from the Wendat politically, rather than culturally (Garrad and Heidenreich 1978). The Wendat and their linguistic relatives the Petun numbered about 20,000 people when first contacted by Europeans (Labelle 2013: 84–85; Trigger 1987: 94).

The Neutral (whom the Wendat called *Attiwandaronk*, or "people who speak a slightly different language") inhabited the region south of the Petun, an area comprising the lower part of the Grand River Valley and the Niagara River between present-day Guelph, London, and Tillsonburg (White 1978). They were called "Neutral" by the French, because they did not engage in warfare with the Wendat or the Haudenosaunee, and they did not permit members of their groups to fight within their own villages.

The Neutral, however, were not entirely peaceful, as they carried out blood feuds with sedentary Algonquian peoples who lived in their vicinity. Much less is known about the Erie, a confederacy of tribes living at the southeastern end of Lake Erie. The Wendat called them *Erieehronon*, and the French referred to this society as the *Nation du Chat*, possibly because of the number of wildcats in their country, although the term *chat* could have also meant raccoon (Labelle 2013: 130–31; Trigger 1987: 27–104; Heidenreich 1971: 156–58).

Swidden Horticulture

The Wendat practised a type of horticulture called **swidden** or **slash-and-burn** agriculture. In this method of cultivation, a section of bark is removed from large trees, which eventually causes their death. Such trees are often toppled over during wind storms, and their branches are then burned, releasing nutrients into the soil. Initially, crops are grown in between the tree stumps as an ever-increasing amount of forest is cleared and put under cultivation. Eventually, however, these fields become depleted of nutrients, a characteristic of forest cultivation of this sort, causing the need for additional fields to undergo the slash-and-burn technique. In time, about every 25 years or so, whole villages will need to be relocated because of the general drop in soil fertility in any given area (Labelle 2013: 107–8).

When a village is moved, new areas where the forest cover is relatively light are sought out, and soil of the sandy-loam type is preferred because it is easily worked. Ideal village locations would also include a possible hilltop position that could be more easily defended, sites with a good source of fresh water nearby, and possibly a swampy area for deer hunting. Horticultural techniques involved a division of labour. Men generally cleared the fields and acted as warriors in defence of their village. Women planted, tended, and harvested the crops. They also were considered to own the fields in which the corn was grown and the longhouses in which people lived.

Longhouses and Clan Membership

Each longhouse was occupied by four or five nuclear families, united by common clan membership and maternal kinship ties. On average the longhouses were about 12 metres wide, 12 metres high, and 25 metres long, although they would vary in size depending upon the number of occupants. A Wendat village might be composed of as many as 50 to 100 of these living structures and could contain 300 to 400 families. Upon entering a longhouse, one would see a long passageway with four or five hearths for cooking and heat. There were often also dividers of poles and mats that roughly separated the individual families inside. As such, each nuclear family had its own cooking and work area.

During the night, people slept on bunks or raised platforms, called *andichons*, which were set along the inside of the walls of the longhouse. These *andichons* were constructed on pole frames raised about 1 metre from a bark-covered floor. The raised platforms were high enough to keep the people above the chill of the ground below, but were low enough to avoid the heavy layer of smoke that tended to hang in the upper reaches of the longhouse. Along the end of each longhouse, storage areas were constructed of large bark baskets in which were stored the year's supply of corn, beans, and squash. Other items, such as snowshoes, fishing nets, and clothing were hung in other available spaces or stored away during seasons in which they were not in use. Large quantities of fish also hung from the rafters to dry.

Each village had a rough design for the position of the longhouses, situated in the path of the prevailing winds, so that if one happened to catch fire it was less likely to light others nearby, which would be the case if the longhouses were sideways to the course of the wind. Later, as space inside

Traditional Iroquois longhouse

Source: Gordy, Wilbur F. 1913. *Stories of American History.* New York: Charles Scribner's Sons, p. 20.

the palisade became more cramped with successive population growth, new longhouses were crowded into any available space.

Inside the longhouses, an accumulation of smoke was a constant problem, causing frequent eye irritation and breathing problems. Although each longhouse had a number of square holes in the roof that permitted the smoke to escape, with each hole covered by a flap of bark that could be opened or closed by long poles, the Jesuits complained in their written journals about the density of smoke inside the houses. The longhouses were in constant need of repair because of their bark construction and the damage caused by wind, rain, and snow storms. In due course, about every 12 to 20 years, whole villages needed to be relocated as the cornfields suffered a depletion of nutrients and firewood became more difficult to obtain within reasonable walking distance from the village (Trigger 1987: 45–46, 151–53).

Marriage and Social Organization

When a couple married, the man went to live with the wife's relatives in her village, a practice referred to as matrilocal residence. The Wendat practised clan **exogamy**, meaning that one had to choose a marriage partner from outside one's own clan. The village social structure was therefore solidified by the kinship ties between related women and children. Children were considered to belong to their mother's clan, rather than the father's kinship group.

Kinship terminology among the Wendat was based on what is called the **Iroquois kinship terminology**. Wendat kinship terms were divided into various classes of relatives. As an example, the term for "mother" also included one's mother's sister and one's father's sister; correspondingly, the term for "father" was extended to include one's father's brother. A separate term was used, however, for one's mother's brother because of the special importance that this maternal uncle played in guiding young males through life. Remember that in a matrilineal system, male children do not belong to the same kinship group as one's father, so male relatives on the mother's side tend to be just as important as one's actual biological father (Labelle 2013: 178–80).

Extending down through the generations in such a matrilineal society, terms for "brother" and "sister" were also extended laterally to include the children of a person's mother's sister and father's brother. This kinship pattern for siblings is what is commonly referred to as **parallel cousins**. Similarly, then, children of cross-sex connecting relatives, such as the children of one's father's sister and mother's brother are termed **cross-cousins**.

This designation, or separation, of parallel cousins from cross-cousins, which is unlike the practice of English speakers, is a relatively common pattern of kinship terminology among the world's societies and plays an important role in regulating marriage. In such instances, one must choose marriage partners from the cross-cousin category, with a preference usually given to those in the **matrilateral** cross-cousin category (i.e., children of one's mother's brother) since these individuals would belong to different clans and are therefore considered preferred marriage partners.

Wendat Marriage Practices

The Wendat were generally monogamous in their marriage practices, although the records of the Jesuit priests would appear to indicate that divorce was commonplace. The Jesuits further reported that a woman might have as many as 12 or 15 husbands during the normal course of her lifetime. One wonders, though, how the term *husband* might be interpreted among the Wendat, since these men could possibly be casual lovers or *paramours* rather than socially recognized or "legal" husbands.

Such misinterpretations were common among the Jesuit missionaries, who often regarded Wendat social practices, especially religious beliefs, in derogatory or **ethnocentric** terms, thinking that such practices were a result of primitive, non-Christian culture. For example, the Jesuits reported that marriage among the Wendat was "nothing more than a conditional promise to live together so long as each shall continue to render the services that they mutually expect from each other" (Labelle 2013: 136–37; Tooker 1964: 126).

Anthropologists might well dispute such a claim, since marriage in non-European societies was often the result of highly structured organizational efforts or structures. The reason for doubting the Jesuit interpretation of Wendat marriage as a transitory affair is that such marriage unites not just two persons but brings together various kinship groups in which valuable property is exchanged, resulting in wider, more permanent social bonds that are difficult to break.

The Social Effects of Divorce

There would no doubt also be other reasons why divorce might not be as common as the Jesuits reported. One of the main reasons for maintaining marriage stability is that the position of men in matrilineal societies is a particularly vulnerable one. If a man was divorced, he would no longer be allowed to reside in the same village as his wife, as he would have no kinsmen there. Alternatively, if he returned to his natal village, this could well be regarded as a matter of disgrace. He would also lose contact with his children. As far as a man is concerned, these various factors would mean that the husband would be "reduced to a wretched life, seeing that it is the women in our country who sow, plant, and cultivate the land, and prepare food for the husbands" (Tooker 1964: 126). However, once a couple had children, it was a rare occurrence that they would separate.

There are also various rules and regulations in place that guided the process of selecting possible marriage partners. First of all, there was a general prohibition against marrying anyone who belonged to the same clan. Couples were also not allowed to marry if there was a direct line of kinship connecting them, even if this line of kinship was quite distant. It was a usual practice for a prospective husband to seek the permission of a girl's parents, although she was at liberty to follow her own inclinations in the choice of a spouse.

The normal daily affairs of the Wendat longhouse were run under the guidance of the clan matron, who was able to exercise authority over her daughters and grandchildren. The matron's brother, who belonged to the same **lineage** (a smaller section of a clan) as her, also had a voice in longhouse affairs, although it was likely that he would live in another village, but could return after a divorce. Her husband also had political influence, even though he was considered an outsider because he belonged to a different clan.

Political Organization

Political organization among the Wendat was based on a person's membership in one of four tribes and eight different clans (Trigger 1969: 54–57). Membership in the clans themselves, however, was not based on any particular territory, as clan membership cut across tribal boundaries. In other words, members of the same clan could be found living in many different villages and in all the various Wendat tribes. Thus, clan membership had an important integrative function in serving to unify political divisions along lines of kinship and descent.

Each Wendat tribe was considered a distinct political unit, had its own territory, and consisted of various villages within this organization. Men did occupy leadership roles and were the only ones who could occupy the role of chief; however, selections for chief often needed to be approved by the clans' matriarchy of elder females.

Village political and leadership structure was divided between civil and war chiefs. The civil chief generally was responsible for the internal affairs of the village, while the war chief presided over war council meetings. The war chief was a position based primarily on charismatic leadership, demonstrations of bravery in raiding parties, and ability as a warrior. The civil chief usually held an office for life, and it could be an inherited position.

The Wendat held councils with other tribal segments, usually attended by chiefs and other representatives of each village. Some chiefs in these councils held more power than others, either because of the larger strength of their particular village, or because of special oratory skills of persuasion. The seat of the council meetings tended to shift from village to village, depending upon the formation of inter-group alliances and the rise and fall of individual leaders. At a higher political level, the Wendat were organized into a confederacy of various clans and villages, suggesting that there was somewhat of a hierarchical basis to the political organization as a whole (Trigger 1987: 58–59, 162–63).

Alliances were formed among various villages, and these agreements shaped important mechanisms of mutual support when disputes arose between segments of the Wendat population. However, as Trigger (1987: 9) notes, the main problems confronting the confederacy as a whole were preventing disputes between members of different tribes from disrupting its unity, maintaining friendly relations with tribes with whom the Wendat traded, and, where possible, coordinating dealings with enemy tribes, in particular the Haudenosaunee.

Inter-Tribal Conflict

Conflict between the Wendat (Huron) of Ontario and the Haudenosaunee (Iroquois) of New York state became a prevalent pattern of tribal relations during the early 1600s (Hunt 1940). The conflicts became accentuated after the crops were harvested and the men, freed from subsistence activities, had more time to devote to raiding parties.

Raids, usually of a retaliatory nature, were carried out on a relatively small scale for many decades; however, the number of such skirmishes increased dramatically during the 1640s. Instead of the previous pattern of raiding villages with the intent of capturing prisoners, probably as part of a cycle of revenge, raiding later entailed the burning of whole villages and ad-joining fields. Eventually, during 1649–50, the Wendat, Petun, and Neutral were completely dispersed from southern Ontario.

Various explanations for the inter-Nation conflicts have been proposed, but there does not appear to be a definitive answer or even any single answer. Hunt (1940), in *The Wars of the Iroquois*, suggests that the conflict between the Wendat and the Haudenosaunee was a result of economic competition in an attempt to control the fur trade. The Haudenosaunee of eastern New York state, Hunt argued, had begun to lose access to the lucrative beaver pelts and trade goods with the demise of the Dutch fur-trading companies on the Eastern Seaboard and especially in the Hudson Valley. As a result, the French gained considerable influence in the fur trade. The Wendat, in turn, were able to control the flow of furs along the Ottawa and St. Lawrence River systems. The Haudenosaunee raiding parties resulted, therefore, be-cause of Haudenosaunee aspirations for materialistic gain and an upper hand in the competition for trade goods and economic influence (Trigger 1985: 203–20, 307–8).

Other explanations are of a primarily psychological nature. This ap-proach suggests that Haudenosaunee men were dislocated from their original home villages because of the matrilocal marriage pattern and thus lacked methods of asserting their male prowess. Warfare provided an outlet for male aggression and a method of gaining prestige (Otterbein 1964).

This psychological explanation, however, is difficult to prove and lacks empirical and historical evidence to support it. It is also thought that warfare has a functional explanation, such that it is a means of solving inter-group conflicts (Coser 1964). According to this approach, group conflict could be considered normal and even have positive social value. Nonetheless, in the Haudenosaunee case, little social value appeared to result from the con-flict, because the Wendat were entirely displaced from their home territory (Labelle 2013: 29–46).

Feuding or Warfare?

In any event, the characterization of the conflict as "warfare" does not appear entirely accurate, as the various expeditions, usually involving perhaps sev-eral hundred warriors, did not appear to have a coherent or strategic focus. "As for social structure," Barrett (2002) explained, "the conventional argu-ment is that warfare involves an entire sociopolitical unit such as a tribe or state against another, while feud involves part of such a unit against another part" (98). Thus, the term *feuding* could be considered a more appropriate term than *warfare* in this case, since both the Wendat and Haudenosaunee had sprung from the same ancestral linguistic and cultural source and had virtually the same village social organization and subsistence economy. In this regard, both the Wendat and Haudenosaunee First Nations could be considered part of the same wider or regional "social structure."

Ultimately, the military success of the Haudenosaunee in their struggles with the Wendat can be related to several important factors. Probably the most important reason was that the Haudenosaunee had greater access to guns than the Wendat. The French were hesitant about allowing the Wendat to trade for guns because they feared inflaming the existing hostilities among the tribes of the St. Lawrence River system. The Haudenosaunee, on the other hand, had a ready source of firearms from Fort Orange (Albany, New York).

The Wendat attempted to counter Haudenosaunee gun attacks by developing new battle strategies, such as dropping to the ground whenever the Haudenosaunee attempted to fire their weapons, and then, when the Haudenosaunee weapons had been discharged, rising and counter-attacking with bows and arrows. Such methods were occasionally successful, but in the long run, they did not prove effective in winning many battles.

Another factor leading to the Haudenosaunee success was the widespread fear generated by the constant state of conflict, reprisals, and counter-attacks that occurred over such a wide area. After each successful campaign, panic began to spread among the Wendat villages, causing a general domino effect with fleeing villagers attempting to avoid ensuing battles.

In 1649, two major Wendat villages were destroyed by the Haudenosaunee, resulting in a full-scale flight from their territory. In May of that year, the Wendat themselves burned 15 of their own villages, and several thousand refugees crowded on Christian Island in Georgian Bay. More deaths resulted during the following winter, attributable to the general lack of food, which, according to some figures, caused more fatalities than the Haudenosaunee raids themselves (Trigger 1987: 725–82).

As the Wendat people abandoned their villages in southern Ontario, many moved to Wisconsin, Michigan, and other northern states. Reserves were established in Quebec, such as Loretteville, or more correctly Village-des-Hurons, in 1697 (Morissonneau 1978). The Huron-Wyandot confederacy consisting of more than 20,000 people became all but forgotten in time, as their longhouses collapsed and their cornfields became overgrown with weeds and brush. Except in the minds of men and women, it did not take long before there was hardly any evidence at all that this once-powerful confederacy had ever existed.

Probably the most important point that could be made is summed up in Labelle's book *Dispersed but not Destroyed*. Her conclusion is that "depictions of Wendat destruction, trauma, dislocation, and violence are not inaccurate portrayals of the circumstances surrounding their dispersal in 1649." However, what should be emphasized is "Wendat determination, renewal, and survival" (Labelle 2013: 214).

The Haudenosaunee of the Grand River

In 1784, Chief Joseph Brant led nearly 2,000 Iroquois Loyalists from New York state into southern Ontario (Weaver 1972, 1978). As British allies, the Haudenosaunee were granted a large tract of land comprising about 675,000 acres, 6 miles deep on either side of the Grand River from it source to its mouth. The land, called the Haldimand Grant, was given to the Haudenosaunee in compensation for their losses during the American Revolution. The Mohawk, Cayuga, Oneida, and Tuscarora originally settled in villages near the present-day city of Brantford. The Seneca settled near the mouth of the river on the opposite bank, but in the 1820s moved upstream to locate near the Onondaga.

Almost from the beginning of this settlement, controversy erupted over the nature, extent, and the exact location of the Haldimand Grant. Further issues revolved around the selling of land by Chief Joseph Brant, who claimed that funds were needed to buy building supplies, farming equipment, livestock, and other necessary purchases related to the new farming life of the Haudenosaunee in southern Ontario. Brant also claimed that the Haldimand Grant had been conveyed to the Haudenosaunee with a title that was "an estate in fee simple, giving the Iroquois not only national recognition but also the right to sell the land at their option. The Crown held that the land was not alienable by the Indians and that the [Haldimand Grant] Proclamation did not recognize political sovereignty of the [Iroquois] League" (Weaver 1978: 525).

In 1793, the lieutenant governor of Upper Canada, John Graves Simcoe, drafted the Simcoe Patent, which stipulated that all land transactions of the Six Nations would have to be approved by the Crown. However, Brant and the other chiefs of the Six Nations rejected the Patent and over the subsequent years sold more than 350,000 acres of the original tract, representing over half of the initial Haldimand Grant. By 1834, various white settlements had grown up along the Grand River on lands sold by Brant, and a decision was made by the Crown that it would be too costly to remove the settlers, thereby legally confirming the Brant land sales.

Farming along the Grand River

Farming by the Six Nations settlers consisted initially of dispersed farms averaging plots of about 20 acres. Agricultural techniques were generally similar to that practised by surrounding white farmers, with corn and potatoes cultivated with a hoe. Before long, larger farms of up to 200 acres

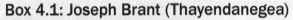

Box 4.1: Joseph Brant (Thayendanegea)

JOSEPH BRANT (THAYENDANEGEA) (1743–1807): SIX NATIONS MOHAWK

- Was perhaps the best known Aboriginal person of his era
- Was on familiar terms with such significant figures of his age as George Washington and King George III
- After the Revolutionary War he relocated most of his people to the Six Nations Reserve
- One of 14 leading Canadian military figures commemorated at the Valiants Memorial in Ottawa

Portrait of Joseph Brant, by George Romney

Source: Wikimedia Commons

emerged, on which wheat, oats, timothy, and peas were grown with plows pulled by oxen. Livestock consisted of cows and hogs, in addition to oxen.

By the 1840s, with the growing presence of emerging frontier towns such as Brantford, farms of the Six Nations people were frequently encroached upon by white settlers. As a consequence, in 1841, the government suggested that the Haudenosaunee surrender their remaining lands of 220,000 acres to the Crown in exchange for a reserve of 20,000 acres in order to prevent the dissolution of contiguous Six Nations land. The Haudenosaunee chiefs convinced the Crown that a reserve of 20,000 acres was not large enough to meet their needs, and in 1847 they were allowed to retain 35,000 acres from their original tract. In addition, in 1848, the Six Nations chiefs gave the Mississauga of the New Credit band 6,000 acres in the southeast corner of the reserve.

From this reserve, each male head of a nuclear family was allotted a 100-acre parcel of land with the intention that it be used for farming and agricultural purposes. In this manner the nuclear family became both the residential and economic unit; however, the matrilineal clans and other

Chiefs of the Six Nations explaining their wampum belts, 1871

Source: Six Nations Public Library-Digital Archive, SNPL000088v00i.

lineage affiliations continued in other social spheres. The clan and lineage associations, for example, continued to function in longhouse social organization, but Christian converts tended not to follow the traditional kinship units. Another difficulty was that the traditional matrilineal affiliation of the Haudenosaunee conflicted with the patrilineal basis of Indian administration and legal status in Canada.

Religious Affiliation and Political Factionalism

Many Mohawks and Oneidas who had a close association with the British had adopted Christianity before they migrated to the Grand River valley. Brant and his friends built a Mohawk Chapel in 1786, which housed a prized Queen Anne Bible and Communion Plate. On the other hand, many Tuscarora became Baptists in the 1840s.

These three First Nations became known as the "Upper Tribes" because of their settlement location upriver and were regarded by the Indian administration because of their adoption of Christianity as "progressive" tribes. Other Six Nation members, such as the Cayugas, Onondagas, and Senecas were referred to as the "Lower Tribes" because of their location downriver on the reserve. They adhered to their traditional religious beliefs, and when the Handsome Lake movement began its rapid spread, they gradually began to adopt these religious beliefs as well.

As time went on, the Upper Tribes became more readily influenced by missionary activity, and their children were educated in missionary-sponsored schools. The Anglican Church became the most powerful mission in the Grand River valley. Itinerant Baptist and Methodist clergy were also active in the area, but tended to lack the financial resources of their Anglican counterparts. The Anglican Church built a day school, called the Mohawk Institute, in 1831. This school offered free formal education, along with farming and domestic training for boys and girls. It later became a residential school in the 1840s and was in operation until 1970.

The Longhouse Religion

The so-called Traditionalists on the reserve (the Cayugas, Onondagas, and Senecas) rejected Christianity and remained adherents to the Longhouse religion. The Longhouse religion began in 1799 as an episode of religious fervour among Senecas (Wallace 1969, 1978). Anthony Wallace referred to such religious movements among North American First Nations, such as the Sioux Ghost Dance religion and the Sun Dance among the Utes and Shoshones, as examples of revitalization (Jorgensen 1972; Wallace 1956). Revitalization movements can be defined as "religious-political movements … aimed at restoring cultural values and eradicating political domination by outsiders" (Sidky 2004: 438).

Such movements among North American First Nations are seen as recourse from the oppression of white society and a sense of powerlessness that results from colonial domination. Revitalization movements are also found in other areas of the world, such as in Melanesia where they are known as "messianic" or "millenarian" movements. In these cases, members of the movement seek a return to a past in which they did not experience the disorientating effects of external domination and were able to exercise control over their daily lives.

Usually, such movements propose a code of ethical behaviour that members are encouraged to follow and feature a charismatic leader who is capable of inspiring followers to adopt a new lifestyle. A proposed reversion to traditional cultural values often involves a rejection of the dominating power's way of life, especially its missionary or evangelical influences, which are seen as a source of corruption among Aboriginal peoples.

The Code of Handsome Lake

The Longhouse religion was based on the revelations of the prophet Handsome Lake. The prophet died in 1815, and during his life, Handsome Lake's gospel had spread to various Haudenosaunee settlements in Canada and the United States. The Longhouse religion still exists today as an organized system of codified beliefs and rituals that functions as a non-Christian alternative to the Protestant and Catholic denominations that have been established in many First Nations communities. It also serves as a forum to assert and preserve the integrity of traditional Haudenosaunee ethnic identity in the face of assimilation pressures from the outside world.

The gospel of Handsome Lake was based on several prominent themes, such as the relinquishing of alcohol, ceasing to practice witchcraft, and a returning to traditional ceremonial practices held on an annual basis. Alcohol was seen as a serious problem in First Nations communities, viewed as responsible for marital discord, fighting, and general social disorganization. In a therapeutic sense, the Handsome Lake code served to reduce personal anxiety brought on by social disorder in Haudenosaunee villages.

There was also a political aspect to the prophet's message. For example, Handsome Lake was actively opposed to the further alienation of Indian land. Economic aspects of his message were also prevalent, in that Handsome Lake encouraged Haudenosaunee men to learn to plow fields and farm in the manner of men in white settlements. There was some controversy around this proposal because it tended to conflict with traditional cultural practice, which viewed horticulture as women's work.

Another proposal was that the Haudenosaunee household in the future should centre around the nuclear family, a practice that conflicted with traditional kinship based on maternal clans and lineages. Accordingly, he was also critical of any interference in family matters by the wife's mother, which was a common occurrence and a source of conflict in traditional families following matrilineal kinship principles.

Handsome Lake therefore also had a social gospel, in addition to his religious teachings. Mother-daughter ties, which were essential aspects of traditional Haudenosaunee social structure, were coming into conflict with the new demands of contemporary reservation life. Related aspects of traditional social organization, such as the manner in which genealogies were determined, the determinants of clan membership, the nomination of various titles and forms of chieftainship, and agricultural cycles, were all cultural and social aspects that were criticized by Handsome Lake. The reason for this criticism was that he regarded the special mother-daughter bond at the matrilineal nexus of Haudenosaunee society as incompatible with the stability of the nuclear family (Wallace 1978).

By about 1900, on the Six Nations reserve, about 78 percent of the band residents regarded themselves as Christians, while 22 percent adhered to the Longhouse religion. This ratio remained essentially unchanged up until the 1960s (Weaver 1972: 23). There has not been any overt conflict between the Christian and Longhouse religious systems as "efforts to Christianize the Longhouse adherents have long been abandoned" (ibid.: 24).

Contemporary Patterns

The Six Nations reserve today remains the largest in Canada, with a population of over 22,000 members (Statistics Canada 2008). Many have moved off the reserve, probably for economic reasons. However, since the reserve is situated in the vicinity of large urban centres, employment is accessible within commuting distance, unlike more isolated First Nations communities in northern

Ontario. Work is available locally in the hospital, on the band council, in road construction or in the operation of stores, restaurants, and gas stations.

Outside of the reserve, residents have found employment in the electronics industry, as welders, mechanics, or as assembly line workers in factories in nearby cities. Employment also exists in the stone quarries of nearby Hagersville and Caledonia, high steel construction, and mining. Food-processing factories and farm machinery plants in Brantford are another source of wage employment. Others travel to larger cities in the area, such as Hamilton, for wage work, while others seek employment in automobile manufacturing plants in other areas of southern Ontario.

Women also augment the family income with various part-time and full-time jobs as family commitments permit, depending upon the ages of their children, especially during the fruit- and berry-picking season of the surrounding Niagara fruit belt. Such seasonal harvesting activities also have

Box 4.2: Tom Longboat

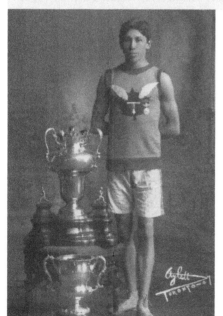

TOM LONGBOAT (1887–1949):
SIX NATIONS ONONDAGA

- Won the Boston Marathon in 1906 in record time
- Won the Olympic Marathon in 1909
- Inducted into the Canadian Sports Hall of Fame in 1955
- The Tom Longboat Award was established in 1951 as a joint effort of the Department of Indian Affairs and the Amateur Athletic Union of Canada

Photo of Tom Longboat, by Charles Aylett, 1907

Source: Library and Archives Canada / C-014090.

the advantage when older children are able to accompany the mother and help with child care.

Summary of Wendat and Haudenosaunee History

Wendat and Haudenosaunee First Nations of southern Ontario had been growing their own food, to some degree or another, for at least a thousand years before the arrival of Europeans. The Wendat, Neutral, and Petun developed sedentary villages based on corn horticulture, supplemented by additional crops of beans, squash, tobacco, and various medicinal plants. They also hunted and fished when time allowed, and engaged in armed conflicts with their linguistic and cultural relatives, the Haudenosaunee League of the Five Nations, to the east in present-day New York state.

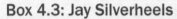

Box 4.3: Jay Silverheels

JAY SILVERHEELS (1912–1980): SIX NATIONS

- Known for his role of Tonto on *The Lone Ranger* television series
- Played in numerous major films such as *Key Largo* with Humphrey Bogart
- Has a star on the Hollywood Walk of Fame
- In 1997 was inducted into the Canadian Lacrosse Hall of Fame

Jay Silverheels as Tonto riding Scout, 1956

Source: Wikimedia Commons

This pattern of inter-tribal feuding apparently was carried on for at least several centuries before the arrival of Europeans. By the early 1600s, the French had formed alliances with the Wendat that included a trade in furs in exchange for goods of European manufacture, a military alliance against the Five Nations, and an arrangement to allow Jesuit missionaries to live in some of the villages. Conversion to Christianity, however, appeared to have been relatively superficial, and the missionaries were tolerated only because of the necessary tie to European trade goods.

The Haudenosaunee had access to European goods, especially firearms

Box 4.4: Charlotte "Edith" Monture

CHARLOTTE "EDITH" MONTURE (1890–1996): SIX NATIONS OF THE GRAND RIVER

- Attended nursing school in New Rochelle, New York, because she was not permitted to train as a nurse in Canada
- Only one of two Aboriginal women to serve overseas as members of the Army Nurse Corps during World War I
- Her recollections of WWI: *"We would walk right over where there had been fighting. It was an awful sight—buildings in rubble, trees burnt, spent shells all over the place, whole towns blown up."*
- She died at Iroquois Lodge, Ohsweken, in her 106th year

Nurse Charlotte Edith Monture

Source: Photo from Veterans Affairs Canada: www.veterans.gc.ca. Used by permission.

that the French were reluctant to trade to their Wendat allies, through Dutch and English traders at Fort Albany on the Hudson River. The Mohawk, probably the most powerful and numerous of the Five Nations, used their position as the easternmost member of the League, and hence the one nearest to European settlements, to take economic advantage by acting as middlemen between the western Haudenosaunee tribes and the traders at Albany. However, several western members of the league, such as the Seneca and Onondaga, were able to use their own geographical position to profit from access to western furs, owing to their proximity to eastern Lake Ontario and the direct St. Lawrence route to the French settlements at Montreal and Quebec City.

All of these various internecine conflicts and alliances eventually culminated in the defeat and dispersal of the Huron Confederacy in 1649–50. The subsequent defeat of the French by the English on the Plains of Abraham in 1759 and the Treaty of Paris of 1763, consolidated the League's position with the English, a position of ascendency among other First Nations of eastern North America.

When the American Revolution broke out, various members of the League could not agree on what course of action should be taken. The Oneidas were sympathetic to the Americans, for example, while the Mohawks were solidly behind the British cause. Eventually each tribe was left to pursue its independent course of action. With the Treaty of Paris of 1783 and the end of hostilities, many Mohawks moved north to settle at the Bay of Quinte, while others under Joseph Brant decided to accept the British offer of land along the Grand River in Ontario, moving to this location in 1784–85. These Mohawks were also joined by a number of Cayugas, some Onondagas, and a few Senecas and Tuscaroras.

Christian influence remained strong among Brant's Mohawks, and as a result, divisions emerged along sectarian lines. On the Grand River reserve, the Council of Hereditary Chiefs formed the local governing body until 1924, when it was subsequently replaced by an electoral system, an event which caused further internal divisions (Fenton and Tooker 1978; Tooker 1978; Weaver 1972).

Suggested Readings

Heidenreich, C. 1971. *Huronia: A History and Geography of the Huron Indians, 1600–1650*. Toronto: McClelland and Stewart.

Labelle, K.M. 2013. *Dispersed but not Destroyed: A History of the Seventeenth-Century Wendat People*. Vancouver: University of British Columbia Press.

Tooker, E. 1964. *An Ethnography of the Huron Indians, 1615–1649*. Bulletin 190. Washington, DC: Smithsonian Institution, Bureau of American Ethnology.

Trigger, B.G. 1969. *The Huron: Farmers of the North*. New York: Holt, Rinehart and Winston.

Trigger, B.G. 1985. *Natives and Newcomers: Canada's "Heroic Age" Reconsidered*. Montreal: McGill-Queen's University Press.

Trigger, B.G. 1987. *The Children of Aataentsic: A History of the Huron People to 1660*. Montreal: McGill-Queen's University Press.

Weaver, S.M. 1972. *Medicine and Politics among the Grand River Iroquois*. Ottawa: National Museums of Canada.

Review Questions

1. Describe how a matrilineal kinship system served to organize Wendat and Haudenosaunee villages.
2. What were the origins of the Longhouse religion? Who was Handsome Lake, and what was his code?
3. What were some of the conflicts between the Haudenosaunee Six Nations political system and the Canadian government?

5 ONTARIO TREATIES AND LAND CLAIMS

Altogether, Ontario is covered by 46 treaties and agreements with the Indigenous inhabitants of the province. These include land purchases by the British Crown prior to Canadian Confederation, as well as those negotiated by the representatives of the Government of Canada, all of which took place historically between 1781 and 1930. This chapter outlines these various treaties, agreements, and purchases, as well as their prominent characteristics and the First Nations involved (see www.ontario.ca/aboriginal/treaties).

The Resettlement of Southern Ontario

The dispersal of the Wendat, Petun, and Neutral by the Haudenosaunee in the 1650s led to a large-scale depopulation of southern Ontario. For the next 50 years, few people were brave enough to venture south of the Lake Nipissing area for fear of Haudenosaunee raiding parties. However, after the early 1700s, the Anishenaabe had gained strength in the Great Lakes region (see Eid 1979: 297–324).

The main reason for this new ascendancy on the part of the Anishenaabe was their pre-eminent role as middlemen in the fur trade, which allowed them to purchase large quantities of firearms and thereby assert their authority against any aggressors. It was after 1700 that the Anishenaabe began a southward expansion out of their settlements in the Georgian Bay area and the southeastern Lake Superior shore region, during which time they began to occupy a large territory between Lakes Huron, Erie, and Ontario.

The advantages that the Anishenaabe enjoyed because of their strategic intermediary position in the fur trade were the result of competition between the French and British to control the flow of beaver pelts. The Anishenaabe were able to successfully play the French against the British in acquiring the best and cheapest trade goods. In turn, the Anishenaabe were being wooed as military allies by both groups such that the "French traded at a loss with the Anishenaabe simply to retain them as military auxiliaries" (Schmalz 1991: x). However, when the English defeated the French in the 1760s, the Ojibwas' position of ascendancy terminated along with the fur-trade rivalry between the two countries.

The Anishenaabe nonetheless remembered how the lack of guns among the Wendat had placed them in a precarious position and was at least a partial reason for their defeat. The French had feared that if the Wendat and their neighbours had secured large quantities of firearms, this could threaten the security of New France.

The Anishenaabe-Haudenosaunee Conflict

With the French defeat, firearms were more readily available through British sources, and the Anishenaabe had every need for an increase in armaments. As Trigger (1987) explains, "With the Huron out of the way, the Seneca could hunt in central Ontario and raid the Algonkian-speaking peoples around the shores of Lake Huron in the same manner that the Mohawk raided the Algonkin, Montagnais, and Abenaki. … The violent attacks that the Iroquois launched against the northern hunting peoples, as soon as the Huron were dispersed, thus was not a mistake, but an integral part of Iroquois strategy. This strategy aimed to provide the Seneca and the other western Iroquois tribes with a northern hinterland in which they could hunt and rob furs" (729).

The threat of Haudenosaunee attacks after the defeat of the Wendat made the Ojibwa realize that they needed to protect themselves in the most effective manner possible. In addition, as Schmalz (1991: 17–19) mentions, the Anishenaabe had several advantages that increased their military capacity, which were not possessed by the Wendat. One of these was that the Anishenaabe were much more mobile than the Wendat, who lived in large, settled villages. The Anishenaabe, as a hunting and gathering society, could move about with greater ease than the Wendat and engage in guerrilla warfare against the Haudenosaunee. The Anishenaabe were elusive targets, as their warriors could live off the land almost indefinitely. With an increase in firearms available through their British connections, the Anishenaabe began to gain military advantages in the shifting power struggle of the Great Lakes region (see Eid 1979).

The Haudenosaunee Expansion into Southern Ontario

The period after the Wendat defeat of 1650 saw a Haudenosaunee expansion into southern Ontario. For the first decades (1650–70), the Haudenosaunee were content to use this area as a hunting ground because of the proliferation of deer and other game that resulted from the dispersal of the previous Wendat population. By the 1680s, the Haudenosaunee began to set up more permanent settlements in southern Ontario in order to trap beaver and establish sites for agricultural production. On the north shore of Lake Ontario, the Haudenosaunee had set up at least a half-dozen villages, and the Anishenaabe were situated just north of the evacuated Wendat territory.

The Five Nations began to assert their dominance over the Anishenaabe in the Georgian Bay area. In 1662, a Haudenosaunee war party attacked an Anishenaabe settlement at Sault Ste. Marie and then proceeded to camp at the mouth of Lake Superior, effectively cutting off Anishenaabe trade to the north. The Anishenaabe pushed back, defeating this Haudenosaunee encampment on Lake Superior and preserving their supply of trade goods with the English. By the 1680s, the Anishenaabe began a period of aggressive offence against the Haudenosaunee, and by the end of the decade the Haudenosaunee had withdrawn from most areas of southern Ontario.

By 1702 the Anishenaabe, which included the Saulteaux from Sault Ste. Marie and the nearby Mississauga, had become established at Toronto and Fort Frontenac, two important trade locations. Soon after, in 1707, the Anishenaabe had established a settlement near Niagara at Chippewa Creek, and by 1720 were firmly ensconced throughout southern Ontario.

Other Anishenaabe settlements were located at such places as St. Clair, Kente, Matchedah, and the head of Lake Ontario by 1736. In 1784, the British purchased land on the Grand River from the Mississaugas, who were apparently only recent arrivals to this area. This land was subsequently transferred to the Haudenosaunee who had become displaced during the American Revolution, thus establishing one of the strange ironies of early Ontario colonial history where, in a sense, the vanquished became the victor.

Early Treaties and Policies

The First Nations of Canada were initially seen as an economic asset to the early Europeans, and as time went on, the Indigenous population also came to be regarded as an important military bulwark against possible American northward expansion. Relationships between Indigenous peoples and the early settlers, however, were posing a problem because of the sale of land to Europeans, often under dubious circumstances.

The British colonial government decided to forestall any further land difficulties between the two groups by enacting the Royal Proclamation of 1763, which became a cornerstone of the so-called protectionist period of colonial policy, stating:

> It is just and reasonable, and essential to our interest, and the security of our colonies, that the several Nations or Tribes of Indians with whom we are connected, and who live under our Protection, should not be molested or disturbed in the Possession of such Parts of our Dominions and Territories as, not having been ceded to or purchased by Us, are reserved to them or any of them as their Hunting Grounds (in Hedican 2008a).

The Royal Proclamation stated furthermore that Indian lands could only be bought or ceded through negotiations with the British Crown, rather than through the previous practice of selling land on an individual basis. This early colonial document is sometimes referred to as the "Indian Bill of Rights" because it is considered the foundation upon which the concept of Aboriginal rights in Canada was built. The reason for this is that the Royal Proclamation recognized that "Indian and Inuit peoples were the original, sovereign inhabitants of this country prior to the arrival of the European colonial powers" (Indian Claims Commission 1975: 6).

Canada's Indian Act of 1876 provided the legal backing for the later treaty period during which reserves were established, and the First Nations people ceded their right to sole ownership of the territories that they had traditionally occupied (Morris 1880). However, a large tract of territory called Rupert's Land, which was the region of the Canadian Shield given to the Hudson's Bay Company under the Royal Charter of 1670, was specifically exempt from the provisions of the Proclamation of 1763.

The influx of settlers into Upper Canada after the Revolutionary War meant that Aboriginal title along the shore of Lake Ontario from Toronto (York) to Kingston (Cataraqui) became an increasingly pressing concern for early colonial administrators. After the defeat of the Wendat, bands of Mississauga began to move south of Sault Ste. Marie into the lands north of Lake Ontario. The first treaty in Ontario was the Treaty of Niagara of 1764, which ceded a four-mile strip of land along the western shore of the Niagara River to the British by 24 signing First Nations. Later, in 1781, a treaty was signed between the Mississauga and the British that alienated a section of land on the Ottawa River, which set the stage for other land cessions in southern Ontario.

The superintendent-general of Indian Affairs at this time, Sir John Johnson, then wrote up a 1787 agreement with the Native leaders, which was signed at the Bay of Quinte. This agreement is sometimes referred to as the "Gunshot Treaty" because the boundary was deemed to be the distance from the shore of Lake Ontario to a location where a gunshot could be heard, although sections of this treaty have gone missing and therefore earlier accounts of certain specifications and boundaries cannot be verified today with any degree of confidence. However, small tracts of land were subsequently ceded on the Etobicoke River in 1805 and along the shore of Burlington Bay in 1806.

The Haldimand Grant to the Six Nations (1784)

The largest transfer of land during the early period of colonial rule in Ontario was known as the Haldimand Grant, named after Sir Frederick Haldimand, who was a governor of Canada (1778–86). The grant of land was made on 25 October 1784, to the Six Nations Haudenosaunee (Iroquois), which comprised the Seneca, Onondaga, Cayuga, Oneida, Mohawk, and Tuscarora, encompassing six miles on either side of the Grand River from its source to its mouth on Lake Erie:

> I do hereby in his Majesty's name authorize and permit the said Mohawk nation, and such other of the Six Nations Indians as wish to settle in the Quarter to take possession of, and Settle upon the Banks of the River commonly called Ours (Ourse) or Grand River, running into Lake Erie, allotting to them for that Purpose Six Miles deep from each Side of the River beginning at Lake Erie, and extending in the Proportion to the Head of said River, which them and their Posterity are to enjoy forever. (Johnston 1964: 50–51; Patterson 1972: 83)

The leader of the Six Nations, Joseph Brant, led nearly 2,000 of his followers onto the Grand River territory soon after this declaration. Several problems were to emerge in the near future, probably the most important of which was that the grant had not been adequately surveyed, leading to general confusion as to the extent of the boundaries involved. For example, nobody seemed to know exactly where the "Head of said River" was actually located. An additional problem was that Brant began to sell off sections of this territory soon after it was settled upon, causing consternation among colonial administrators, who began to wonder how much of the grant would be left for posterity (see Paxton 2010; Kelsay 1984).

Who Owned the Haldimand Tract?

There was also a legal issue involved about which party, the British colonial administration or Joseph Brant and his followers, actually owned the property in the Haldimand Tract. Brant claimed that the Six Nations people were the owners of the property in fee simple (ownership of land without limitations or encumbrances as to use). The colonial government had a different opinion, as Lieutenant-Governor Simcoe opposed any sale of land from the grant, suggesting that if the sales continued, there would be little property left for future generations of Six Nations people.

The colonial government treaded lightly over this issue for fear of alienating the Six Nations people. There was still concern that war could erupt with the Americans at just about any time, and so the Six Nations warriors were seen as a bulwark against expansionist plans from the south. In addition, an antagonized Six Nations population could possibly attack the fledgling British settlement at York (now Toronto) on Lake Ontario, which would forestall future development of Upper Canada.

Ultimately, the British colonial government withdrew their opposition to the land sales. In any event, the land speculators who had bought the Six Nations property had difficulty selling the lots so that by 1801, all of the new purchasers had fallen into arrears of their payments for land. Of the original 570,000 acres that had been bequeathed to the Six Nations, nearly 380,000 acres had been sold, representing two-thirds of the initial land grant and a potential huge monetary loss if the speculated land failed to sell. A further complication was that large numbers of white settlers began to illegally occupy Six Nations lands along the Grand River with little recourse by the colonial authorities as to how these squatters might be removed.

Box 5.1: Roberta Jamieson

ROBERTA JAMIESON (b. 1953): SIX NATIONS MOHAWK

- The first Aboriginal woman ever to earn a law degree in Canada (1976)
- The first non-Parliamentarian to be appointed an *ex officio* member of a House of Commons Committee, the Special Task Force on Indian Self-Government
- Ontario's provincial Ombudsman (1989–99), the first woman to be appointed to this position
- First woman elected Chief of the Six Nations of the Grand River (2001); President and CEO of Indspire (2004); Officer of the Order of Canada (2016)

Roberta Jamieson

Source: Photo used by permission of Indspire.

"New Arrangements" Implemented

These sorts of issues dragged on for decades. In 1841, the Indian Affairs Office of the colonial government claimed that it had the right to administer the Six Nations land. The Indian Affairs Office even sold Six Nations land, claiming that the proceeds would be held in trust. Six Nations leaders protested the sales, arguing that they only agreed to lease the land, not sell it outright.

As it turned out, some of this land had been allocated by the colonial government for the purpose of building a road through the wilderness, which eventually became Highway 6. The lieutenant-governor of Upper Canada, Sir Francis Bond Head, approved the sale of this disputed land, claiming that such a move was necessary so as not to "impede progress" of the colony and to "protect" the Aboriginal nations.

Bond Head delivered a speech at Manitoulin Island to a gathering of Anishenaabe and Odawa leaders in August of 1836, upon the signing of a treaty by which these Algonquian First Nations alienated their traditional territory. He addressed the issue of white encroachment, stating:

> As an unavoidable increase in white population as well as the progress of cultivation have had the natural effect of impoverishing your hunting grounds it has become necessary that new arrangements should be entered into for the purpose of protecting you from encroachment of the whites. (Patterson 1972: 86)

It was never made entirely clear what these "new arrangements" would entail and the manner in which they would affect the Aboriginal inhabitants at this time.

The Huron Tract Treaty (1827)

An important early treaty of Ontario was the Huron Tract (or Amherstburg) Treaty of 1827. According to this treaty, more than 2 million acres of land (2,748,000 acres, to be precise) were ceded to the British Crown by the Chippewa (or Anishenaabe) of southern Ontario; it is known officially as Treaty No. 29 (Canada 1891 [1971]: 62–69). Initially the British Indian

Department treated the Chippewas as one large band that had a shared interest in four reserves, namely, Walpole Island, Sarnia, Kettle Point, and Stony Point. In later years, between 1860 and the 1880s, these various bands began to separate from one another (Surtees 1969, 1982).

An annuity of 642 pounds, 10 shillings, was to be paid for the land ceded to the Crown, to be divided accordingly to the various band members. The land involved was of an immense size, as it covered much of southern Ontario, from the town of Nepean near the Ottawa River, to the Grand River and the township of London, to the rapids at the St. Clair River, and to the shore of Lake Huron.

The initial territory designated for reserves was fairly substantial by today's standards, but probably not so in contemporary times because the area had few inhabitants and was needed for subsistence hunting and fishing. For example, the reserve territory comprised four square miles below the rapids of the St. Clair River; two square miles at the River aux Sable, which empties into Lake Huron; and two miles at Kettle Point, Lake Huron, containing about 23,054 acres for the 4,400 individuals of the Chippewa Nation.

For the Kettle Point First Nation, further land surrenders followed in 1912 when beachfront property was ceded, which band members claim was done under duress by the local Indian agent of the Department of Indian Affairs. Similarly, a portion of the Stony Point Reserve was surrendered in 1928, under the rationale that this land could not be used for agricultural purposes and therefore was of little use to the band.

Ipperwash Provincial Park

Eventually, in 1936, Ipperwash Provincial Park was created from the preceding surrendered land. At the time, both the members of the Kettle and Stony Point First Nations indicated that the park property contained burial sites and that these should be protected. In 1950, the park superintendent's wife photographed human remains in the park. The discovery was subsequently reported to authorities in the Ontario government, although no action was ever taken to protect the burials (Hedican 2013: 155–61).

A Ministry of Natural Resources memo from 1972 claimed that there was no evidence of a burial mound, although a later memo cautioned that the methodology of the investigation "does not agree with current archaeological survey standards." The Ipperwash Report (Linden 2007: 59) notes that many government letters from the 1930s made mention of First Nations graves on the park property, in addition to the park superintendent's wife's discovery of the human bones in the 1950s.

World War II brought further erosions of land belonging to the Kettle Point and Stony Point First Nations. The Department of National Defence decided that an army cadet training base should be established on reserve property. Accordingly, on 14 April 1942, 2,240 acres of Stony Point First Nation property was appropriated under the War Measures Act. Residents of the Stony Point reserve who were living on the land appropriated by the Defence Department were relocated to the Kettle Point Reserve, and some houses were bulldozed while others were removed using skids pulled by tractors or moved on flatbed trucks.

Box 5.2: Francis Pegahmagabow

FRANCIS PEGAHMAGABOW (1891–1952): SHAWANAGA

- The most highly decorated for bravery First Nations soldier in Canadian military history
- Three times awarded the Military Medal and seriously wounded
- Expert marksman and scout, credited with killing 378 Germans and capturing 300 more
- Was an activist and leader in several First Nations organizations, including serving as chief for the Wasauksing First Nation near Parry Sound

Francis Pegahmagabow in 1945

The Relocation of Stony Point Residents

There were many social and economic problems that resulted from the relocation of Stony Point residents to the Kettle Point Reserve. The main problem was that the Kettle Point Reserve was not large enough to house the new community members, lacked jobs for the new residents, and did not have the housing to accommodate the displaced Stony Point band members.

Stony Point soldiers returning home after the war found that some of their houses had been demolished, effectively rendering them homeless as a reward for serving their country. All of these difficulties acted as a further basis of contention and strife between members of the two communities who had previously lived in amicable proximity to one another.

Residents of both reserves were promised that this new living situation would be short-term, and that after the war, the appropriated land would be returned. The promise stated, in fact, that "if, at the termination of the war, no further use of the area is required by the Department of National Defence negotiations will be entered into with the Department of Indian Affairs to transfer the lands back to the Indians at a reasonable price determined by mutual agreement." Nonetheless, the Department of National Defence insisted that it had a continuing need for the land in question for military training. An occupation of Camp Ipperwash in May 1993 by the residents of the Stony Point Reserve resulted in a subsequent move of the cadet camp to facilities at CFB Borden.

During another protest over land that the Stony Point residents claimed was inappropriately removed from their control, on 6 September 1995, Aboriginal protester Dudley George was shot and killed by an OPP officer. It took until November 2003 for an inquiry to be initiated under Commissioner Sidney Linden, with a final report released by the Government of Ontario in May 2007. Finally, on 28 May 2009, control of Ipperwash Provincial Park was signed over to the Stony and Kettle Point First Nations (*London Free Press*, 2009; Hedican 2008b, 2013).

The Robinson-Huron and Robinson-Superior Treaties (1850)

Until the end of the 1840s, Upper Canada experienced an increasingly large influx of settlers seeking agricultural land. This population expansion extended up to the Bruce Peninsula, north of which the climate was deemed unreliable for crop production. However, plans were nonetheless underway for settlement of the more northerly sections of the province, not so much for agricultural reasons but because of the vast mineral resources that were presumed to exist north of Lakes Huron and Superior.

By the early 1800s, prospectors had already begun to explore the mineral-rich Canadian Shield country in the Lake Superior region of northern Ontario. However, Aboriginal peoples objected to this intrusion into their territory, which had not been ceded to the British Crown, and in one instance, violence erupted at a mining site near Sault Ste. Marie in the 1840s. This incident probably did as much as anything to precipitate the treaties of the 1850s.

Box 5.3: Elsie Knott

ELSIE KNOTT (1922–1995): CURVE LAKE

- The first woman in Canada to be elected as a chief of a First Nation, serving from 1954–76
- Was elected Chief of the Curve Lake First Nation in 1954, just three years after amendments to the Indian Act gave Native women the right to vote in band elections
- Served as an Elder with the Union of Ontario Indians
- In 1999, she posthumously received a Lifetime Achievement Award, given by the Union of Ontario Indians to recognize her service to her community and to her nation

Elsie Knott

Source: The Aboriginal Multi-Media Society (AMMSA): www.ammsa.com/content/elsie-knott-footprints. Used by permission.

During the course of planning for the northern areas of Ontario, a more comprehensive approach was adopted for treaty negotiations, contrary to the piecemeal negotiations that had characterized earlier efforts. The Robinson-Superior and Robinson-Huron Treaties of 1850 involved an extensive tract of land, larger than the previous treaties combined.

The area over which Aboriginal title was ceded by these treaties extended from the north shores of Lakes Huron and Superior up to the height of land and the territory of Rupert's Land. The Hudson's Bay Company held monopoly trading and administrative rights to that territory by virtue of a royal charter. The Robinson Treaties provided for annual payments or annuities, for hunting and fishing on unoccupied Crown lands, and for the establishment of reserves for the settlement of Aboriginal peoples. Thus, the Robinson Treaties established a basic formula that would later act as a guide for additional treaties.

The Numbered Treaties

The British North America Act, now known as the Constitution Act of 1867, conferred on the federal government the responsibility for "Indians, and Lands reserved for Indians." In other words, the First Nations peoples became wards of the Canadian federal government. At this time they were not regarded as Canadian citizens, a legal status they did not gain until the 1960s, but were placed under separate legislation (the Indian Act of 1876), which positioned them in a different legal category. Thus, it is fair to say that the post-Confederation period was one in which the First Nations peoples became increasingly marginalized in the Canadian political system, and subsequent treaties tended to solidify this situation of isolation and neglect. For the vast territories that were surrendered by the First Nations peoples, the Canadian government gave little in the way of compensation.

The Province of Ontario was created in 1867 when it entered Confederation. At this time, the northernmost boundary of the province extended to the height of land, or the northern boundary of the Robinson-Superior Treaty. In 1870, the Hudson's Bay Company relinquished its monopoly rights in the region, for which it was financially compensated. The first of the so-called Numbered Treaties were negotiated in 1871 with the signing of Treaties Nos. 1 and 2, which mainly involved the southern portion of Manitoba and territory to the north and west of this province. The lands between Manitoba and Lake Superior were ceded with the signing of Treaty No. 3, focusing on the Lake of the Woods or Kenora District; this treaty is also known as the North-West Angle Treaty. A further "adhesion" was also negotiated in this interprovincial area in 1929–30, thus effectively ending the treaty process in the province, except for specific claims that emerged in later decades.

The Numbered Treaties had more specific provisions than those that were included in the Robinson Treaties. Reserve lands, for example, became more standardized, based on the granting of 160 acres per family. Schools were to be established on every reserve, and an annuity of $3 per person was granted, subject to future increases when warranted. Treaty No. 3 departed from the previous treaties by allowing a reserve allotment of 640 acres per family of five (Frideres and Gadacz 2008: 194–95).

In 1889, Ontario's northern boundary was revised, extending the province to the Albany River. Treaty No. 9 was signed in 1905 with the northern Anishenaabe and Cree, which further stretched the northern boundary of

The Indian Chiefs Medal, presented to commemorate Treaties Nos. 3, 4, 5, 6, and 7, bearing the image of Queen Victoria

Source: Library and Archives Canada, account number 1986-79-1638.

the province to Hudson Bay and James Bay. This new territory added to the province thereby allowed for the construction of the Canadian National Railway north of Lake Nipigon in 1911.

Finally, in 1923, the Williams Treaties were signed, whereby the Anishenaabe and Mississauga of southeastern Ontario between Georgian Bay and the Quebec border were compensated for the surrender of their hunting and fishing rights. The Williams Treaties were the last treaties negotiated in Ontario, except for the previously mentioned small plots of land that were subsequently added to Treaty No. 3 in northwestern Ontario in 1929–30.

Dick King, Potawatomi, on the Parry Island Reserve, holding a war club and dance rattle, 1928

Source: Photo by Frederick Johnson, Smithsonian Institution

In summary, Ontario provides an example of an extended period, from 1784 to 1923, during which treaties were negotiated with the First Nations inhabitants of this province. The Royal Proclamation of 1763 provided the initial foundation for the treaty process, establishing that the British Crown, and then the later Government of Canada, had the sole responsibility for extinguishing Aboriginal title to the lands possessed by First Nations people (Poelzer and Coates 2015: 52, 81).

As time passed after the negotiation of the initial treaties, a pattern was established whereby certain Aboriginal rights to hunting, fishing, and trapping on Crown lands were recognized; reserves were allotted on the basis of either 160 or 640 acres per family depending upon circumstances; and the payment of annuities at "treaty time" were instituted.

As one might expect, however, the treaty process was an ongoing series of negotiations that had certain inherent difficulties associated with it, leading at various times to legal contestations. These legal challenges to the treaties often involved differences of opinions between Aboriginal negotiators and government officials over what was promised in the treaties, and at other times the issues involved Aboriginal groups who claimed that their members had been unjustly left out of the treaty process.

The St. Catharines Milling Case (1888)

It did not take long after various treaties were signed in Ontario for disputes to arise over the nature of Aboriginal title. The most significant early case concerning Aboriginal rights was adjudicated in 1888 by the Judicial Committee of the Privy Council, the highest court in the British Empire. In *St. Catharines Milling and Lumber Company v. the Queen*, an important ruling was made regarding Aboriginal title. In this case, the ruling stipulated that Aboriginal title involved a "right to possess" or what could be regarded as a "usufructory right"—in other words, a right to use and occupy (Morse 1985: 96–99, 127–36).

This case had important implications for the future interpretation of Aboriginal rights. Aboriginal title in this case was considered to be dependent upon the goodwill of the sovereign and not on any inherent rights developed from treaties, Aboriginal concepts of land use, or other related matters. In the St. Catharines Milling case, the dispute was essentially between the federal government and the Province of Ontario over timber licences pertaining to lands in Ontario. The federal government's argument was that it had acquired title to the lands in question from First Nations peoples.

Eventually, the Judicial Committee of the Privy Council ruled in Ontario's favour, on the basis of its opinion that Aboriginal peoples could not be regarded as actually "owning" their land. It was argued that Indigenous concepts of "ownership" differed from prevailing European perceptions of proprietorship, and as such, clear title could not be conveyed from Aboriginal peoples to the federal government via the various treaties in Ontario. This decision indicated, therefore, that any interest that Aboriginal peoples had in their land prior to the treaties was extinguished at that time, and the beneficial interest in these lands was transferred immediately to the province upon signing. It would take many years before this issue of Aboriginal title would again be considered by the Canadian courts.

Box 5.4: Daphne Odjig

DAPHNE ODJIG (1919–2016): WIKWEMIKONG

- An artist whose work fuses together elements of Aboriginal pictographs and First Nations arts
- A founding member of the Professional Native Indian Artist Association in 1973, along with Norval Morriseau
- Member of the Order of Canada (1986); elected to the Royal Canadian Academy of Arts (1989)

Daphne Odjig

Source: Misterlobat, 21 October 2008 / Wikimedia Commons.

The Nature of Aboriginal Claims

Aboriginal claims, generally speaking, tend to fall into two categories: specific claims and comprehensive claims. Specific claims arise from problems with treaty implementation, whereas comprehensive claims arise in cases where no treaties were signed. There are instances, for example, in which Aboriginal peoples claim that specific treaty terms were not fulfilled. The negotiations for Treaty No. 3 and Treaty No. 9 in northern Ontario were remembered by the Aboriginal persons in attendance in oral accounts that differ in certain regards from the accounts that were eventually written down in the official records (Macklem 1997).

Treaty No. 3, which covers an extensive area in northwestern Ontario near the Manitoba border, is an important and historically significant case in this regard because of the differences of opinion regarding the written texts and the oral accounts. In this case, the Aboriginal peoples actually have their own written accounts, called the Paypom Document. This document comprises transcripts of the treaty negotiations that were kept for Chief Powasson during ongoing discussions, and include most importantly the promises that were apparently made to the First Nations signatories to the treaty in 1873. The Paypom Document demonstrates that the differences are not merely instances of written versus oral accounts, but concrete differences in the written records of both Aboriginal and government negotiators.

The Paypom Document

The Paypom Document consists of 18 points with the names August Nolin and Joseph Nolin written in the bottom portion of the text. It emerged under peculiar circumstances, as explained by Paypom, the First Nations elder who obtained the document:

> Linde was a photographer and a friend to the Indian people. One day, about 40 or 50 years ago, he told me he had a paper and the Government wanted to buy it from him. He said that they would give him $5,000 for it. But he wanted me to have it, "for your children," he said. That winter I saved all the money from my trapline. … I saved my money and in the spring I gave it to Linde. He moved south, but he sent me a parcel in the mail. He sent it like a parcel

of clothes so nobody would suspect it was the treaty [i.e., the document they had talked about].

The notation below appears in pencil on the back of the original:

This copy was given to me in 1906 by chief Powasson at Bukety—the Northwest Angle—Lake of the Woods.
(Signed)
C.C. Linde

(Grand Council Treaty #3, www.gct3.ca/about/history/paypom-treaty)

Disputes, such as those arising from Treaty No. 3, have emerged over not so much matters of interpretation but over the apparent neglect to include certain items discussed orally at the time of the treaty negotiations and their eventual absence from the written record. In fact, the Indian Claims Commission recognized these difficulties when it noted that

Treaty Indians have a number of claims that relate to the agreements for the cession of their lands through treaty. Some of these [claims] rest on an insistence that specific treaty terms have not been fulfilled, and that the broader spirit of the treaties has not been assumed by the government. A frequent claim is that verbal promises made at the time of negotiations were not included in the written texts. In some areas, Indian people also emphasize in their treaty claims that these transactions constituted inadequate settlements, even if all their terms were fulfilled. These claims involve assertions about the way in which treaties were negotiated, the disparities between the two contracting parties and the alleged unfairness of the terms. (1975: 5)

The James Bay Treaty (Treaty No. 9)

The territory covered by Treaty No. 9, also known as the James Bay Treaty, extends north of the area of the Robinson-Superior Treaty of 1850, to Hudson Bay and James Bay in the north, the Quebec boundary in the east, and the boundary of Treaty No. 3 in the west. Essentially then, this is the area formerly within the boundaries of Rupert's Land, which was controlled by the Hudson's Bay Company and transferred to the Dominion of Canada in 1870. Therefore, for some 35 years this large mass of land represented an ambiguous matter as far as Aboriginal rights were concerned, since it was not part of the Province of Ontario but was technically owned by Canada, yet was under the sole influence of HBC for practical purposes (Long 2010).

As far as the Aboriginal peoples of this area were concerned, they wished for some clarification as to which of these parties had sole jurisdiction over their hunting and trapping territories. Further ambiguities revolved around issues pertaining to natural resource development and exploitation and what access third parties might have, such as non-Aboriginal trappers who were moving northward into this territory (Long 1989: 19–54, 2006: 1–29).

There were discussions concerning the possibility of a law forbidding trapping by non-Aboriginal people. By the advent of the 20th century,

Fort Hope (Eabametoong) members at Lansdowne House, 13 July 1930. Councillors Mishell and Moonias are on the right.

Source: Canada, Department of Indian Affairs and Northern Development / Library and Archives Canada / C-068927.

Aboriginal peoples were petitioning the federal government for clarification of their concerns (see Abel 2006: 46–47, 278–84). Some Aboriginal people were in favour of negotiating a treaty with the Crown, while others were not so inclined. HBC officials attempted to articulate the nature of these disparate views in 1902:

> Whatever is done in the matter by the Department the sooner the better. The Osnaburgh Indians are anxious for it. There may be some little difficulty with the Fort Hope Indians now but it may not be insurmountable. They were alright last year. Unless they have changed their minds the Indians as far as the Attawapiskat River northward from the Albany were inclined to accept it. The R[oman] C[atholic] Attawapiskat Indians are led by Kachang who is not anxious for government control. (quoted in Macklem 1997: 101–2)

In the context of the concerns mentioned above by the Indian Claims

---

Box 5.5: Obediah (Johnny) Yesno

OBEDIAH (JOHNNY) YESNO (1938–2010): EABAMETOONG

- Starred in Walt Disney movie *The King of the Grizzlies*
- Won acting award at Monte Carlo Film Festival for role in *Wojeck*
- Member of the Order of Canada (1976)
- Director of the Chiefs of Ontario and met with Queen Elizabeth II

Actor Johnny Yesno

Source: *The Sault Star*, 26 March 2010.

Commission, the signing of Treaty No. 9 further illustrates the difficulties of concretely establishing the nature of Aboriginal rights. The negotiations and various meetings pertaining to Treaty No. 9 took place between 1905 and 1906. Representing the federal government was Commissioner Duncan Campbell Scott, and Commissioner David Martin represented the Province of Ontario. The various Cree and Ojibwa bands were represented by leaders from a variety of locations, such as Osnaburgh House (Mishkeegogamang), Fort Hope (Eabametoong), Moose Factory, and Long Lake.

The territory in question involved some 130,000 square miles, over which the Aboriginal people would agree to surrender certain rights, but retain rights to hunting, trapping, and fishing on Crown land under certain

Chief Robert Fiddler of the Deer and Sandy Lake Bands at the time of Treaty No. 5, 9 June 1930

Source: Indian and Northern Affairs Canada / Wikimedia Commons.

conditions, and relocate to various reserves covering a total of 524 square miles. In 1929–30, various alterations or adhesions were subsequently made to the original territory, which added a further 128,000 square miles when Ontario's western boundary was extended to its present position (Macklem 1997; Calverley 2006; Long 2006, 2010; Asch 2014: 109–10).

Interpreting Treaty Provisions

A central issue during the negotiation process pertained to the nature of the agreements—what was discussed, by whom, and when? "An examination of the nature, scope, and status of Treaty 9," Macklem (1997) explains, "raises complex questions regarding the relationship between oral and written understandings of the treaty's term" (98). Furthermore, the

Box 5.6: James Bartleman

JAMES BARTLEMAN (b. 1939): CHIPPEWAS OF MNJIKANING

- Distinguished 35-year career in Canada's Department of Foreign Affairs, including Director of Security and Intelligence (1967–2002)
- National Aboriginal Achievement Award for public service (1999)
- Lieutenant-Governor of Ontario (2002–7)
- Chancellor of the Ontario College of Art (2007–12)
- Officer of the Order of Canada (2011)

James Bartleman

Source: Photo by Bert Crowfoot. Used by permission of the Aboriginal Multi-Media Society (AMMSA). Retrieved from www.ammsa.com/sites/default/files/html-pages/old-site/achieve/AA99-J.Bartleman.html.

treaty also "raises more general questions concerning the constitutional status of treaty rights and the extent to which treaty rights trump governmental and third party activity" (ibid.). The problem is that when there are discrepancies between the oral accounts of treaty negotiations and their written counterparts, it is often an unspoken rule that the printed account takes precedence over the verbal one. As far as Aboriginal peoples themselves are concerned, oral traditions should bear as much credence as the government's written versions.

With regards to the various aspects of Treaty No. 9, a central point of contention involves the Aboriginal peoples' "right to pursue their usual vocations of hunting, trapping, and fishing throughout the tract surrendered" (Macklem 1997: 109). Aboriginal people's abilities to pursue their traditional subsistence activities under the stipulations of Treaty No. 9 have come with two qualifications or provisos.

The first of these is that Aboriginal hunting, fishing, and trapping is constrained by the various government regulations and laws, such as restriction on hunting or fishing certain species considered threatened or endangered or restrictions on seasonal taking of species during particular time periods. A second restriction on traditional subsistence is that these activities cannot take place in areas "as may be required or taken up for settlement, mining, lumbering or other purposes" (ibid.).

A century ago, these sorts of restrictions may have appeared to be of little concern, especially since there were very few Europeans venturing into northern Ontario, except for missionaries or fur traders. However, this is not the case today, when the pulp and paper industry has virtually denuded the northern forests, and there have been large-scale mining activities conducted in the Ring of Fire for several decades now.

The point here is that there is an apparent contradiction in the treaty process when the Aboriginal signatories agreed to "cede, release, surrender and yield up ... rights, titles and privileges whatsoever" (ibid.) on the one hand, yet are also granted the right to hunt, fish, and trap on their ancestral lands on the other. The nature of these various "rights" have been left in an ambiguous state. There have never been any clarifications as to the characteristics of these rights or the legal basis under which they might be exercised. One might conclude, then, that as far as Treaty No. 9 is concerned, the nature of Aboriginal rights is fraught with the difficulties of multiple interpretations and legal uncertainties.

Conclusion

The first and foremost aspect of the treaties that have been negotiated in Ontario is that Canadian law acknowledges the rights and interests of the First Nations peoples based on the recognition that they were the original occupants of the land. In other words, the treaties of Ontario formalize the relationship between the Crown and First Nations based on principles of mutual respect and trust.

Treaties are not just dusty documents from the past, as some might erroneously think, but are living legal entities that obligate the Crown and the various provincial governments to fulfill the stipulations laid out in the treaties in return for a relinquishing of control over the territories occupied by First Nations. (For further details, refer to the Ontario Ministry of Indigenous Relations and Reconciliation, www.ontario.ca/aboriginal/treaties.)

In this sense, the treaties are legally binding agreements that set out the rights, responsibilities, and relationships of First Nations and the federal and provincial governments. Ontario is covered by 46 treaties and other agreements, such as land purchases by the Crown. The agreements were signed between 1781 and 1930, a period of 150 years. Originally "the Crown" referred to the British Crown, the reigning monarch such as Queen Victoria, but today it refers to the federal and provincial governments.

It is important to note also that each treaty is unique and represents a specific relationship between individual First Nations and the Crown. While each treaty has its own specific characteristics, in general terms the elements of Ontario treaties usually include payments of goods and cash, often in the form of annuities paid on the "Treaty Day," which commemorates the original signing of a treaty and at which time annuity payments are made.

Other aspects would probably include cession of First Nations title to certain lands and the creation of reserves, and protection of fishing, hunting, and trapping rights. In some treaties, stipulations are also made for the establishment of schools and the provision of clothing and farming equipment. In summary, as the Ontario government states on the Ministry of Aboriginal Affairs website, "Treaties are foundational legal documents in the relationship between First Nations and the Crown. Even though many of the treaties were signed over a century ago, they remain as relevant today as on the day they were signed."

Suggested Readings

Asch, M. 2014. *On Being Here to Stay: Treaties and Aboriginal Rights in Canada.* Toronto: University of Toronto Press.

Hedican, E.J. 2013. *Ipperwash: The Tragic Failure of Canada's Aboriginal Policy.* Toronto: University of Toronto Press.

Linden, S.B. 2007. *Ipperwash Inquiry.* Toronto: Publications Ontario. www.ipperwashinquiry.ca.

Long, J.S. 2006. "How the Commissioners Explained Treaty Number 9 to the Ojibway and Cree in 1905." *Ontario History* 98 (1): 1–29.

Long, J.S. 2010. *Treaty No. 9: Making the Agreement to Share the Land in Far Northern Ontario in 1905.* Montreal: McGill-Queen's University Press.

Poelzer, G., and K.S. Coates. 2015. *From Treaty Peoples to Treaty Nation.* Vancouver: University of British Columbia Press.

Review Questions

1. Using the example of specific treaties, describe the nature of Aboriginal rights in Ontario.
2. Why did the Ipperwash protest lead to the death of Dudley George?
3. What does it mean that treaties in Ontario should be regarded as "living documents"?

6 SOCIAL MOVEMENTS AND CURRENT EVENTS

The purpose of this chapter is to discuss some of the prominent contemporary issues involving the First Nations people of Ontario. There are far too many issues currently happening to discuss them all, but nonetheless the present discussion is meant to provide an overview of several of the more significant ones. These fall into many categories, such as land claims, resource and economic development issues, the Indian status problem, and the reconciliation process involving residential schools. Many of these current movements and issues have lately been the topic of television, radio, and print media coverage.

There are many significant situations, movements, or events that are occurring across Canada that have important implications or impacts on the First Nations of Ontario. Accordingly, this chapter has been divided into two broad sections. The first of these discussions concerns Canada-wide movements; more Ontario-specific occurrences follow in the second section.

Canada-Wide Movements and Events

The Royal Commission on Aboriginal Peoples

The concept of Aboriginal rights in Canada was explored extensively in the Report of the Royal Commission on Aboriginal Peoples, which was released on 21 November 1996. RCAP, as it is commonly referred to, was co-chaired by George Erasmus, the former national chief of the Assembly of First Nations (1976–83), and the Honourable Rene Dussault, a former Quebec deputy minister of justice (1977–80). Altogether, the Commission published four special reports, concerning land claims, justice, suicide, and relocation of the Inuit, along with two commentaries on self-government. Reputed to be the most expensive federal inquiry in Canadian history, costing nearly $60 million, the report of the Commission comprised 5 volumes and heard over 3,500 witnesses.

To set RCAP in historical context, it was founded on a survey of First Nations communities commonly referred to as the Hawthorn-Tremblay Report (Hawthorn 1966/67). The result of this survey was a wide array of

Box 6.1: Marlene Brant Castellano

MARLENE BRANT CASTELLANO (b. 1935): MOHAWKS OF THE BAY OF QUINTE

- First Aboriginal Full Professor in a Canadian university (Trent University, 1973)
- Chairperson of the Department of Native Studies at Trent University (1978–80)
- Co-Director of Research for the Royal Commission on Aboriginal Peoples (1992–96)
- National Aboriginal Achievement Award in Education (1996); Order of Ontario (1995)
- Officer of the Order of Canada (2005)

Marlene Castellano

Source: Photo used by permission of Marlene Castellano.

recommendations centring on the educational, social, and political conditions of Aboriginal communities in Canada, the most famous of which has been referred to as "citizens plus," meaning that "Indians should be regarded as 'citizens plus'; in addition to the normal rights and duties of citizenship, Indians possess certain additional rights as charter members of the Canadian Community" (p. 13).

RCAP put forward more than 400 recommendations, such as the suggestion that Parliament issue a royal proclamation admitting to past mistakes on the part of the Canadian government. It also called for the establishment of an Aboriginal parliament, to be called the "House of First Peoples," which would represent Aboriginal peoples from across the country and function as an advisory body to the federal government. This recommendation envisaged that the many reserves across Canada, numbering about 2,000, would come together as some 30 to 50 Aboriginal Nations. The suggestion was that these Aboriginal Nations would function somewhat along the same lines as provincial governments.

In the opinion of one commentator, "The *Report* provides the most thorough Aboriginal constitutional vision to have appeared since the defeat of the 1969 White Paper. Although we do not know the inner workings of the Commission, we may reasonably assume that the *Report* reflects an Aboriginal perspective, as four of the seven commissioners including the co-chair were Aboriginal" (Cairns 2000: 116). In all, despite the time and expense of the Commission, the federal government did not seem enthusiastic about the Commission's recommendations. Members of Aboriginal First Nations were no doubt disappointed that Prime Minister Harper declined an offer to attend an all-chiefs conference to discuss the implications of the Report. This failure to invoke a response from governments, or even to stimulate any sort of public discussion on the plight of Canada's First Nations, has been described as "disturbing and astonishing" (Cairns 2000: 5).

Idle No More

Idle No More is a grassroots protest movement started in November 2012, comprising Aboriginal people and their non-Aboriginal supporters. The name "Idle No More" is derived from the railway station in Saskatoon where a teach-in was conducted in response to the Harper government's introduction of Bill C-45. This movement has been described as the most powerful demonstration of Aboriginal identity in Canadian history. Thousands of Aboriginal people and their supporters took to the streets, shopping malls, and other venues, drumming, dancing, and singing in a collective voice (Coates 2015).

Bill C-45 is referred to as an "omnibus bill" because it comprises many bills together. The idea is that it is more efficient for the government to attempt to pass one large bill composed of many smaller ones than debating each bill individually. The resulting protest against this bill included "round" dances in public places, the blockade of rail lines, and the celebrated hunger strike by Attawapiskat Chief Theresa Spence, all of which was coordinated via social media and the Idle No More website (www.idlenomore.ca).

Among the various aspects of this omnibus bill that were of concern to Aboriginal people and environmental activists was the apparent removal of protections for forests and waterways and, in particular, the removal of the term *absolute surrender* in Section 208 of Bill C-45. Bill C-45, in particular, was intended to recast the Navigable Waters Protection Act (NWPA) of 1882 and change the name to the Navigation Protection Act (NPA). Under the new NPA, the previous stipulation of a necessary consultation process involving any kind of constructions on navigable waterways was removed, leaving a vast list of deregulated waterways, many of which passed through the lands of Aboriginal peoples.

As far as First Nations people were concerned, this process of deregulating waterways was a direct challenge to their treaty rights. In addition, the new NPA would appear to allow for the construction of pipelines in territory previously protected from such developments. The bill was therefore seen by Aboriginal peoples and environmental groups as a threat to the preservation of northern wilderness areas. Many Aboriginal people also felt slighted by the Bill C-45 initiative because they had not been consulted about the legal changes taking place, leading to the assumption that negotiating with the federal government was a waste of time and new tactics were needed.

Idle No More Tactics

One of the more significant tactics of Idle No More supporters was to engage in a concerted media campaign against the omnibus bill. As an example, the official Idle No More website issued a press release on 10 January 2013, indicating the following:

The Conservative government bills beginning with Bill C-45 threaten Treaties and [the] Indigenous Vision of Sovereignty. The movement promotes environmental protection and indigenous sovereignty. It plans to accomplish these goals by: (A) Implementing leadership structure and councils (Such as the Council of Women) (B) Taking training in coordinating rallies, media, messaging and safety issues as well as identifying provocateurs, misinformation shill, and propaganda. (C) Placing key spokespeople and connecting with experienced experts in different areas; i.e. treaty research, indigenous rights and governance, environmental activism, writers, international spokesperson, national etc.

As of 5 December, 2014, a modified Vision statement is now in place; Idle No More calls on all people to join in a peaceful revolution, to honor indigenous sovereignty, and to protect the land and water. INM has and will continue to help build sovereignty & resurgence of nationhood. INM will continue to pressure government and industry to protect the environment. INM will continue to build allies in order to reframe the nation to nation relationship; this will be done by including grassroots perspectives, issues, and concern. (www.idlenomore.ca, retrieved 5 December 2014)

Idle No More Protests

The Idle No More movement is particularly opposed to resource exploitation, especially as this takes place on Aboriginal lands, threatens First Nations' sovereignty of their territory, and degrades the sustainability of the environment. A related issue is that resource development projects, according to Idle No More supporters, do not generally benefit First Nations communities.

On 30 December 2012, the CNR line between Toronto and Montreal was blocked for three hours, although it was not officially confirmed that the blockade was affiliated with the Idle No More movement. In addition, on 5 January 2013, multiple border crossings were shut down, including the Blue Water Bridge in Sarnia, the International Bridge in Cornwall, and the Peace Bridge between Fort Erie and Buffalo (*CBC News* 2013a, 2013b).

One of the co-founders of the movement, Sylvia McAdam, indicated later (on 13 January 2013) that she does not support the blockade of highways and railroads, preferring instead that demonstrators use avenues of peaceful protest that are "within the legal boundaries" (*CTV News* 2013).

In addition, Conservative Senator Patrick Brazeau, a former First Nation chief, told the media that the Idle No More protests seemed to lack focus and suggesting that democratic processes were available to air their grievances. He also offered the opinion that Attawapiskat Chief Theresa Spence's hunger strike didn't set "a good example for Aboriginal youth" (*APTN National News* 2012).

On 11 January 2013, a meeting was held between Prime Minister Harper and a delegation of First Nations leaders, including representatives of the Assembly of First Nations. This meeting was considered a follow-up to the Crown–First Nations Gathering held on 24 January 2012. In the announcement of the meeting, no mention was made of Idle No More.

Box 6.2: Shirley Ida (Pheasant) Williams

SHIRLEY IDA (PHEASANT) WILLIAMS: WIKWEMIKONG FIRST NATION, MANITOULIN ISLAND

- Her Aboriginal name is *Migizi ow-kwe*, meaning "that Eagle Woman."
- Attended St. Joseph's Residential School in Spanish River, Ontario, at the age of ten
- Professor Emerita from Native Studies Department at Trent University
- A member of the Bird Clan of the Ojibwa and Odawa First Nations
- Is a consultant with the Elder at Sweetgrass First Nation Language Council for the Woodland Cultural Centre in Brantford

Shirley Williams
Source: Used by permission of Shirley Williams.

Assembly of First Nations Reaction

Clearly, a rift had begun to form between the Idle No More supporters and the Assembly of First Nations representatives. While the AFN was initially a supporter of INM protests, the latter's founders emphasized their intention to remain a grassroots movement. They also indicated that their vision is a different one from that of the leadership of First Nations Chiefs, saying "we have been given a clear mandate ... to work outside of the systems of government" (*National Post* 2013).

It was becoming evident, however, that National Chief of the Assembly of First Nations Shawn Atleo and other chiefs were utilizing the "protest's momentum to press Ottawa on treaty rights and improving living standards" (*Globe and Mail* 2013b). It should also be noted that Idle No More spokesperson Pam Palmater had previously run against Atleo for the position of National Chief of the AFN. Palmater, a Mi'kmaq lawyer, was the Academic Director of the Centre for Indigenous Governance at Ryerson University at the time. Despite the protests, Bill C-45 was passed and received royal assent on 14 December 2012. It is now known as the Jobs and Growth Act, 2012.

Idle No More Update

A collection of essays by Indigenous authors has been written, entitled *The Winter We Danced* (2014). This collection was put together by the Kinonda-niimi Collective, which comprises such well-known Indigenous authors as Taiaiake Alfred (Wet'suwet'en Nation), Glen Coulthard (Yellowknives Dene Nation), Isadore Day (Chief of the Serpent River First Nation), and Winona Duke (Anishenaabe), among others.

Several of the more significant articles in this collection include that by Jessica Gordon and the Idle No More founders, entitled "The Idle No More Manifesto," in which it is stated that "We believe in healthy, just, equitable, and sustainable communities and have a vision and plan on how to build them" (2014: 73). Additionally, in "Idle No More and Indigenous Nationhood," Taiaiake Alfred asserts that this movement "embodies principled opposition to the destruction of the land and the extension of social justice to Indigenous peoples" (2014: 347). He also states that "we need to focus our activism on the root of the problem facing our people collectively: our collective dispossession and misrepresentation as Indigenous peoples" (p. 348). Even more to the heart of the issue is Pamela Palmater's belief that "the failure of Canada to share the lands and resources as promised in the treaties has placed First Nations at the bottom of all socio-economic indicators—health, lifespan, education levels and employment opportunities" (2014b: 37–39).

The Debate over Indian Status

As far as Canada's Indian Act is concerned, there are a number of stipulations under Section 6(1) pertaining to "a person who is entitled to be registered." In other words, the designation of *Indian* really has nothing to do with Aboriginal status or heritage at all, but simply pertains to a legal definition of who may be "entitled to be registered" regardless of their cultural background.

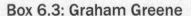

Box 6.3: Graham Greene

GRAHAM GREENE (b. 1952): SIX NATIONS ONEIDA

- Graduated from Toronto's Centre for Indigenous Theatre program in 1974
- Nominated for Academy Award as Best Supporting Actor for role of Kicking Bird in *Dances with Wolves* (1990)
- Won two Gemini Awards for Best Performance in *The Adventures of Dudley the Dragon* and *North of 60*
- Awarded an honorary Doctor of Law degree from Wilfrid Laurier University (2008)

Graham Greene at the Gemini Awards in 1998

Source: Jared Purdy / Wikimedia Commons.

Prior to 1985 and the passage of Bill C-31, the Indian Act was clearly discriminatory against women because if a "status" or "registered" woman married a man without status then she and her dependent children would lose their Indian status. Correspondingly, a status man who married a non-status woman would not lose his status, and his wife, regardless of her cultural background, would subsequently gain the status of her husband.

The revision to the Indian Act in 1985 under the provisions of Bill C-31 attempted to eliminate this inequity. For example, after 1985, a "registered" or "status" person would no longer either gain or lose status as a result of marriage. In addition, it allowed for persons who previously had lost their status to apply for a reinstatement of their Indian status.

Problems with Status Reinstatement

On the surface, this all sounded like a great plan: prevent the loss of status in the future for women and restore lost status for those who once had it. In addition, it prevented non-Aboriginal women from gaining Indian status. The problem was that the plan was not thought through very well. While restoration was a good idea, does this mean that persons with "restored" status would then be allowed to live on a reserve? If so, who will pay for this, since housing and jobs are already in short supply on reserves? As a result of these sorts of questions, critics of the Bill C-31 legislation would no doubt contend that it lacked sincerity and would find it disingenuous at best, or even racist at worst.

Another problem was that Bill C-31 created two classes of legal "Indians." Those who originally had status that was subsequently reinstated were classified under Section 6(1) of the Indian Act. On the other hand, those who would have obtained status from a parent who lost it applied under Section 6(2).

Thus, different categories of reinstatement were possible, and the ability to pass on Indian status was different in each case. For example, if a person obtained status through Section 6(2) and subsequently married a non-Indian, then their children would be considered to be non-Indians and would not be allowed to be registered. On the other hand, if the same person—someone registered under Section 6(2)—were to marry an Indian (someone registered as an Indian under the Indian Act), then their children would also then be considered to be Indians under the terms of the Indian Act.

In any event, the success rate for applicants (one needed to apply for status, which was subsequently adjudicated by the Department of Indian Affairs' Indian Registration Unit) was not very high. Out of the initial pool of 42,000 applications for reinstatement in 1985, only 1,605 were accepted that year. Over the subsequent 5 years (1985–90), more than 75,000 applications were received, affecting about 135,000 individuals.

By 2001, just over 105,000 persons had been added to the status Indian population, which had the effect of increasing the total status Indian

Box 6.4: Ted Nolan

TED NOLAN (b. 1958):
GARDEN RIVER

- Left winger for the Detroit Red Wings and Pittsburgh Penguins (1978–86)
- As head coach of the Sault Ste. Marie Greyhounds (1988–94), he led the team to three consecutive Memorial Cup tournament berths, winning the National Junior title in 1993
- Won the Jack Adams Award as the NHL's top coach when he led the Buffalo Sabres to the Northeast Division title (1996–97)
- In 2011, became head coach of the Latvian men's national hockey team, which lost a hard-fought 2-1 match against Team Canada, the defending Olympic champions, during the 2014 Winter Olympics

Ted Nolan

Source: Buchanan-Hermit, 2006 / Wikimedia Commons.

population in Canada to 623,000 persons. As such, even with the low re-instatement rate, nearly one-seventh of the registered Indian population consists of reinstated persons (Hedican 2008a: 229).

Such a dramatic increase in the status Indian population created immense problems over a fairly short period of time. The existing housing crisis was one of the main issues that prevented reinstated persons from returning to their home reserves—it was estimated that only 2 percent of Bill C-31 persons were successful in securing reserve housing between 1985 and 1990 (Cairns 2000: 74). It did not help that the Assembly of First Nations was opposed to Bill C-31, lending credibility to the view that the reinstated status Indians were not welcome and were not the equals of those who had managed to retain their status.

The Lynn Gehl Court Challenge

One may argue that Bill C-31 served to eliminate sexual discrimination in the Indian Act. However, this legislation also created many new problems that have not been seriously dealt with by both Aboriginal and non-Aboriginal groups. These problems were particularly magnified by the Lynn Gehl court challenge to the status Indian provisions of the Indian Act.

Lynn Gehl is an Algonquin-Anishenaabe First Nations woman from Ontario. *CBC News* (2014a) reported that Gehl was challenging the federal government in court because her application for Indian status was denied in 1995 since she did not know the identity of one of her grandfathers. "They made the assumption that this unknown grandfather was a non-Indian man, and through the process of that assumption I was denied Indian status registration," Gehl said.

Pamela Palmater, a First Nations lawyer and prominent figure in the Idle No More movement, finds Gehl's case interesting in light of Canada's Aboriginal policies, which she claims discriminate against Indian women and children. "Imagine," Palmater (2014a) asks, "if Canadians had to worry about losing their Canadian citizenship or the right to live in their home province based on who they married or their gender."

In Gehl's case, without status she cannot live on a reserve and has less say in important decisions of her community, such as current land claims negotiations between the Algonquins of Pikwakanagan First Nation (formerly Golden Lake Band) and the federal government. Palmater estimates that nearly 50,000 children of First Nations women have been denied status because of the way Aboriginal Affairs now assumes the unnamed father on their birth certificate is non-Aboriginal (*CBC News* 2014a).

Both Palmater and Gehl argue that political motives are behind the denials of Indian status. Gehl claims that "it's obvious Canada wants to get out of making status Indians and they want to get out of the treaty responsibilities that they have to provide for status Indians." Palmater states the case in even stronger terms, adding "even if they [the federal government] lose a court case and have to reinstate Indians back to the Indian register, they make sure to incorporate other rules so that you're losing other Indians by some other rule and the ultimate goal is so that at the end of the day there will be no Indians" (*CBC News* 2014a). The CBC reports that technical arguments will be heard in Ontario Superior Court, which will determine whether Gehl's case can continue in the court system.[1]

The UN Declaration on Indigenous Rights

In 2007, the United Nations Declaration on the Rights of Indigenous Peoples passed easily, by a vote of 143 to 4. The countries that voted against this UN Declaration were the United States, Australia, New Zealand, and Canada, while 11 countries abstained from voting. One factor involved in the voting is that all four of the countries against the Declaration have sizable Indigenous populations who would no doubt wish to use the UN Declaration as a means of advancing their own causes and to use media coverage of the Declaration as a platform to bring to the public's attention their own grievances (see Asch 2014: 65–68; United Nations 2007).

In Canada, the Declaration was not supported by the federal government because it would appear to give wide-ranging powers to Indigenous groups that, according to the government, would contravene existing laws. For example, according to Minister of Indian Affairs Chuck Stahl, the Declaration is "inconsistent with the Canadian Constitution, with Supreme Court decisions and with our own treaty negotiations and obligations. ... We'd have to consult with 650 First Nations to do that [support the vote]. I mean, it's simply not doable" (*Toronto Star*, 2007).

Eventually, on 12 November 2010, Canada did become a signatory to the UN Declaration; however, Canada is not legally bound by its terms. There are significant aspects of the UN Declaration that are worth mentioning. For example, the Declaration states that Indigenous peoples "have the right to maintain and strengthen their distinctive political, legal, economic, social and cultural institutions." However, former Indian Affairs minister Stahl commented that such wording is unworkable, because "some people ... say that means we can have our own legislatures, our own council in our own language. But no one's quite sure, and that's the trouble with language like that" (Cannon and Sunseri 2011: 273).

One way to look at the UN Declaration is to see it as a form of resistance by which Indigenous groups attempt to push back against larger colonial powers that can be seen to oppress them. Indigenous groups claim that they have inherent rights that a central government is obligated to protect. Often, these inherent rights derive from the lands that Indigenous peoples once lived on but ceded to larger powers through treaties or other forms of property surrender. Sometimes Indigenous groups claim that they were tricked into giving up their land, because colonial powers misworded the treaties in

Box 6.5: Harry LaForme

HARRY LAFORME (b. 1947): MISSISSAUGAS OF NEW CREDIT

- First Aboriginal person to be appointed to sit on any appellate court in Canadian history
- Chair of the Royal Commission on Aboriginal Land Claims (1991)
- Appointed a judge of the Ontario Superior Court of Justice (1994)
- National Aboriginal Achievement Award in the area of Law and Justice (1997)
- Chair of the Residential Schools Truth and Reconciliation Commission (2008)

Honourable Justice Harry LaForme

Source: Photo from the Law Commission of Ontario: www.lco-cdo.org/en/justice-harry-laforme. Used by permission.

such a way that a treaty of peaceful relationships was the prominent thrust of negotiations, only for the Indigenous group later to find that what was happening was the dominant power was taking control of Indigenous lands.

Indigenous Rights and the State

In cases such as these, Indigenous groups, whether their lands were taken illegally or not, argue that central governments have a fiduciary obligation to protect the rights of the members of these groups. As Christie (2007) suggests, there are "strong guiding principles laying out general restrictions on how the fiduciary can act, and guiding the fiduciary towards a narrow range of acceptable options. Ranging over the particular principles and guideposts is one over-arching fiduciary principle: the fiduciary must act in the best interests of the beneficiary" (159).

In other words, when colonial powers take over Indigenous lands, these powers have an inherent obligation to deal fairly with the original inhabitants of these lands and not exploit them by taking their resources. Resistance on the part of Indigenous groups can therefore be understood, at least partly, as a reaction against what is perceived to be suppression and a denial of their inherent rights.

It is this perception, that the colonial-Aboriginal relationship is an unjust one, that could lead Indigenous groups to dispute the jurisdiction of the state in their internal affairs. The very relationship between the state and First Nations is therefore in itself a particularly contentious issue. The role of the judiciary in conceptualizing state-Indigenous relationships further complicates matters, because not all Aboriginal peoples are willing to accept the premise that they live under the sovereignty of the state government. Aboriginal peoples might hold the position that various treaties did not necessarily lead to a relinquishing of their sovereignty and on this basis dispute state intervention in their internal affairs.

When the state-Indigenous relationship is a contested one, jurisdictional matters are particularly problematic, especially when the police, on behalf of the state, attempt to exert the enforcement of state laws on Indigenous lands. What is evident in such cases is a form of neo-colonialism as the treaty rights and land claims of Aboriginal groups are controlled by the state and its courts. In such a relationship, it is difficult to imagine that the rights of Aboriginal groups could be protected on the assumption that these are guarded by the courts, which are supposed to act as impartial agents of the state.

It therefore would appear inevitable that conflicts would develop between Indigenous groups and the state when the judicial system is purported to simultaneously act in the best interests of *both* the state and the Indigenous inhabitants. If reconciliation is to take place between the two parties—the state and Indigenous groups—then institutional structures need to be put in place that would allow for the expression of conflict that does not result either in the suppression of Indigenous groups by the police forces of the state or in armed insurrection by the less dominant groups. These sorts of structures are what Williams and Murray (2007) have referred to as "a decolonizing framework of action" (176). This framework, they explain, embodies the core values identified by Aboriginal peoples: truth, reconciliation, reparation, and the reconstruction of the relationship between Aboriginal peoples and the state.

Restorative Justice and Reconciliation

In the late 1800s, the Department of Indian Affairs and various churches took approximately 24,000 children from their homes to attend residential schools. The desired government outcome was for them to become self-sustaining members of the non-Aboriginal community. Nearly 50 percent of the students that attended these residential schools never returned home, according to a statement made by the Grand Chief's Office of the Ontario Grand Council Treaty #3 (www.gct3.ca/administrative-departments/indian-residential-school-i-r-s/).

The students who did not return home either died at the residential schools from disease, neglect, or corporal punishment and abuse, or they were no longer able to function in their home communities because of the loss of language and cultural skills as a result of the enforced policy of assimilation to non-Aboriginal society that was prevalent at the time.

The Indian Residential Schools Truth and Reconciliation Commission (TRC) was officially established on 2 June 2008 (www.trc-cvr.ca). The residential school system is often considered the most outstanding act of cultural genocide ever inflicted on Aboriginal peoples in Canada. The truth and reconciliation approach is seen as a form of restorative justice, which differs from adversarial and retributive justice based on fault-finding and punishment of the guilty parties (see Hedican 2013: 46–47; Henderson and Wakeham 2013; Niezen 2013).

Prime Minister Harper's Apology
Shortly after the announcement that the TRC had been constituted, Prime Minister Stephen Harper delivered a historic speech in the House of Commons, on 11 June 2008, in which he apologized on behalf of all Canadians for the harm that was done to Aboriginal peoples of this country because of the Indian residential school system. Prime Minister Harper noted in particular that "the government of Canada sincerely apologizes and

Box 6.6: Tara Hedican

TARA HEDICAN (b. 1981): EABAMETOONG

- Only Canadian to ever win a gold medal at the World Junior Wrestling Championships (2001)
- Won Tom Longboat Award as the Canadian Aboriginal Athlete of the Year (2001)
- Won multiple Canadian Wrestling Championships; won Pan-American Championship (2001)
- Master's Degree from Queen's University; former Principal of Shoal Lake Reserve Elementary School in northwestern Ontario; presently teacher and sports director at the Wabaseemoong (Whitedog) First Nation school in northern Ontario
- Inducted into the University of Guelph's Sports Hall of Fame (2016)

Tara Hedican

Source: Photo by Lori Bona Hunt, "Guelph Wrestler Sets Her Sights on the 2004 Olympics," *Guelph Alumnus*, Fall 2003 (vol. 35, Issue 3). Used by permission.

asks the forgiveness of the aboriginal peoples of this country for failing them so profoundly. We are sorry." He also added that "today, we recognize that this policy of assimilation was wrong, has caused great harm, and has no place in our country" (Harper 2008).

Restorative justice is an approach that seeks to heal or "restore" the relationships between offenders, community members, and the victims of the offences that have taken place. This approach is especially favoured by Aboriginal peoples living in small, relatively isolated communities, because the offending persons often return to their communities and need to be integrated back into the social settings so that they are forgiven for their offences.

"Remembering the Children" Tour

The TRC is part of the court-approved Indian Residential School Settlement Agreement (IRSSA), which was negotiated between the legal counsel of former students, government representatives, church members, the Assembly of First Nations, and other Aboriginal organizations. It was in March 2008 that Aboriginal peoples and church officials embarked on the "Remembering the Children" tour, which travelled from city to city listening to Aboriginal people's experiences with the residential school system. In addition, in January 2009, King's University College of Edmonton, Alberta, convened an interdisciplinary studies conference on the subject of the Truth and Reconciliation Committee.

Remembering these past horrific events was not easy for the former students of residential schools. The various hearings revealed physical and even sexual abuse of Aboriginal students on a hitherto unimaginably wide scale. Since Aboriginal students often spent long periods of time away from their parents, siblings, and other community members, there were also the experiences of what could be termed "cultural disassociation" that prevented traditions from being passed down to succeeding generations.

TRC Political Conflicts

Unfortunately, it did not take long for conflicts to emerge in the TRC hearings. Harry LaForme, who was a justice of the Ontario Court of Appeal, was appointed the first commission chair (*Toronto Star* 2008), but he resigned in October 2008. A member of the Mississauga of the New Credit First Nation in southern Ontario, Justice LaForme cited what he thought was undue political interference by Grand Chief Phil Fontaine of the Assembly of First Nations, the organization that represents all status Indians in Canada.

Justice LaForme claimed that Grand Chief Fontaine wanted the TRC to abandon the reconciliation approach and take a more political stance against the federal government. In the midst of this controversy, several of the commissioners resigned. However, in June 2009, a reconstituted Commission was established, headed by Justice Murray Sinclair, the first Aboriginal judge in Manitoba history. A conclusion that could be made here is that attempts at societal reconciliation have important political dimensions. Or, as Niezen (2010) states, "Public apologies and truth and reconciliation commissions have become like confessionals for states" (179).

Ontario-Specific Themes and Issues

The Caledonia Conflict

There have been many disputes in Ontario over treaty rights. Many of these disputes have involved land that First Nations claim was unjustly taken from them, and then protests were initiated in an attempt to reclaim these lost territories. In 1974, for example, the Ojibway Warrior Society took over Anicinabe Park near Kenora in northwestern Ontario (Hedican 2013: 97–100). The Teme-Augama Anishnabai (Temagami) First Nation set up a blockade in 1988 on a logging access road to protest the Robinson-Huron Treaty (1850), which they claim they did not sign and therefore the land in question has not been properly ceded to the Canadian government (Hodgins and Benedickson 1989; Bray and Thomson 1990).

The Caledonia dispute of 2006 involved First Nation protesters who blocked construction workers from entering a housing development in southern Ontario, about 20 kilometres from Hamilton. The protestors were then confronted by a group of townspeople calling themselves the Caledonia Citizens Alliance, and insults and punches were traded between the two parties. Eventually, the OPP arrived to break up the skirmish. However, confrontations continued throughout the day on April 20, with an escalation of violence, culminating with a burning truck being sent into a hydroelectric power station, causing a power outage in the area (Devries 2011: 8–11).

The basis of the protest was the Haudenosaunee Six Nations' claim that 40 hectares of land purchases, called the Douglas Creek Estates, had never been surrendered to the Crown. In February 2006, Haudenosaunee members set up tents and a wooden building on the protested site, an action that prompted a local sheriff to attempt serving an eviction notice. The OPP then arrested 21 First Nation protestors. The protestors responded by erecting a barricade on the main road into Caledonia. In June 2006, Premier Dalton McGuinty arranged for the purchase of the disputed property by the Government of Ontario for $21.1 million, but this did not resolve the situation, and tensions continued. In June 2009, some residents of Caledonia announced that they were forming unarmed "militias." By 2011, according to a study of this dispute by Laura Devries, "the story has not simplified at all. Caledonia is largely peaceful on the surface ... but tensions remain" (2011: 165).

Northern Ontario's Ring of Fire

The *Ring of Fire* is the name given to a vast region of mineral deposits in northern Ontario, situated about 400 kilometres northeast of Thunder Bay, in the James Bay Lowlands. The Ring of Fire region was named after Johnny Cash's famous country and western ballad when Richard Nemis, founder and president of Noront Resources, first made significant mineral finds in the area. The region is near the Attawapiskat River in the Kenora District, extending about 70 kilometres east of the First Nation community of Webequie and due north of the Albany River, west of James Bay.

There are three First Nations communities in this area that would be directly impacted by mineral exploration and development, namely Marten Falls, Webequie, and Neskantaga. There are other First Nations on the edge of the Ring of Fire that would also be impacted by this proposed mineral development, such as Constance Lake, Nibinamik, Aroland, Long Lake 58, Ginoogaming, Eabametoong, and Mishkeegogaming (see Appendix A for more information on the specific First Nations involved).

All of these First Nations suffer from depressed economic conditions in one way or another, such as high unemployment, low per-capita incomes, and lack of employment possibilities. For example, as Tony Clement, former Treasury Board president and FedNor minister, acknowledged on 4 February 2013, the Ring of Fire area is home to some of the "most socioeconomically disadvantaged communities in all of Canada."

Clement stated, in addition, that "chronic housing shortages, low education outcomes and lack of access to clean drinking water jeopardize the ability of local First Nations to benefit from significant economic, employment and business development opportunities associated with the Ring of Fire developments." Nonetheless, the Ring of Fire, according to Clement, represents a "once-in-a-life opportunity to create jobs and generate growth and long-term prosperity for northern Ontario and the nation" (Ontario Ministry of Natural Resources 2013).

Economic Salvation or Political Football?
The Ring of Fire development, therefore, is seen as a possible significant economic benefit to the area, but there are infrastructural challenges that could blunt the possible benefits that the mining activities could bring to the region. Bob Rae, former Ontario premier, was appointed to represent the First Nations impacted by the mining developments as their chief negotiator (*Globe and Mail* 2013b).

Major questions about the development and its supposed benefits remain. For example, how prepared were the region's First Nations people for the employment opportunities that were expected to be available? According to the Grand Chief of the Nishnawbe Aski Nation, Les Louttit, two or three years was not enough time for the skills training that would be required to prepare local workers for the constructions jobs. He also noted the gap in secondary and post-secondary educational levels between First Nations people in northern Ontario and the rest of the country. The implication is that Ring of Fire mining may not benefit First Nations in northern Ontario as much as originally hoped (*CBC News* 2013c). As such, the Ring of Fire's potential for economic development in northern Aboriginal communities may be derailed by political conflicts among the various parties involved (see Wightman and Wightman 1997; Bray and Epp 1984).

Negotiating Benefits for First Nations
If the First Nations people in the Ring of Fire region are to benefit from the mining proposals, then there is a long road ahead. Potential developers, for example, are required to negotiate an Impact Benefit Agreement with the First Nations communities before any mining development can take place. There is also other legislation that could potentially benefit the First Nations' bargaining position.

The Government of Ontario's Far North Act, for example, received assent and became law on 25 October 2010. The Far North Act provides a "legislative foundation to support Far North land use planning as a joint process between First Nations and Ontario." According to the Ontario government, the Hudson Bay Lowlands, which is the primary region affected by the mining proposals, is the "third largest wetland in the world," with a population of 24,000 First Nations residents in 34 communities.

Negotiations between the mining companies and the First Nations residents initially did not go smoothly. In 2003, Noront Resources began using two frozen lakes as landing strips without consulting Marten Falls and Webequie First Nations. The Ontario Mining Act only allows exploration activities, rather than the construction of permanent structures. In 2010, Marten Falls Chief Eli Moonias explained that Noront Resources did not have "permits to construct landing strips on the string bog or roads to the nearby airstrip." The chief described how, over a seven-year period, Noront Resources "sunk machines here and they have done outrageous acts here" (Garrick 2010).

Environmental Assessment

In response, members of Marten Falls and Webequie First Nations set up a blockade on the landing strips at Koper and McFaulds Lakes (Garrick 2010). Further impediments to the negotiating process developed when, on 20 October 2011, Matawa First Nations Management, a regional Chiefs council, removed its support for the Ring of Fire development unless the federal government agreed to a joint review of the Environmental Assessment process, which would allow First Nations communities to have a voice in the assessment.

The problem with the Environmental Assessment process, according to a notice posted on the Neskantaga First Nation website, is that it "is a generic public process with no distinct or government-to-government engagement with the First Nations that will be affected by the proposed projects. ... All who have something to say should be given an opportunity to speak and have their say in our own language, in our own communities." The website also mentions that the Ontario government decides "what's best for First Nations and implement policies and programs in line with that determination," rather than consulting directly with the First Nations involved (www.neskantaga. com/, retrieved 15 November 2014).

Matawa Chiefs Sign Ring of Fire Framework

On 26 March 2014, nine Matawa-member First Nations and the Province of Ontario moved towards reaching an agreement that would ensure First Nation communities would benefit from the proposed Ring of Fire development. The regional framework agreement was a first step in a community-based negotiation process that began in July 2013, at the request of Matawa-member First Nations. The agreement ensured that First Nations and Ontario would work together to advance Ring of Fire opportunities.

Key aspects of the agreement were the regional long-term environmental monitoring and enhanced participation in Environmental Assessment processes, resource revenue sharing, economic supports, and regional and community infrastructure (Ginoogaming First Nation 2014).

The Wabauskang Challenge

Another mining development is related to the Wabauskang First Nation near Kenora in northwestern Ontario, who used its hearing with the Supreme Court of Canada to challenge the Province of Ontario's ability to delegate the carrying out of Aboriginal consultation to mining companies, rather than having the Ministry of Mining and Northern Development deal with First Nations themselves.

The hearing at the Supreme Court was granted to Wabauskang First Nation so that it might settle its long-standing fight with Rubicon Minerals over a proposed mining project inside the First Nation's territory. Waubauskang, the provincial government, and Rubicon all submitted outlines of their arguments to the Court for the justices to consider (*Kenora Daily Miner and News* 2014).

The situation was complicated by the fact that federal government approval is required before treaty land can be appropriated for development use, something the Crown is allowed to do according to Treaty No. 3. In this context, First Nations lawyers argued that the provincial government went too far when it delegated the responsibility for conducting mandatory consultations with them, and so the plan for the Rubicon mine project, which had been approved by Ontario, is invalid.

According to the Rubicon submission, the delegation of aspects of the process did not deprive the Aboriginal community of the consultation they are entitled to. However, Wabauskang's Chief Leslie Cameron disagreed, saying that giving the proponents of a project the responsibility to consult with First Nations is very problematic. As Chief Cameron indicated, "it makes for a very one-sided form of consultation process where the provincial government just takes for granted what the company is telling them, saying they've dealt with us. And some of the things they say happened [during consultation] are out-and-out lies" (*Kenora Daily Miner and News* 2014).

The Supreme Court Decision on Treaty Rights

In a landmark decision on 11 July 2014, the Supreme Court of Canada indicated that the Province of Ontario is burdened with legal responsibilities when making land-use decisions in the Treaty No. 3 area. This decision is a result of the challenge brought by the Wabauskang First Nation to the Ontario Court of Appeal, which indicated that there is no role for the federal government in ensuring the protection of treaty rights when Ontario makes decisions about lands and resources in the Treaty No. 3 region.

The Supreme Court disagreed with Ontario's position, arguing that Ontario is directly responsible for ensuring that treaty rights are protected. According to Wabauskang Chief Martine Petiquan, "Our Treaty is with Canada. It is Canada that is responsible for fulfilling the promises made to the people of Treaty 3. We have always maintained, and will continue to affirm, that the federal government needs to be involved in ensuring that our treaty rights are respected" (Wasbauskang First Nation 2014).

The Wabauskang First Nation challenge, however, clearly indicates that Ontario has an obligation to respect treaty rights in the province. It also points to the complicated jurisdictional concerns involving Ontario's First Nations, the federal government, and provincial/territorial responsibilities (Wabauskang First Nation 2014).

The Algonquin Land Claim

By the beginning of 2015, the **Ontario Ministry of Indigenous Relations and Reconciliation** was dealing with more than 64 land claims in the province. Fifty of these have been accepted for negotiations, three are being researched and assessed, and a further eleven settlement agreements are being implemented. Many of the land claims are relatively small in size, as they pertain to disagreements over the size of reserves resulting from possible errors in surveying done during the Robinson-Superior and Robinson-Huron Treaties of 1850. It is possible that the surveying methods used during the negotiation of the treaties were less accurate than those employed today, and also that certain geographical features of 150 years ago no longer exist (Ontario Ministry of Indigenous Relations and Reconciliation 2014).

The Algonquin land claim is the largest land claim currently being negotiated in Ontario. If successful, it will be the province's first modern-day, constitutionally protected treaty. Approximately 10,000 people of Algonquin descent live in the land-claim territory, comprising ten First Nations and communities.

The claim covers a territory of 36,000 square kilometres in eastern Ontario, which is populated by more than 1.2 million people. The Algonquin of Ontario assert that they have Aboriginal rights and title that have never been extinguished and have continuing ownership to the Ontario portions of the Ottawa and Mattawa River watersheds and their natural resources. The boundaries of the claim are based largely on the watershed, which was historically used and occupied by the Algonquin.

The key terms of a possible settlement agreed to by the negotiators for the Algonquin of Ontario, the Government of Canada, and the Government of Ontario are as follows:

- the transfer of 117,500 acres of Crown lands to Algonquin ownership
- $300 million as settlement capital provided by Canada and Ontario
- defined Algonquin rights related to lands and natural resources

It has also been agreed by the negotiators that no new reserves will be created, Algonquin Park will be preserved for the enjoyment of all, and land will not be expropriated from private owners as a result of the settlement. As far as hunting and fishing are concerned, Algonquin harvesting rights will be subject to provincial and federal laws necessary for conservation and public health and safety. In addition, a key aspect of the settlement will be that no lands will be transferred from Algonquin Park. A new 30,000-acre provincial park near Crotch Lake, in the North Frontenac Park lands west of Smiths Falls, is being recommended.

Buttressing Neo-Colonial Trends
The Algonquin land claim is also the basis for an insightful study by Bonita Lawrence (2013) called *Fractured Homeland*, which centres on Algonquin identity in Ontario. This book focuses on the Algonquins of Pikwakanaga and the comprehensive land claim they launched in 1992, during which it was discovered that two-thirds of Algonquins have never been recognized as Indian.

Lawrence's account documents the Algonquins' 20-year struggle for identity and nationhood through the use of family histories and extended interviews with elders who were witness to the dispossession of traditional territory.

As indicated in the book's title, the Algonquin have suffered from a "fractured" identity because of the neo-colonial pressures asserted over them and their traditional lands across the Ottawa River watershed. This struggle to reassert jurisdiction over their traditional lands has been caused by the imposition of a provincial boundary, which divided the Algonquin across two provinces, and the Indian Act, which denied federal recognition for many of the members of this First Nation. In turn, the land claim forced many of the Algonquin people to struggle with questions of identity during times when they were facing disruption by settlers and the state.

Bonita Lawrence's theme of fractured identity caused by colonial forces furthermore resonates with another similar work, *Red Skin, White Masks*, by Glen Coulthard (2014), who is a member of the Yellowknives Dene Nation. Subtitled *Rejecting the Colonial Politics of Recognition*, this work makes the argument that at the heart of colonial relationships between Indigenous peoples and the nation-state is the false promise of recognition, which is promoted by liberal pluralism and attempts at reconciliation. Coulthard challenges the assumption that contemporary difference and past histories of destructive colonialism between the state and Indigenous peoples can be reconciled through a process of acknowledgement. Alternatively, he suggests a political process that seeks to "revalue, reconstruct, and redeploy" Indigenous cultural practices based on self-recognition, rather than seeking approval from the agents of colonialism. In summary, he argues that "this orientation [of liberal politics] to the reconciliation of Indigenous nationhood with state sovereignty is still *colonial* insofar as it remains structurally committed to the dispossession of Indigenous peoples of our lands and self-determining authority" (2014: 151).

Conclusion

The current events discussed in this chapter are not meant to provide comprehensive coverage of the topic. There are many other land claims, protests, resource matters, community problems, and economic development issues that could be considered as well. The discussion in this chapter is only meant to provide the reader with a broad sampling of current events and issues that involve the First Nations of Ontario in order to illustrate the wide range of concerns.

Certainly, land claims are one of the most prominent current issues involving Aboriginal-provincial negotiations. Past treaties, many of which are now several hundred years old, are often indeterminate with regards to their provisions, exact boundaries, and reserves promised, or hunting and trapping rights. The Ontario Ministry of Indigenous Relations and Reconciliation has for many years been conducting negotiations with the First Nations of the province, but the process is at times stretched out over many decades, causing dissatisfaction on both sides of the negotiating table.

Resource issues are becoming ever more prominent as mining companies are discovering the untapped mineral wealth of Ontario, especially in northern areas. The Ring of Fire is such a situation involving mining companies anxious to move beyond the exploration stage, while First Nations people in the area argue for a slower process in which the Aboriginal rights promised by past treaties are honoured.

Other important contemporary issues involve the status of First Nations people, especially as this is defined in the Indian Act. Many Aboriginal people in the past lost their Indian status because of unjust practices, such as eliminating women (and at times their children as well) from band rolls because of their marriage to men without status. The Bill C-31 provisions of 1985 served to reinstate some of the many persons who had previously lost their status, but many First Nations people argue that the process of adjudication, controlled by the federal government, has not been a fair one.

Suggested Readings

Cairns, A.C. 2000. *Citizens Plus: Aboriginal Peoples and the Canadian State.* Vancouver: University of British Columbia Press.

Cannon, M.J., and L. Sunseri, eds. 2011. *Racism, Colonialism, and Indigeneity in Canada.* Oxford: Oxford University Press.

Coulthard, G.S. 2014. *Red Skin, White Masks: Rejecting the Colonial Politics of Recognition.* Minneapolis: University of Minnesota Press.

DeVries, L. 2011. *Conflict in Caledonia: Aboriginal Land Rights and the Rule of Law.* Vancouver: University of British Columbia Press.

Henderson, J., and P. Wakeham, eds. 2013. *Reconciling Canada: Critical Perspectives on the Culture of Redress.* Toronto: University of Toronto Press.

Niezen, R. 2013. *Truth and Indignation: Canada's Truth and Reconciliation Commission on Indian Residential Schools.* Toronto: University of Toronto Press.

Review Questions

1. Describe the importance of the United Nations Declaration on Indigenous Rights.
2. What do resource development projects such as the Ring of Fire in northern Ontario tell us about the nature of Aboriginal rights?

Note

1. In a decision of Ontario's Court of Appeal, Lynn Gehl was granted Indian status on 20 April 2017.

AFTERWORD

PRESENT AND FUTURE CHALLENGES: FIRST NATIONS IN TRANSITION

This book has traced the history of the First Nations people of Ontario for the last 10,000 years. The most significant conclusion that could be drawn from this history is that the Aboriginal peoples of Ontario have demonstrated an amazing resiliency when it comes to overcoming diversity and meeting the challenges of their time.

The demise of the last ice age brought about climatic changes, which in turn led to new patterns of animal migrations, new waterways, and new lifestyles. The Aboriginal peoples were not only able to cope and survive but even thrive despite the challenges they faced throughout their history. The arrival of Europeans brought further changes, which often led to de-population caused by disease and loss of habitations and traditional lands. Residential schools and oppressive and assimilative government policies pressured First Nations people to adopt new ways of living. However, even today, their traditional languages, beliefs, and community patterns continue to persist in spite of these adversities.

First Nations people have organized themselves in various ways—some-times politically, at other times socially and economically—to confront the threats to their traditional lands and the resources coveted by the settler population. Facing the challenges today and into the future will not be an easy task. First Nations people lack the wealth that outsiders possess, and their communities often face grave problems without adequate housing and employment. Their leaders, however, continue to push forward, challenging the outside powers that would deny them their inherent Aboriginal rights guaranteed by treaties, negotiations, and other long-term settlements.

One can see even today the future challenges in the north with the Ring of Fire developments: the relatively pristine traditional territories of Ontario's

First Nations will be put under tremendous stress. The quest for minerals and other resource initiatives in forestry and hydroelectric power will no doubt change the face of northern Ontario. These developments will also have significant environmental impacts, possibly as great as the oil sands project in northern Alberta. Will First Nations people benefit in any significant way from these schemes, or will their lands be further torn apart by an apparently insatiable industrial economy? This is the main question for the First Nations of Ontario in the future.

In summary, there are several important points that should be made in terms of the topics covered in this book. Despite the idea, in the minds of some Canadians, that First Nations people were perhaps important aspects of the past, but are no longer so today, it cannot be asserted strongly enough that the Aboriginal populations of this country today are as functioning and vibrant as they ever were. They have lived in this country for over 10,000 years and continue to cope with today's challenges.

It is also important to indicate that colonialism has had a very harmful impact on First Nations. The treaties have taken traditional lands away from the First Nations, and the Aboriginal people were provided very little in return. Instead, for the most part, they were relegated to small parcels of land, called reserves, that had insufficient resources for the people to make an adequate living. As has been pointed out, if Canadians were to share the resources of this bountiful country with First Nations in an equitable manner, this would almost certainly improve the social and economic situation.

Another significant point that must be made is that the treaties that were negotiated with First Nations and the British and Canadian governments are not just historical relics that have no relevance to contemporary times. In fact, the treaties are "living documents" that are as relevant today as ever. All Canadians have a responsibility to ensure that the terms of the treaties are honoured, because the very land and resources used by the people of this country were given freely by the Aboriginal peoples and were not taken away from them in any wars.

When the first European settlers arrived in Canada, the Aboriginal peoples shared their land, food, and whatever other resources they had with the newcomers. The time is well past that Canadians should engage in a spirit of reciprocity, sharing the riches of this country with the Aboriginal populations who were here first and will no doubt continue to thrive into the future.

Review Questions

1. In your opinion, what are the greatest challenges that First Nations face at the present time?
2. How has colonialism influenced the manner in which First Nations people can determine the course of their own future?
3. What changes should the Canadian government make so that First Nations people can make a better life for themselves, both presently and in the future?

APPENDIX A

THE FIRST NATIONS OF ONTARIO

The following descriptions of the First Nations of Ontario are derived from information provided by the Ontario Ministry of Indigenous Relations and Reconciliation, Aboriginal Affairs and Northern Development Canada (2014 Census), the Assembly of First Nations, the Union of Ontario Indians, and the reports provided by the 2006 Census (Statistics Canada 2008). The webpages of individual First Nations are also utilized as an information source.

This information, where available, indicates the geographical location of bands, the total registered population, associated names or other designations (in parentheses), number of reserves, and larger ethnic or linguistic affiliations. In some cases, the First Nation community may be composed of both status and non-status people, or may not be considered a reserve (non-status) under the provisions of the Indian Act. It is possible that the members of two or more bands may also reside on the same reserve.

In 2011, the total registered Indian (status) population of Ontario was 141,165 people, composed of 67,685 males (48%) and 73,480 females (52%). In total, Canada currently recognizes 617 First Nations for the entire country. For Ontario, there are 139 First Nations listed by the Department of Indigenous and Northern Affairs Canada, 22.5% of the Canadian total.

As such, in Ontario, there is an average number of 1,016 people per First Nation. In addition, there are 444 reserves, settlements, or villages listed, not all of which are presently occupied, for an average of 318 persons per reserve or settlement. Indigenous and Northern Affairs Canada (INAC) lists 2014 population figures for most, but not all, First Nations. In the event that 2014 population figures are not available for a particular First Nation, alternative sources of information, possibly not officially recognized, are utilized.

Aamjiwnaang (Chippewas of Sarnia)

www.aamjiwnaag.ca

One reserve located on the shores of the St. Clair River, directly south of Sarnia in southwestern Ontario, across the American border from Port Huron, in Lambton County. This First Nation community consists of about 850 Chippewa (Ojibwa; Anishenaabe) Aboriginal people. *Aamjiwnaang* means "at the spawning stream." Concerns have been expressed about their proximity to the chemical plants in the area and the possible adverse effects of maternal and fetal exposure to the effluent and emissions of these plants. According to studies in environmental health, this is the only community in the world to have a birth rate of two girls for every boy.

Abitibi. See Wahgoshig

Akwesasne. See Mohawks of Akwesasne

Albany. See Fort Albany

Alderville

www.aldervillefirstnation.ca

One reserve located near the south shores of Rice Lake in southern Ontario, which has been this First Nation's home since the 1830s. Prior to this, the community had lived 90 kilometres east of this location, around the Bay of Quinte, which subsequently became home to the Mohawks of the Bay of Quinte First Nation as this land had been promised to Joseph Brant by the British after the American Revolution. Residents consider themselves a band of Mississaugas, a sub-nation of the Ojibwas or Anishenaabe. In 2014, the total registered population was 1,119, of which the on-reserve population was 316 people.

Algonquins of Pikwakanagan (Golden Lake First Nation)

www.algonquinsofpikwakanagan.com

Pikwakanagan is an Algonquin word meaning "hilly country covered in evergreens." This First Nation consists of one reserve situated in the Ottawa Valley on the shores of the Bonnechere River and Golden Lake in Renfrew, about 40 kilometres south of Pembroke. In 2014, the total registered population was 2,502 people, of which 467 live on their reserve. Enforced residential schooling has caused a partial loss of traditional language and culture.

Angling Lake. See Wapekeka

Animbiigoo Zaagi'igan Anishinaabek (Lake Nipigon Reserve)

www.aza.ca

When the Robinson-Superior Treaty was signed in 1850, only three reserves in total were set aside for the First Nations people (Gull Bay, Pic Mobert, and

Fort William). The reasoning for this limited number of reserves was that the Aboriginal people in this treaty area were still hunters and gatherers who lived a seasonal, migratory way of life. When they were ready to adopt a more sedentary lifestyle in the future, additional reserves would be set aside. The problem was that it took many generations for these reserves to be created. "The Nipigon Band of Indians," as the people living around Lake Nipigon were called, was not even recognized by the Government of Canada as a distinct community until 1921. During this time, the ancestors of the Animbiigo Zaagi'igan Anishinaabek First Nation were living around the northeastern shore of Lake Nipigon, primarily in the Ombabika and Auden area. In 1985, the community elected its first chief, whose main priority was to bring the various dispersed people together in order to discuss the creation of a reserve. An office was created at Beardmore in 1989. Finally, after 158 years of wandering about the Lake Nipigon area, the community celebrated the creation of their new reserve on 24 May 2008, at Partridge Lake near the southeastern shore of Lake Nipigon. In 2014, the total registered population was 476 persons, of which 96 live on-reserve. The community is affiliated with the Nokiiwin Tribal Council, which represents six First Nations in the Lake Nipigon area and along the north shore of Lake Superior.

Anishinaabeg of Naongashiing

www.bigisland.ca

This First Nation consists of 12 reserves in the Lake of the Woods area, all situated about 40 to 80 kilometres southeast of the town of Kenora. The total registered population in 2014 was 414 people, of which 192 live on-reserve. The community is affiliated with the Anishinaabeg of Kabapikotawangag Resource Council, which represents six First Nations in the Kenora–Sioux Narrows region. The people were signatory to Treaty No. 3, usually referred to as the North-West Angle Treaty of 1873. They reached legal band status in the 1920s, and in 1982, the majority of the band members relocated to the Saug-a-gaw-sing Reserve on the southeast shore of the Lake of the Woods, situated about 77 kilometres from Kenora.

Anishinabe of Wauzhushk Onigum (Rat Portage)

www.firstnation.ca/wauzhushk-onigum-rat-portage

This is an Ojibwa (Anishenaabe) First Nation located in northwestern Ontario on Lake of the Woods, near Kenora. It consists of two reserves. Agency 30 is on the Aulineau Peninsula of Lake of the Woods and is shared by the members of 13 First Nations. The other reserve, which is the most populated site, is Kenora 38B, situated three kilometres southeast of Kenora. As of 2014, the total registered population was 743, of which 368 persons live on-reserve. Community members belong to the Grand Council Treaty #3 and are members of the Anishinaabeg of Kabapikotawangag Resource Council, which represents six First Nations in the Kenora–Sioux Narrows region.

Ardoch Algonquin (Omamiwinini, or "people of the wild rice")

www.aafna.ca

A non-status Algonquin (Anishenaabe) community situated around the Madawaska, Mississippi, and Rideau watershed, north of Kingston. Ardoch is considered a non-status community because its members choose to continue to organize themselves around the extended family model wherein they determine their own membership, and thus population figures are not officially available. This is opposed to those First Nations who have status under the Indian Act, which defines band membership under Canadian law. *Manomin*, or wild rice, has always been a strong component of Ardoch identity, and the community has struggled to preserve *manomin* from commercial harvesters. Community members have also been involved in protests to block a prospective uranium mining site near Sharbot Lake, considered part of traditional Ardoch territory.

Aroland

www.firstnation.ca/aroland

This community gained status under the Indian Act on 15 April 1985. It is located along the Canadian National Railway (CNR) line in northwestern Ontario, approximately 25 kilometres west of Nakina and 350 kilometres northwest of Thunder Bay. Originally, the Aroland Settlement was named after the Arrow Land and Logging Company, which operated in the area from 1933 to 1941. The membership of Aroland is composed of former members of other First Nations in the area, such the members of Long Lac (now Ginoogaming First Nation), Fort Hope (now Eabametoong First Nation), Marten Falls First Nation, and Fort William First Nation, who settled on the Kowashkagama River to the south of the existing village. The population in 2008 was a total of 700 members of Ojibwa- and Oji-Cree-speaking people, 300 of whom live on-reserve. The community today is served by the Nishnawbe Aski Police Service and Tikinagan Child and Family Services. It is also affiliated with the Matawa First Nations Management, a tribal council that services ten other First Nations in northern Ontario in the area of Long Lac, Webequie, and Ogoki Post. For a study of Aroland's struggles with land tenure, see Paul Driben and R.S. Trudeau, *Aroland Is Our Home* (1986).

Ashkibwaanikaang. See Seine River

Asubpeeschoseewagong. See Grassy Narrows
Atikameksheng Anishnawbek (Whitefish Lake)

www.atikamekshenganishnawbek.ca

This First Nation is composed of the descendants of the Ojibway, Algonquin, and Odawa Nations and is located approximately 19 kilometres southwest of the city of Sudbury. It consists of one reserve situated at the east end of Whitefish Lake. In 2014, the total registered population was 1,178, of which 412 persons lived on-reserve. The community belongs to Mamaweswen, the North Shore Tribal Council representing seven First Nations in the Sault Ste. Marie–Thessalon region. It is also associated with a variety of other Aboriginal political organizations, such as the Assembly of First Nations and the Chiefs of Ontario. A resolution passed in 2006 changed the name of the First Nation from Whitefish Lake to Atikameksheng Anishnawbek, which officially took effect in 2013. In 2008, the chief and council announced litigation against Canada and Ontario for violating the Robinson-Huron Treaty (1850), stating that the First Nation should be granted a reserve much larger than Whitefish Lake. In 2010, the community was selected as the host community for Building Homes and Building Skills, a project by television personality Mike Holmes to train First Nations people in construction and building trades (*Northern Life* 2010).

Attawapiskat

www.attawapiskat.org

This First Nation is named after the Cree *Ahtawapiskatowi ininiwak*, which means "people of the parting of the rocks." It is located in the Kenora District of northern Ontario, at the mouth of the Attawapiskat River at James Bay. The people live on two reserves: one 165 kilometres west of James Bay on both banks of the Ekwan River, and the other near the west shore of James Bay on the left bank of the Attawapiskat River. In 2014, the total registered population was 3,514, of which 2,014 live on-reserve. The community is served by a seasonal ice road, constructed each December, that links it to the towns of Kashechewan First Nation, Fort Albany, and Moosenee; the road spans altogether about 310 kilometres over what is at times very hazardous terrain. The people are members of the Mushkegowuk Tribal Council, which represents six First Nations of primarily Cree speakers from Moose Factory to Cochrane.

In 2008, the De Beers Victor Diamond Mine was opened, which generates about $400 million in annual revenue for the company. Although De Beers has acknowledged that the mine is on Attawapiskat traditional land, the royalties from the Victor Mine flow to the Province of Ontario, not to the Attawapiskat First Nation. However, the mine does employ about 100 Attawapiskat personnel. As of 2011, the De Beers company has also transferred about $10.5 million to a trust fund held by Attawapiskat. The beneficiary of the trust includes "all members of Attawapiskat on a collective and undivided basis" (Attawapiskat First Nation 2012: 4).

Aundeck Omni Kaning (Ojibways of Sucker Creek)

www.aokfn.com

The name of this First Nation in Anishenaabe means "where the crows nest." It is located five kilometres west of the town of Little Current along Highway 540, on the shores of Georgian Bay, which is on the main land-access point to Manitoulin Island. The current total membership is 700, with an average of 340 members residing within the community. The community is relatively young, with an estimated 57 percent of the population under 30 years of age. One of the community's successful economic ventures is Wabuno Fish Farm and Processors, which was established in 1992 as a production facility to raise rainbow trout. Another venture is Endaa-aang Tourism, an eco-tourism business opened in 2001 with cabins and teepees on the mainland and traditional occupied islands situated on the north shore of Georgian Bay.

Bamaji Lake. See Slate Falls

Batchewana. See Ojibways of Batchewana

Bay of Quinte. See Mohawks of the Bay of Quinte

Bear Island. See Temagami

Bearskin Lake

www.firstnation.ca/bearskin-lake

Three settlements make up the Bearskin Lake First Nation. In 2014, the total registered population was 904, of which 466 live on-reserve. Originally located on Bearskin Lake, their main community moved to its present site on Michikan (Fish Trap) Lake in the 1930s. The main village is situated on the west shore of the lake, and all three communities are tied together by all-weather gravel roads that traverse the area from Windigo Lake north to Muskrat Dam. Prior to achieving full band and reserve status in 1975, Bearskin was a satellite community of Big Trout Lake First Nation. Today, Bearskin Lake First Nation is a member of the Windigo First Nations Council, a regional tribal council that is a member of the Nishnawbe Aski Nation, and is policed by the Nishnawbe Aski Police Service. The Bearskin community participates in the Junior Canadian Rangers Program for youth (12–18 years), which teaches various skills such as first aid, using rifles safely, Aboriginal customs, and traditions, along with hunting and fishing skills. The Michikan Lake Business Centre operates several economic enterprises in the community, including a five-unit motel.

Beausoleil

www.chimnissing.ca

Located on the southern tip of Georgian Bay in Simcoe County, this First Nation consists of three reserves situated on Christian, Beckwith, and Hope Islands, which are close to the communities of Midland and Penetanguishene. Traditional Aboriginal languages spoken include Ojibwa, Odawa, and Potawatomi, which are all members of the Algonquian (Algonkian) language family. In 2014, the total registered population was 2,300, of which 647 lived on these reserves. A member of the Ogemawahj Tribal Council. See also *Moose Deer Point* for further details.

Beaverhouse (non-status)

www.wabun.on.ca/first-nation-profiles/beaverhouse-first-nation

Located on the banks of the Misema River system northeast of Kirkland Lake. The name of the community is derived from the Algonquian name of the river, *Maaseema Qweesh*, where *Qweesh* refers to a "beaver's nest or house." The site of the community is on a remote peninsula that does not have direct road access and is only accessible by boat in the summer and snowmobile in the winter. Beaverhouse First Nation was not included as a community in the Treaty No. 9 document of 1906 or in the adhesions of 1929–30, which accounts for its designation as a "non-status" First Nation. The Beaverhouse community has worked on developing relationships with regional First Nation organizations, such as the Nishnawbe Aski Nation, the Chiefs of Ontario, and the Wabun Tribal Council. Population statistics are not officially available at this time.

Begetekong Anishinabek. See Ojibways of the Pic River

Big Grassy

www.biggrassy.ca

Mishkosiminiziibiing Anishinaabeg is the Ojibwa name for the Big Grassy First Nation, which is located in the Kenora District, about 50 kilometres north of the Canada/US border and 450 kilometres west of Thunder Bay. Together with the Ojibwa of Onigaming First Nation, the Big Grassy First Nation is a successor to the former Assabaska Band of Saulteaux. The Assabaska Band had initially chosen a reserve site, Little Grassy River 35E, along with two additional sites (Little Grassy River 35E1 and Windy Point 35E2, comprising together 800 acres), but these were never surveyed. Without consultation with the Assabaska Band, all three reserves were disposed of upon creation of the Lake of the Woods Provincial Park. The total registered population in 2014 was 769, of which 321 people live on-reserve. This First Nation is composed of six reserves in the Kenora, Lake of the Woods, and Sioux Narrows area. One of these, Agency 30, is shared with 12 other First Nations. The Big Grassy community is a member of the Anishinaabeg of Kabapikotawangag Resource Council, a regional tribal council that is a member of the Grand Council Treaty #3.

Big Trout Lake. See Kitchenuhmaykoosib Inninuwug

Biinjitiwabik Zaaging Anishinabek (Rocky Bay)

www.rockybayfn.ca

This is an Ojibway First Nation bordering on the community of MacDiarmid, consisting of one reserve called the Rocky Bay 1 Indian Reserve. In 2014, the total registered population consisted of 715 people, of which 339 live on-reserve. Since the early 1950s, various Aboriginal people from such locations as Gull Bay, Red Rock, and Sand Point were living at Rocky Bay, and they were formally constituted as the Rocky Bay Band in 1960. In 1963, an Ontario Order-in-Council transferred 32 acres of MacDiarmid to the federal government to be set aside as a reserve for the Rocky Bay Band. The First Nation television series *Spirit Bay* was filmed here in the 1980s, and a school in Rocky Bay has been named Spirit Bay School after the series. The community is a member of Nokiiwin Tribal Council and the Union of Ontario Indians. This First Nation is also a signatory to the Robinson-Superior Treaty of 1850.

Bingwi Neyaashi Anishinaabek (Sand Point)

www.bnafn.ca

Formerly known as the Sand Point First Nation, this is a relatively new reserve located on the shores of Lake Nipigon. There is no housing or infrastructure in place at the present time. The proposed community site being considered for residential development has the potential to be developed as a green community with an emphasis on renewable energy options. The site is located on the east shore of Pijitawbik Bay on Lake Nipigon and is situated approximately 17 kilometres south of the town of Beardmore. The community of MacDiarmid and the Biinjitiwaabik Zaaging Anishinaabek (Rocky Bay) First Nation are located on the southern border of this site. The junction of Highways 11 and 17, as well as the community of Nipigon, are approximately 50 kilometres farther south, about 170 kilometres northeast of the city of Thunder Bay. The site includes the property most recently known as the Lake Nipigon Provincial Park. As of 2014, the total registered population was 255 persons, of which 90 persons are listed as living on-reserve. While the Sand Point Aboriginal settlement dates back to at least 1850, the documented tenure of the subject property begins in 1890 when a Hudson's Bay Company post was constructed on this site; it was later abandoned about 1930. A relatively undisturbed cemetery still remains at this location. In the early 1900s, the residents of the HBC post constructed a saw mill to provide an economic foundation for the community, which employed 180 men until it burned down in 1925. Today, the community is a member of the Nokiiwin Tribal Council, which represents six First Nations in the Beardmore–Thunder Bay area near Lake Nipigon, as well as the Union of Ontario Indians.

Bizhiw-zaaga'iganiing Nitam Anishinaabeg. See Cat Lake

Bkejwanong Territory (Walpole Island)

www.bkejwanong.ca

Occupants live on one reserve located in southwestern Ontario on the border between Ontario and Michigan in the United States, on the mouth of the St. Clair River on Lake St. Clair, in Lambton County. Aside from Walpole Island, the reserve encompasses Squirrel, St. Anne, Seaway, Bassett, and Potawatomi Islands. Bkejwanong means "where the waters divide." This First Nation is considered unceded territory because of a boundary dispute over the Canadian-American border and is inhabited by Ojibwa, Potawatomi, and Odawa speaking peoples. Walpole Island is considered the final resting place of Tecumseh, a prominent 19th-century leader of the Shawnee. The total registered population in 2014 was 4,706 persons, of whom 2,332 live on the reserve.

Brunswick House

www.brunswickhousefirstnation.com

An Ojibwa-Cree-speaking First Nation located in the Sudbury District about 5 kilometres from the town of Chapleau and 97 kilometres from Sault Ste. Marie. The community consists of two reserves with a registered population in 2014 of 768 members, of which 202 persons live on-reserve. Policed by the Nishnawbe Aski Police Service, an Aboriginal community service. The name of the First Nation derives from the fur-trade era when the Ojibwa people traded at posts at Brunswick and Missinabi Lakes. With the signing of Treaty No. 9, a reserve was designated for the band, but the people relocated in 1925 when the Ontario government established the Chapleau

Game Reserve, which was closed to all hunting and trapping. In 1947, the band moved to the present Duck Lake and Mountbatten reserves, closer to Chapleau. The community is a member of the Nishnawbe Aski Nation and the Wabun Tribal Council.

Caldwell (Chippewas of Pelee)

www.caldwellfirstnation.com

Located in Southern Ontario, this is an Anishenaabe-speaking First Nation comprising three tribes: the Potawatomi, Odawa, and Ojibwa. Historically, they have been referred to as "the Chippewas of Point Pelee and Pelee Island." Their traditional territory encompassed a broad area extending from the Detroit River to Long Point, Ontario, and the Lake Erie Islands. At present, the Caldwell First Nation is the only federally recognized Indian band in southern Ontario without reserve land of its own, although a settlement agreement was signed with Canada in 2011. In 2014, the total registered population was listed as 352 persons, all of whom live off-reserve.

Cape Croker. See Chippewas of Nawash

Cat Lake

www.firstnation.ca/cat-lake

This is an Ojibwa community situated approximately 180 kilometres northwest of Sioux Lookout in northwestern Ontario. The population in 2014 was 711 people, with 591 living on-reserve. It calls itself Bizhiw-zaaga'iganiwininiwag, meaning "The First Nation at Wild-Cat Lake," with "wild-cat" referring to the Canadian lynx. The community of Cat Lake was originally established as a Hudson's Bay Company trading post in 1788 and later belonged to the Osnaburgh Band of Ojibwa. The Cat Lake Reserve is within the boundaries of the territory described by the James Bay Treaty (Treaty No. 9) of 1905. The reserve was formally established on 22 June 1970. Wasaya Airways runs a daily schedule of flights in the area. The community has no year-round road access; however, winter roads connect Cat Lake to Pickle Lake, via the Northern Ontario Resource Trail, which takes an average of four to five hours to travel. The Band Council is a member of the Windigo First Nations Council, a non-political regional chiefs council. The community is also a member of the larger Nishnawbe Aski Nation, a tribal organization that represents many of the First Nations in northwestern Ontario. It is also policed by the Nishnawbe Aski Police Service, an Aboriginal-based policing network.

Chapleau Cree (Fox Lake)

www.chapleaucree.ca

This Mushkegowuk Cree First Nation consists of two reserves (Fox Lake and Chapleau #75) situated in the Sudbury District approximately 5 kilometres southwest of the town of Chapleau and 160 kilometres west of Timmins. INAC does not list a population total, but the Chapleau First Nation webpage (n.d.), under "community profile," indicates a total registered population of 337 persons, 73 of whom live on-reserve. Statistics Canada (2008) indicates an on-reserve population of 92. A reason for the relatively low on-reserve population mentioned on the Chapleau Cree webpage is that the town of Chapleau had built a sewage reservoir only 1,000 feet from the settlement boundaries from the #75 reserve, resulting in land that was of poor quality, and so band members have chosen not to settle there. In 1989, both the federal and provincial governments agreed to set aside lands for the Chapleau Cree First Nation and to establish a new permanent community. The community is a member of the Mushkegowuk Tribal Council, the Nishawbe Aski Nation, and a signatory to Treaty No. 9. The Fox Lake reserve is accessible by road five kilometres southwest of Chapleau on Highway 129. The Nishnawbe Aski Police, an Aboriginal police service, serves the community, which employs three full-time officers.

Chapleau Ojibway

www.chapleauojibwe.ca

One of three First Nations in close proximity to the town of Chapleau (Chapleau Cree and Brunswick House are the others), situated approximately 160 kilometres northeast of Sault Ste. Marie. It consists of three reserves in the Sudbury District, of which the main reserve (Chapleau 74A) is located two kilometres south of Chapleau, off Highway 101. In 2014, the total registered population was 41, of which 32 persons live on-reserve. It is a member of the Wabun Tribal Council, which represents five First Nations in the Chapleau–Gogama region; the Nishnawbe Aski Nation; and is a signatory to Treaty No. 9. According to the memory of First Nation elders, there was originally a fairly large community on the shores of the Chapleau River, which included Anglican and Catholic churches. However, over time the population has declined as younger people moved to other communities, and only a few older people live along the river.

Chi Genebek Ziibing Anishinabek. See Serpent River

Chippewas of Georgina Island

www.georginaisland.com

An Ojibwa (Anishenaabe) people living on the southern shores of Lake Simcoe, situated approximately 30 kilometres south of Parry Sound. The reserve consists of three islands, namely, Georgina, Snake, and Fox Islands. In 2014, the total registered population was 863 people, of whom 199 live on-reserve. Access to the reserve consists of a ferry service in the summer months. The First Nation is a member of the Ogemahwahj Tribal Council, which represents five First Nations in the Port Perry–Mactier region.

Chippewas of Kettle and Stony Point

www.kettlepoint.org

An Anishenaabe-speaking people living on the Kettle Point Reserve, situated 35 kilometres northeast of Sarnia on the southern shore of Lake Huron. In 1942, the federal government appropriated land at Stony Point under the War Measures Act, which forced the members of both the Stony and Kettle Point communities onto one reserve. In 1995, a land claim protest took place at Ipperwash Provincial Park, resulting in the killing of band member Dudley George by OPP officer Kenneth Deane. The Ontario government initiated an investigation into this incident, referred to as the *Ipperwash Inquiry*, the results of which were released in 2007 (Linden 2007). The disputed land was returned to the First Nation in 2009. As of 2014, the total registered population was 2,400, of which 1,350 live on the reserve. The community is a member of the Southern First Nations Secretariat, which represents seven First Nations in the Sarnia–Thamesville region. For a study of the Ipperwash Provincial Park dispute in which Dudley George was killed, see Edward Hedican, *Ipperwash: The Tragic Failure of Canada's Aboriginal Policy* (2013).

Chippewas of Nawash (Cape Croker)

www.nawash.ca

Located on the eastern shore of the Saugeen (Bruce) Peninsula on Georgian Bay, approximately 26 kilometres from Wiarton. The First Nation was initially named "Nawash" after Chief Nawash, who fought beside Tecumseh in the war of 1812. In 1992, the Cape Croker reserve was officially named *Neyaashiinigming*, meaning "point of land surrounded on three sides by water." Band membership was listed at approximately 2,080 on its website (INAC does not list population figures for this First Nation). In 2001, the community formed a formal research partnership with the University of Guelph to study fisheries and other resource management issues.

Chippewas of Pelee. See Caldwell

Chippewas of Rama (Mnjikaning)

www.mnjikaning.ca

An Anishenaabe (Ojibwa) First Nation located about five kilometres northeast of Orillia between Lake Simcoe and Lake Couchiching. Around 1830, this community was moved to the Coldwater Narrows area by the Crown, part of an "experiment" that shaped "Indian Reserves." Forced to move again, by the terms of what the Rama First Nation members refer to as an "illegal surrender," the First Nation purchased land in Rama Township in 1836. The land there was difficult to farm, so the First Nation pursued other entrepreneurial opportunities in the tourist market. A community referendum has recently resumed the name of Chippewas of Rama, replacing the previous name of Mnjikaning First Nation. The community comprises 1,500 total members, with approximately 750 living on the Mnjikaning Reserve, according to the First Nation's webpage (INAC does not have a population listing). It is well known for the Casino Rama and Entertainment Complex, and is a member of the Ogemawahj Tribal Council.

Chippewas of Sarnia. See Aamjiwnaang

Chippewas of Saugeen

www.saugeenfirstnation.ca

Located on the shores of Lake Huron about three kilometres northeast of Southampton. Has formed an alliance with the Chippewas of Nawash First Nation, which collectively is known as the Saugeen Ojibway Nation Territories. While predominately Ojibway (Anishenaabe), because of the influx of refugees from the south and west after the War of 1812, there are also people whose ancestry can be traced to Odawa and Potawatomi people. INAC does not list any population figures for this First Nation; however, the band's own website indicates that a population of 427 people live in the community. The total band population is not indicated.

Chippewas of the Thames

www.cottfn.com

An Anishenaabe (Ojibwa) First Nation consisting of one reserve 24 kilometres west of St. Thomas, on the west bank of the Thames River in southwestern Ontario. The population as of 2014 was 2,761 people, with 961 living on the reserve. The community is a member of the Southern First Nations Secretariat, which represents seven First Nations in the Sarnia–Thamesville region, and the Union of Ontario Indians. In 1763, Chief Seckas of the Thames River brought 170 warriors to the siege of Detroit during Pontiac's uprising. The reserve was established in 1819, as part of a treaty by which the Chippewas of the Thames agreed to share 552,000 acres of land with the British for an annuity of 600 pounds and the establishment of two reserves. In 1840, the Chippewas reached an agreement with the Munsee-Delaware Nation to share the reserve. The Munsee portion of the reserve became part of the new Munsee-Delaware Nation No. 1 Reserve in 1967.

Cockburn Island. See Zhiibaahaasing

Collins. See Namaygoosisagagun

Constance Lake

www.clfn.on.ca

Located on the shores of Constance Lake, near Hearst in the Cochrane District in northeastern Ontario. In 2014, it was home to 1,672 people of Cree and Ojibwa ancestry, with approximately 860 living on two reserves. One, Constance Lake 92, is located on the Kabinakagami River, and the other, English River 66, is on the east bank of the Kenogami River. A member of the Nishnawbe Aski Nation, a tribal political organization representing many of the First Nations in northern and northwestern Ontario, especially those living in the Treaty No. 9 area. The community is also a member of the Matawa First Nations Management, which represents ten First Nations in northwestern Ontario. This First Nation is also situated in the mineral-rich Ring of Fire, and there is a proposed massive chromite mining and smelting development project in the James Bay Lowlands. Tony Clement, former president of the Treasury Board, has claimed that the Ring of Fire area will be the economic equivalent of the Athabasca oil sands project, with a potential to generate $120 billion. This development would be of immense economic benefit to the First Nations people of the area as they are some of the most socio-economically disadvantaged communities in all of Canada, according to Mr. Clement. Former Ontario premier Bob Rae has been appointed as chief negotiator to represent the different First Nations governments (Marten Falls, Webequie, Neskantaga, Nabinamik, Aroland, Long Lake 58, Ginoogaming, Eabametoong, Mishkeegogamang, and Constance Lake) in this region.

Couchiching

www.couchichingfirstnation.com

This is a Saulteaux (Ojibwa) First Nation consisting of two reserves in the Rainy River District near Fort Francis. The total registered population in 2014 was 2,422 people, of whom 738 live on-reserve. The community is a member of the Pwi-Di-Goo-Zing Ne-Yaa-Zhing Advisory Services, which is a regional tribal council representing seven First Nations near Fort Francis, Emo, and Mine Centre. It is also a member of the Grand Council Treaty #3. Certain members of the Anishenaabe Nation in Treaty No. 3 lived at what was then known as Frog Lake with Chief Mikiseesis (Little Eagle). In 1875, two additional reserves were surveyed for the "light-skinned Anishenaabe," or *Waasaakode Innini*, as part of what Canada called the "half-breed" adhesion of Treaty No. 3. In 1965, all three reserves were amalgamated as the community of Couchiching First Nation.

Curve Lake

www.curvelakefirstnation.ca

Located in Peterborough County on the Trent waterways, consisting of Mississauga Ojibway peoples who live on three reserves about 14 kilometres north of Peterborough. One of these reserves (Trent Waters Indian Reserve 36A) is also shared with the Hiawatha and Scugog First Nations. In 2014, the total registered population living on these reserves numbered 791 people, with an additional 1,458 registered band members living off-reserve. The community traces its origins to 1829, when a small band settled around Curve and Mud Lakes, but the area did not officially become a reserve until 1837. Other reserves were added in 1964.

Dalles. See Ochiichagwe'babigo'ining

Deer Lake

www.deerlake.firstnation.ca

This is an Oji-Cree First Nation in northern Ontario, located approximately 180 kilometres north of Red Lake. The total registered population in 2014 was 1,259 people, of whom 1,053 live on-reserve. It is one of the few First Nations in Ontario to have signed Treaty No. 5 in 1910. The community is part of the Keewaytinook Okimakanak Council of Northern Chiefs, which represents six First Nations between Fort Severn and Red Lake, and is also policed by the Nishnawbe Aski Police Service. The people of Deer Lake are closely related to the people of Sandy Lake First Nation and North Spirit Lake First Nation. However, in 1985, the Deer Lake First Nation formally split from the Sandy Lake First Nation, with each achieving full band status. The two reserves maintain close relations, given the people's shared history and number of family connections. The people living on the reserves in this area speak a unique dialect of the Anishenaabe language that combines elements of Berens River Ojibway, as spoken in nearby Pikangikum and Poplar Hill, and Severn Ojibway (Oji-Cree), as spoken in Island Lake in Manitoba. Fluency in the Oji-Cree language is relatively high, as nearly 70 percent of Deer Lake people have learned their native language as their first language. The Deer Lake community has an interesting history as well. In 1906, the North-West Mounted

Police arrived to arrest Chief Jack Fiddler and his brother Joseph. The elderly Fiddler brothers were charged with the murder of an elderly woman, who was thought to be possessed by a windigo, an evil cannibalistic spirit. This incident is recounted in *Killing the Shamen* (1985) by Chief Thomas Fiddler and James S. Stevens.

Deleware Nation at Moraviantown

www.delawarenation.on.ca

Located on the southern shores of the Thames River, near the town of Thamesville in the Chatham–Kent area, approximately three hours west of Toronto. Moraviantown is located on the south shore of the Thames River, east of Thamesville. In 2014, the total registered population was 674 people, with 440 living off-reserve. A part of the Munsee branch of the Lenape-Delaware people with one of the oldest settlements in the region, founded in 1792. This First Nation played an important role alongside both First Nations and British forces in the War of 1812. During this time, their original village, on the north side of the Thames River, was burned by retreating American soldiers at the Battle of the Thames, which is also the site at which the Shawnee leader Tecumseh was killed. Today, community members operate the Lenape Radio Society, 104.3 FM (CKBK), broadcasting old-time stories, often in the Delaware language, with a mixture of news, music, and weather reports.

Dokis

www.dokisfirstnation.com

This Ojibwa (Anishenaabe) First Nation consists of one reserve located on the boundaries that separate the districts of Parry Sound, Sudbury, and Nipissing, approximately 16 kilometres southwest of Lake Nipissing on the French River. The community is accessed by a 25-kilometre gravel road from Highway 64, to the nearest urban centres of North Bay, via Highway 17, and Sudbury, via Highway 69. Both are approximately 170 kilometres from the community. Michel "Eagle" Dokis signed the Robinson-Huron Treaty in 1850, which created the present First Nation boundaries. The main settlement is located on a large island called Okikendawt Island, which means "Island of the Buckets/ Pails." These "buckets" are rock formations created by centuries of flowing water and were often utilized for tobacco offerings for safe passage through the territory. In 2014, the total registered population was 1,168, of which 174 members reside on-reserve. The community is a member of the Waabnoong Bemjiwang Association of First Nations, which represents six First Nations in the Parry Sound–Capreol region.

Eabametoong (Fort Hope)

www.eabametoong.firstnation.ca

This First Nation consists of one reserve (Fort Hope 64) located in the Kenora District of northern Ontario, on the shore of Eabamet Lake in the Albany River system, approximately 300 kilometres north of Thunder Bay. The name *Eabametoong* in the Anishenaabe language means "the reversing of the water place." This phenomenon refers to the water flow from Eabamet Lake into the Albany River, which reverses each year resulting from runoff, such that water flows into Eabamet Lake from the Albany River for a short period of time, before resuming its normal flow. The total registered population in 2014 was 2,525 people, of whom 1,526 live on-reserve. It is a member of the Matawa First Nations Management, which is a tribal council representing ten First Nations in the Webequie and Ogoki Post area of northern Ontario. The reserve is only accessible by airplane to the Fort Hope Airport or by the winter road that connects the community to the Northern Ontario Resource Trail. Eabametoong originated during the fur-trade era when the Hudson's Bay Company built a trading post by Eabamet Lake in 1890. The Fort Hope Band came into existence in 1905 when Treaty No. 9 was signed by about 500 people. In 1976, a cooperative store and police station were opened, and eventually the community came under the jurisdiction of the Nishnawbe Aski Police Service. The new community of Eabametoong started in 1982, with the official name of Eabametoong First Nation being adopted in 1985. For an anthropological study of economic development issues in the mid-1980s, see Paul Driben and R.S. Trudeau, *When Freedom is Lost: The Dark Side of the Relationship between Government and the Fort Hope Band* (1983).

Eagle Lake (Migisi Sahaigan)

www.eaglelakefirstnation.ca

The Eagle Lake community is located in northwestern Ontario, approximately 25 kilometres southwest of Dryden on the northeast shores of Eagle Lake and is accessible via Highways 502 and 594. As of 2010, the total population was 574 persons (INAC does not list current membership figures for this First Nation). It is a member of the Bimose Tribal Council, which represents ten First Nations in the Dryden–Kenora region. The people are also a part of the Grand Council Treaty #3, which was signed in 1873 and covers 55,000 square miles. Cultural activities are an important element of Eagle Lake society, which includes powwows, community sweats, sharing circles, traditional healing and elders' activities, and school and community feasts. This is also a sports-oriented community with two baseball diamonds and an arena. It has been a co-host and participant in the All Ontario High School Championships for men's and women's hockey and figure skating.

Flying Post

www.flyingpost.ca

Flying Post was a Hudson's Bay Company trading post located on the *Kukatush* or Groundhog River, a tributary of the Mattagmi River, built by Donald McKay in 1800. The Flying Post Reserve is located 40 kilometres from Smooth Rock Falls and had a total registered population in 2014 of 213 people, of whom all are living off-reserve. The band office is located in Nipigon, Ontario, and is a signatory of Treaty No. 9 (16 July 1906). On 10 July 2008, Flying Post Chief Murray Ray, along with the chiefs of the Mattagami and Brunswick House First Nations, in conjunction with the Wabun Tribal Council, signed an exploration agreement with the Augen Gold Corporation in Timmins as part of the development of the Jerome Mine site west of Gogama.

Fort Albany

www.firstnation.ca/fort-albany

Situated on the southern shore of the Albany River on Sinclair Island in the Cochrane District of northeastern Ontario and named after a Hudson's Bay Company post originally built in 1670. The community is only accessible by air, water, or winter road, and is policed by the Nishnawbe Aski Police Service. Air Creebec provides Fort Albany residents with daily passenger flights, with connecting flights to Toronto. The majority of the population speaks Mushkegowuk Cree, although there is a mixture of languages spoken, such as French, English, and Ojibwa. In the 1950s, the original reserve was divided into two communities along religious lines, with Fort Albany remaining largely Roman Catholic and members of the Kashechewan First Nation mainly Anglican. Since the 1970s, both First Nations have been treated as separate bands with their own band councils. In 2014, the total registered population of both First Nations combined (since INAC does not recognize Kashechewan as a separate First Nation) was 4,774, with 3,086 persons living on-reserve. The community is a member of the Mushkegowuk Tribal Council, which represents six First Nations in the Cochrane–Moose Factory region.

Fort Hope. See Eabametoong

Fort Severn (Washaho Cree Nation)

www.fortsevern.firstnation.ca

This is the most northerly First Nation in Ontario and consists of two

Cree-speaking reserves located at the mouth of the Severn River. The total registered population in 2014 was 676 people, of whom 529 live on-reserve. The community is linked by an ice road, called the Wapusk Trail, in the winter, to Peawanuck in the east and Shamattawa and Gillam to the west in Manitoba. It is policed by the Nishnawbe Aski Police Service and is a member of the Keewaytinook Okimakanak Council of Northern Chiefs, which represents six First Nations in the Red Lake and Fort Severn region. In 1689, the Hudson's Bay Company built Fort Severn at this site, and it was one of the earliest English fur-trading posts in the New World. In 1782, the French attacked the outpost and pillaged it as they were allies of the Thirteen Colonies during the American Revolutionary War. The people of the area were joined into treaty with the 1930 adhesion to Treaty No. 9. In 1973, the original reserve, situated at the confluence of the Severn and Sachigo Rivers, was relocated to the mouth of the Severn River on Hudson Bay for more direct access to shipping. The reserve achieved full status in January 1980. Important cultural events include the Washo Cree Nation Elder's Canoe Trip, which visits ancestral villages and riverbank graves along the *Weeshinago Siipi* (Beaverstone River) and *Atchigo Siipi* (Sachigo River) waterways.

Fort William

www.fwfn.com

This is an Ojibway First Nation situated in close proximity to Thunder Bay on the north shore of Lake Superior. In 2014, the total registered population was 2,203, of which 981 live on-reserve. The community is a member of the Nokiiwin Tribal Council, which represents six First Nations in the Thunder Bay–Beardmore area, and the Union of Ontario Indians. It is also home to the head offices of Wasaya Airways, which provides air transport to many First Nations in northern Ontario. The Fort William Reserve was originally set aside under the provisions of the Robinson-Superior Treaty of 1850 and created in 1853. Under this treaty, the British Crown promised cash payments and trade goods, as well as annuities beginning in 1851; freedom to hunt and fish in the traditional manner, except on private land; and a reserve at Fort William. In return, the Fort William Band agreed to surrender their traditional territory, which extended from Pigeon River to the south at the United States bound-ary, east to Lake Nipigon, and north to the Treaty No. 9 boundary, as well as agreeing not to interfere with foreign settlers in this area. Nearby Mount McKay, originally known as *Animikii-wajiw* or the "Thunder Mountain" in the Ojibwa language, is often utilized as a site for sacred ceremonies and other community cultural activities. Between 2007 and 2009, a non-profit environmental group called *Anishinabek Gitchi Gami* Environmental Programs (AGG) was formed, comprising Thunder Bay citizens and members of the Fort William First Nation, in order to address threats to human and environmental health caused by industrial pollution in the Thunder Bay area.

Fox Lake. See Chapleau Cree

Garden River (Ketegaunseebee)

www.gardenriver.org

Located near Sault Ste. Marie, the reserve consists of two non-contiguous areas; the larger one is situated along the St. Mary's River and Highway 17, the other on the Garden River, which is a tributary of the St. Mary's River. The Garden River First Nation signed the Robinson-Huron Treaty on 29 November 1850, and was represented by Shingwaukonse, who was generally recognized as an Ojibwa Grand Chief by other bands in the Lake Huron and Lake Superior watersheds. In 1833, a combined schoolhouse and Anglican church was constructed at Garden River, and in 1873, the Shingwauk Industrial Home was opened, but was destroyed by fire shortly after. It was subsequently rebuilt at Sault Ste. Marie as an Indian Residential School, drawing mostly boys from distant Walpole Island, Sarnia, and Muncey, as well as Garden River. In 1877, a separate residential school for girls was opened, named the Wawanosh Home for Girls, but by 1962, all of the students were "living out." In 2014, Garden River had a total registered population of 2,776, with 1,262 members who reside on the reserve, and the others (1,514) living mainly in Sault Ste. Marie. This community is a member of the Mamaweswen, the North Shore Tribal Council, which represents seven First Nations in the Sault Ste. Marie–Thessalon area.

Gasabaanakaa Nistam Anisininiwaad. See Kasabonika Lake

Georgina Island. See Chippewas of Georgina Island

Gibson Reserve. See Wahta Mohawks

Ginoogaming (Long Lake 77)

www.ginoogaming.ca

This First Nation consists of one reserve located in northern Ontario, approximately 40 kilometres east of Geraldton on the north shore of Long Lake, close to the town of Longlac. The total registered population is 816, of which 173 live on-reserve. The community is within the boundaries of the territory described by the James Bay Treaty of 1905 (Treaty No. 9). The Long Lake Reserve was officially created when the band signed an adhesion to Treaty No. 9 in August

1906. Ginoongaming First Nation is a member of the Matawa First Nations Management, which is a regional tribal council representing ten First Nations in the Long Lake, Webequie, and Ogoki Post area. The community's primary tribal organization is the Nishnawbe Aski Nation, which represents most of the First Nations of northern Ontario. An important current issue for the community is the Ginoogaming Timber Claim Trust, which was established in April 2002 following negotiations and an agreement between Ginoogaming and the Government of Canada for compensation resulting from illegal taking of timber on Long Lake Reserve #77. The overall goal of the Timber Claim Trust is to provide social, economic, and cultural benefits to all members of the Ginoogaming First Nation, no matter where they happen to live. In conjunction with the Timber Claim Trust initiative, in January 2013 the Ginoogaming community also started the Giizhagaakwe (Cutting Wood) program in order to harvest conifer pulpwood from the Kenogami Forest, which is the second largest area of forest resources in Ontario.

Golden Lake Algonquin. See Algonquins of Pikwakanagan

Grassy Narrows (Asubpeeschoseewagong)

www.grassynarrows.ca

The Grassy Narrows First Nation is also known as the *Asabiinyashkosiwagong Nitam-Anishinaabeg* in the Anishenaabe or Ojibwa language. It is located 80 kilometres north of Kenora along the Wabigoon-English River, northeast of Lake of the Woods. As of 2014, it had a total registered population of 1,519 people, of whom 986 live on-reserve. The community is a member of the Bimose Tribal Council, which represents ten First Nations in the Kenora–Dryden region of northwestern Ontario, and of the Grand Council Treaty #3. With the signing of Treaty No. 3, sometimes referred to as the North-West Angle Treaty, each family was to receive as much as a square mile of land; tribal members were allowed to hunt, fish, and trap on unused portions of their former domain; and the government undertook to establish schools and provide ammunition for hunting, along with a small amount of money to the tribe in the form of annuity payments. From 1876 to 1969, schooling was at the McIntosh Residential School situated at McIntosh, Ontario.

This First Nation was inflicted with a major tragedy when community members were poisoned by mercury originating from the Dryden Chemical Company, which was discharged into the Wabigoon–English River system. Fish were the major source of protein for the Grassy Narrows people, and when their commercial fishery was closed down in 1970, unemployment rose to 90 percent in the community. The closure also affected the tourism industry, in which local people acted as guides for out-of-town fishermen. Grassy Narrows First Nation received a settlement in 1985 from the Canadian government and the Reed Paper Company, which had bought out the Dryden Chemical Company, but the mercury was never removed from the water. A 2012 study found that the mercury content of pickerel in the river had been reduced, but a health advisory remains in effect. Deforestation has been another important community issue, and in 2011, the Grassy Narrows First Nation won a victory in Ontario's Superior Court when it was ruled that the Province of Ontario cannot authorize logging operations when they infringe on federal treaty promises that protect Aboriginal rights to traditional hunting and fishing. *See* Anestasia Shkilnyk, *A Poison Stronger than Love: The Destruction of an Ojibwa Community* (1985).

Gull Bay (Kiashke Zaaging Anishinaabek)

www.firstnation.ca/gull-bay-kiashke-zaaging-anishinaabek

The Gull Bay community consists of one reserve on the western shore of Lake Nipigon, on Highway 527 about 175 kilometres north of Thunder Bay in northwestern Ontario. In 2014, the total registered population was 1,327, of which 382 live on-reserve. The people are a signatory to the Robinson-Superior Treaty of 1850 and members of the Nokiiwin Tribal Council, which represents six First Nations in the Thunder Bay–Beardmore area. They are also members of the Union of Ontario Indians, a political territorial organization that represents many of the Anishenaabe First Nation governments in Ontario situated about Lake Superior and Lake Huron. On 10 November 2014, the Gull Bay First Nation ratified a $12.5 million settlement with Ontario Power Generation that will offer compensation and a formal apology to community members. The settlement is the result of flooding of Lake Nipigon caused by the construction of dams on the Nipigon River and the diversion of the Ogoki River. The flooding, which dates back to 1918, eroded the Gull Bay Reserve boundaries, desecrated traditional burial sites, and resulted in a loss of livelihood because of a diminished access to hunting, trapping, and fishing areas.

Henvey Inlet

www.hifn.ca

This community is located on the northeast shore of Georgian Bay, about 90 kilometres west of Sudbury and 71 kilometres north of Parry Sound. It consists of three separate reserve properties of Ojibwa-speaking people. The registered population is about 600 people, of whom approximately 450 live off-reserve.

The people belong to the Waabnoong Bemjiwang Association of First Nations, which represents six First Nations in the Parry Sound–Capreol area. A major initiative of the Henvey Inlet First Nation is a wind farm project run by the Nigig Power Corporation. On 4 June 2010, this corporation submitted an application to the Ontario Power Authority for a 300-megawatt wind farm. Construction is expected to begin in 2017. It is estimated that the wind project could generate revenues of about $150 million per year. Nigig Power's share of the net revenue is expected to be in the range of $15–$35 million per year over a 20-year period. The Henvey Inlet First Nation would then manage this revenue in order to provide for a wide range of community needs, such as education and training, business development, and other community initiatives.

Hiawatha

www.hiawathafirstnation.com

Located on the north shore of Rice Lake, east of the Otonabee River, approximately 30 kilometres south of Peterborough. There are extensive archaeological remains on this First Nation reserve relating to the Point Peninsula Complex, consisting of a series of earthen mounds constructed for ceremonial, religious, and burial purposes. Serpent Mounds Park includes an effigy mound, as well as nine other burial mounds, some nearly 200 feet long. In 2014, the total registered population was 606, of which 205 persons lived on-reserve.

Hornepayne

www.hpfn.ca

This is a non-status Ojibwe First Nation that does not have a reserve, nor is it recognized by Indigenous and Northern Affairs Canada as a First Nation, although its membership has apparently applied for such status. Total membership is difficult to determine, but the First Nation's website lists a total population of 11 people who speak both Ojibwe and Cree and are seeking other possible members. The First Nation is located near the town of Hornepayne in northwestern Ontario and is a member of the Matawa First Nations, a non-profit regional chiefs council, and is recognized as a Native community by the Nishnawbe Aski Nation. It is within the territory recognized by the James Bay Treaty (Treaty No. 9) of 1905. According to the members' webpage, the people of this First Nation were situated around Nagagami and Obakimaga Lakes in northern Ontario about 1760, and by the 1930s, started to move to a settlement on the Morrison (Shekak) River. By the 1940s, they had moved to their present Hornepayne location in order to work for a timber company and the Canadian National Railway.

Iskatewizaagegan #39 (Shoal Lake)

www.shoallake39.ca

An Anishenaabe (Ojibwa) First Nation located along the northwestern shores of Shoal Lake, situated near the Manitoba border. Consists of four reserves with a total registered population of 621 in 2014, of which 348 live on-reserve. One of the reserves (Shoal Lake #39) is partly located in Manitoba, and another (Agency 30) is shared with 12 other First Nations. The community is part of the Grand Council Treaty #3 territory. An ongoing issue, as indicated on the First Nation's website (n.d.), is that "Shoal Lake has been the primary drinking water supply for Winnipeg since 1919 but Shoal Lake 39 receives absolutely no compensation for the water supply." As of March 2012, the matter of water usage, and Winnipeg's proposed plan to sell its water to outlying communities, was brought to the Manitoba Court of Queen's Bench. The community is a member of the Bimose Tribal Council, which represents ten First Nations in the Kenora–Dryden region of northwestern Ontario.

Kasabonika Lake (Gasabaanakaa Nistam Anisininiwaad)

www.kasabonikafirstnation.com

This is an Oji-Cree First Nation located 448 kilometres northwest of Sioux Lookout in northern Ontario. It is a remote community accessible only by air through Kasabonika Airport or by winter road. The total registered population in 2014 was 1,116 people, of whom 1,065 live on-reserve. It is part of the Shibogama First Nations Council, which represents five First Nations in the region north of Sioux Lookout, and a member of the Nishnawbe Aski Nation. The local detachment of the Nishnawbe Aski Police Service was closed in February 2008 because of the lack of running water and a reliance on firewood to heat the facility. Prisoners now must be flown to Sioux Lookout at great expense. Community members developed the Kasabonika Resource Policy in 2007 to facilitate dealing with any possible mineral development in their area.

Kashechewan (Keeshechewan)

According to the records of the Department of Indigenous and Northern Affairs Canada, the survey information for the Kashechewan First Nation is combined with that of Fort Albany, which is located near James Bay in northern Ontario. Therefore, Kashechewan does not have a separate website or separate population totals, although they are considered locally as two separate communities. For both Fort Albany and Kashechewan First Nations, the total registered population in 2014 was 4,774, of which 3,086 live on-reserve; both First Nations share the same reserve (Albany Reserve #67). A further source of confusion resulted when the name "Keeshechewan" was chosen for the name of the community, which means "where the water flows fast," but the sign for the new post office arrived with the misspelling "Kashechewan," which has no real meaning in the Cree language. It nonetheless has become the community's official name. Its members are represented by the Mushkegowuk Council, along with seven other First Nations in northern Ontario, and the Nishnawbe Aski Nation, which is a political territorial organization that represents the 49 First Nations that are part of the Treaty No. 9 area. In 2007, the Government of Canada signed a memorandum of agreement with the Kashechewan community for a grant of $200 million to improve and repair settlement infrastructure, housing, and flood control services. However, in May 2014, Kashechewan residents were once again forced from their homes due to flooding, which resulted in 2,000 persons being evacuated to Thunder Bay, Kapuskasing, Timmins, and other northern locations.

Keeshechewan. See Kashechewan

Keewaywin

www.keewaywin.firstnation.ca

This is a relatively isolated Oji-Cree community located about 200 kilometres northeast of Red Lake, situated on the eastern shore of Sandy Lake in northern Ontario. It was once a part of the Sandy Lake First Nation but later separated and has separate reserve status, even though both First Nations are situated on the same lake. In 2014, the total registered population was 760 persons, of whom 552 live-on reserve. It is only accessible by air, presently serviced by Adventure Air and Wasaya Airways, or by winter road. The community is a member of the Keewaytinook Okimakanak Council of Northern Chiefs, which represents six First Nations in the Red Lake–Fort Severn region of northwestern Ontario.

Ketegaunseebee. See Garden River

Kettle and Stony Point. See Chippewas of Kettle and Stony Point

Kiashke Zaaging Anishinaabek. See Gull Bay

Kingfisher Lake

www.kingfisherlake.ca

Located 350 kilometres north of Sioux Lookout in northwestern Ontario, this First Nation consists of three reserves around Kingfisher Lake. The people consider themselves speakers of the Oji-Cree language. It is accessible by air all year round, waterways during the summer, and ice roads in the winter. In 2014, the registered population was 562 people, with an on-reserve population of 520 people. The community is policed by the Nishnawbe Aski Police Service. The origins of the community have been associated with the 1808 establishment of a Hudson's Bay Company post at Big Beaver House, 12 kilometres southwest of the present Kingfisher Lake reserve. During 1929–30, the leaders of the Kingfisher First Nation gathered at Big Trout Lake to participate in the signing of the adhesion to Treaty No. 9, at which time the band was considered a part of the Big Trout Lake Band. In 1964, the leaders of the Kingfisher Lake population decided to establish a permanent community and moved to the current location of the reserve lands. Formal recognition of the band's status was achieved in 1975. In 2011, the residents of Kingfisher Lake were temporarily housed in Ottawa due to the threat of forest fires in the surrounding area.

Kitchenuhmaykoosib Inninuwug (Big Trout Lake)

www.bigtroutlake.firstnation.ca/

This community consisting of one reserve is located on the north shore of Big Trout Lake, from which the Anishenaabe (Oji-Cree) name of the community is derived, and is situated about 580 kilometres north of Thunder Bay. It is a fly-in settlement, accessible by air with regularly scheduled flights by Wasaya Airways to the Big Trout Lake Airport. During the winter months, the community is accessible by the winter road to Pickle Lake, which is serviced by Ontario Highway 599, the northernmost highway in the province. The total registered population in 2014 was 1,598 people, of whom 1,110 reside on-reserve, which makes it the largest First Nation in the region. When Treaty No. 9 was first signed at Osnaburgh in 1905, the Trout Lake Band was located on land that was, at the time, not considered part of Ontario. When band members learned of the signing, they requested treaty terms so that they could be included in the provisions of Treaty No. 9. Subsequently, in 1929–30, an adhesion was made to Treaty No. 9, which eventually led to the granting of full reserve status for Big Trout Lake in 1976. Marion Anderson, who became a band councillor for Big Trout Lake in 1950, was the first woman ever to serve as a First Nation councillor in Ontario. She was later awarded the Order of Ontario in honour of this distinction. In 2008, the chief and five councillors of the Big Trout Lake First Nation were sent to jail in Thunder Bay over a dispute with the Platinex mining company, which the band claimed was prospecting and conducting exploration activities without the consent of the band. The leaders were given temporary parole and then permanently freed by the Ontario Court of Appeal two days later. In 2012, Chief Donny Morris and his wife were invited to New Zealand for a speaking tour to discuss the band's experience with Platinex and the Government of Ontario.

Koocheching

www.firstnation.ca/koocheching

Located about 400 kilometres north of Sioux Lookout in northwestern Ontario, and accessible by air to Sandy Lake, 65 kilometres to the southwest, on a year-round basis, or by a 12-kilometre seasonal road from Keewaywin First Nation, which also connects Pickle Lake and Cat Lake. Population figures are not available at this time. This First Nation does not have official status (non-status) because of a jurisdictional dispute with the federal government that has been going on for nearly two decades. According to Chief William Harper, the federal department of Indigenous and Northern Affairs (INAC) has indicated that a reserve for the Koocheching First Nation must come from the adjacent Keewaywin First Nation, a Cree community who received official reserve status in 1985. As a result of this dispute, the Koocheching elementary school, attended by eight children, was closed in 2010 due to lack of funding. The Koocheching community is a member of the Nishnawbe Aski Nation and a signatory to Treaty No. 9.

Lac des Mille Lacs (Nizaatikoong)

www.lacdesmillelacsfirstnation.ca

The Saulteaux Ojibwe name of this First Nation is derived from *Neazaadiikaang*, meaning "at a point of land abundant with poplars." It has two reserves in the Thunder Bay District of northwestern Ontario. One of the reserves is on the northeast shore of Lac des Mille Lacs, 55 kilometres northwest of Thunder Bay, and the other is 132 kilometres northwest of Thunder Bay at the junction of the Seine and Firesteel Rivers. Its members are affiliated with the Bimose Tribal Council, which represents ten First Nations in the Kenora–Dryden area, and the Grand Council Treaty #3. As of 2014, the total registered population was 602 people; however only 5 persons live on-reserve. The reason for this situation is that because of past flooding by various dam projects in the region, members of this First Nation are mostly dispersed throughout northwestern Ontario and other parts of Canada. However, it does have a governance office located on the territory of the Fort William First Nation near Thunder Bay. The goal of the members of this First Nation is to rebuild their own community on the Seine River site, and in 2006, they released a site analysis feasibility study. They also have an outstanding land claim with the federal government over the loss of their reserve territory. In 2012, Leo Baskatawang, an Iraq

War veteran and a registered member of the Lac des Mille Lacs First Nation, staged a 4,400-kilometre march from Vancouver to Ottawa with a copy of the Indian Act chained to his body in order to raise awareness of the plight of the community and other First Nations peoples.

Lac La Croix (Neguaguon Lake)

www.firstnation.ca/lac-la-croix

The name of this First Nation derives from the French designation, meaning "the Lake of the Cross"; however, for the Ojibway people this location is traditionally known as *Zhingwaako Zaaga'igan,* meaning "Lake of the Pines." This community consists of one reserve on Neguaguon Lake in the Rainy River District, along the Ontario-Minnesota border, about 200 kilometres northwest of Thunder Bay and approximately 95 kilometres east of Fort Francis in northwestern Ontario. Access to the community is by Flanders Road, an 80-kilometre long, all-weather road that is accessed by Highway 11 about 40 kilometres west of Atikokan. Originally, this First Nation also had another reserve, Sturgeon Lake Indian Reserve 24C, but through the Ontario Provincial Park Act of 1950, this second reserve was made part of Quetico Provincial Park. As of 2014, the First Nation had a registered population of 451 people, of whom 351 reside on-reserve. Community members were signatory to Treaty No. 3 and are members of the Pwi-Di-Goo-Zing Ne-Yaa-Zhing Advisory Services, a regional chiefs council that represents seven First Nations in the Fort Francis–Emo–Mine Centre area.

Lac Seul (Obishikokaang)

www.lacseul.firstnation.ca

An Anishenaabe First Nation located on the southeastern shores of Lac Seul, 56 kilometres northeast of Dryden and 38 kilometres northwest of Sioux Lookout in northwestern Ontario. The Lac Seul reserve is made up of three communities: Kejick, Whitefish Bay, and Frenchman's Head. The French name for the lake and the reserve is possibly a mistranslation of *Obishikokaang,* meaning "White Pine Narrows." A signatory to Treaty No. 3 and a member of both the Nishnawbe Aski Nation and the Independent First Nations Alliance, which is a regional tribal council representing five First Nations over a wide area, from Big Trout Lake to Armstrong in northern Ontario. In 2014, the total registered population was 3,323, of which 902 live on-reserve. In 1929, Ontario Hydro constructed a dam at Ear Falls to produce hydroelectricity, which caused the flooding of Lac Seul. The flooding caused the area known as Kejick Bay to become an island, permanently separating it from the mainland

and splitting the community into two parts. The island portion retained the name Kejick Bay, and the portion of the community on the mainland became Whitefish Bay.

Lake Helen. See Red Rock

Lake Nipigon Reserve. See Animbiigoo Zaagi'igan Anishinaabek

Lansdowne House. See Neskantaga

Long Lake #58

www.longlake58fn.ca

An Anishenaabe (Ojibwa) First Nation situated close to Highway 11 along the northeast shore of Long Lake, adjacent to the town of Longlac, which is located 35 kilometres northeast of Geraldton. It is also immediately north of the Ginoogaming (Long Lake 77) First Nation. In 2014, the total registered population was 1,460, of which 482 live on-reserve. The community is associated with Matawa First Nations Management, a regional tribal council representing ten First Nations widely dispersed, from Long Lac to Webequie and Ogoki Post and other reserves. This First Nation lies within the boundaries of the Robinson-Huron Treaty of 1850 and has been located on a one-square-mile tract of land since 1905, although the community contends that they have never signed a treaty with the Crown. The surrounding territory on which the people of this First Nation have lived, hunted, and fished has been reduced considerably by railway and highway construction and the development of hydroelectric projects, which have flooded and eroded even more of the land.

Long Lake 77. See Ginoogaming

Magnetawan

www.magnetawanfirstnation.com

One reserve of Anishenaabe-speaking people located six kilometres east of Georgian Bay, south of Sudbury in the Parry Sound District. Total registered population of 253 in 2014, of which 82 band members live on-reserve. Elementary students attend school locally, but secondary students attend the Parry Sound High School. The reserve is within the boundaries of the Robinson-Huron Treaty of 1850. The reserve was first surveyed in 1853; however, in 1907 an additional tract of land in the township of Wallbridge was added to compensate for an error in the original survey. The community is a member of the Waabnoong Bemijiwang Association of First Nations, which represents six First Nations in the Parry Sound–Capreol region.

Manitou Rapids. See Rainy River

Manitoulin Unceded Indian Reserve. See Wikwemikong Unceded

Marten Falls (Ogoki Post)

www.firstnation.ca/marten-falls-ogoki-post

This Anishenaabe First Nation consists of two communities in two different districts. Marten Falls is located on the north bank of the Albany River in the Kenora District, and Ogoki Post (*Ogooking* in Ojibwa), on the south bank of the Albany River, is in the Cochrane District. Both communities are located about 170 kilometres northeast of Nakina, situated on the Canadian National Railway to the south, and about 300 kilometres northeast of Thunder Bay. As of 2014, the total registered population was 742, of which 376 live on-reserve. It is a member of Matawa First Nation Management, a regional tribal council representing ten First Nations ranging from Long Lac to Webequie to Ogoki Post, as well as others, and is a signatory to Treaty No. 9. This First Nation is only accessible by air via Nakina Air Service. The winter road has not been in service since 2000. Large freight is shipped on barges on the Albany River in the summer when water levels permit. The community has its own radio station, CKFN 89.9 FM (a repeater of CKWT-FM). The on-reserve version of Children's Aid is provided through Tikinagan Child and Family Services, and the community is policed by the Nishnawbe Aski Police Service.

Matachewan

www.matachewanfirstnation.com

Consists of one reserve of Ojibwa- and Cree-speaking people located in the Timiskaming District of northern Ontario, approximately 30 kilometres southeast of the town of Matachewan and about 60 kilometres west of Kirkland Lake. As of 2014, the total registered population was 733 people, of whom 46 people live on their own reserve. This First Nation is a signatory to Treaty No. 9. It is a member of the Wabun Tribal Council, which represents five First Nations in the Chapleau–Gogama region, and the Nishnawbe Aski Nation.

Mattagami

www.mattagami.com

Consists of one reserve, which is situated along the Mattagami River (which means "meeting of the waters" in Ojibwa) in the Sudbury District, 20 kilometres northeast of Gogama and 80 kilometres from Timmins. In 2014, the total registered population was 557, of which 180 live on-reserve. The community is a mixture of Ojibwa, Oji-Cree, and Odawa speakers. Mattagami First Nation is a member of the Wabun Tribal Council and the Nishnawbe Aski Nation. In 1962, the Mattagami First Nation made history by electing the first all-women chief and council for their community. Chief Helen Naveau served for eight terms all together, and her father, Henry Kitchibra, was part of the infantry unit that fought at Vimy Ridge during World War I.

McDowell Lake (Misi-zhaaga'iganiing)

www.firstnation.ca/mcdowell-lake

This is a small Oji-Cree First Nation located in northern Ontario, approximately 155 kilometres northeast of Red Lake on the central western shore of McDowell Lake. The community was established by trapper Johnny Kenequanash in the 1940s at McDowell Lake, which was a main waterway for people travelling by canoe north to Windigo Lake or east towards Cat Lake. Kenequanash and his family were joined by the James family, and then by former members of the North Caribou Lake (Weagamow Lake) Band. The main economic activity of the community for many years was commercial fishing. In 1985, McDowell Lake, along with six other First Nations, was awarded official band status. As of 2014, the total registered population was 58, of which 25 people live on-reserve. Those community members living off-reserve primarily reside in Thunder Bay and Red Lake. Access to the community is by float plane or ski-equipped aircraft. There is no ice road that connects to this community in the winter. The McDowell Lake Council and staff coordinate trips to the community village so that the people can remain connected to their lands. Band members are kept up-to-date through a monthly newsletter and a Facebook group. The community uses a saw mill and chainsaws to renovate homes. Ice is collected in the winter months and stored in an ice shed for summer use. McDowell Lake First Nation is also working with Bell Canada to clean up hazardous waste that was left on the reserve lands.

M'Chigeeng (West Bay)

www.mchigeeng.ca

An Ojibwa First Nation located on one reserve on Manitoulin Island. Total registered population in 2014 was 2,527 people, of which the on-reserve population was 972. In 2010, a new English- and Aboriginal-language radio station (CHYF-FM) began broadcasting with a format completely devoted to the recovery and sustainment of the Ojibwa language. In addition, the community has initiated the Anishinaabemowin Revival Program (ARP), which aims to develop proficiency in conversational Ojibwa. The ARP team has worked at recording elders in the community, translating old stories into Anishenaabemowin, and then rendering them into curricular resources. The M'Chigeeng website also has recordings of elders recounting various stories in the Anishenaabe language. The community is a member of the United Chiefs and Councils of Mnidoo Mnising, which represents six First Nations in the Little Current–Sheguiandah area.

Michipicoten

www.michipicoten.com

Located 24 kilometres south of Wawa, along a beach on the northeast shore of Lake Superior. The community is registered under Gros Cap Indian Reserve #49 and has additional reserve land located in Missinabie and Chapleau, Ontario. In 2014, there was a total registered population of 1,092, of which 62 reside on-reserve. The Michipicoten population went through several forced moves during the 19th and 20th centuries that have caused significant disruption to the community. After the signing of the Robinson-Superior Treaty of 1850, the people settled in a village on their ancestral lands at the mouth of the Michipicoten River. However, with the discovery of gold in 1897 at Wawa, the Michipicoten village site was sold to a development company. Further reserve lands were subsequently sold to the Algoma Central Railway in 1899, resulting in a dispersal of the population after 1900. Thirty years later, the federal government purchased some of the original reserve property from the Algoma Central Railway, but in the 1970s it became evident that this village was not suitable due to sanitation reasons, and once again the community was forced to move. Eventually, a village was established along the Lake Superior shoreline where the Gros Cap (IR#49) reserve is situated today.

Migisi Sahgaigan. See Eagle Lake

Mishkeegogamang (Osnaburgh)

www.mishkeegogamang.ca

Variously referred to in the past as New Osnaburgh, Osnaburgh House, or as simply Osnaburgh, this First Nation is located in northwestern Ontario along Highway 599, about 315 kilometres northwest of Thunder Bay and 20 kilometres south of Pickle Lake. This is the area where the Albany River meets Lake St. Joseph. The first historical record of this First Nation dates to the founding of a Hudson's Bay Company trading post near the northeast end of Lake St. Joseph in the early 1800s. Treaty No. 9 was signed in 1905, at which time two reserves were established. In 1954, Highway 599 was completed, from Savant Lake to an earlier mine road located several kilometres from the Osnaburgh village, so the government encouraged the people to move to a new village, known as New Osnaburgh. Until 1993, the band was called the Osnaburgh First Nation. In 2014, the total registered population was 1,800 people, of whom 1,151 live on-reserve. At one time, the community was a member of the Windigo First Nations Council, but today the band is not part of any regional tribal council, although the community retains a membership in the Nishnawbe Aski Nation. Mishkeegogamang is policed by the Nishnawbe Aski Police Service. The land base consists of two reserves, although this First Nation is made up of separate and somewhat geographically disconnected communities. For example, on the main reserve (Reserve No. 63B) are the communities of Bottle Hill, Popular Heights, and Sandy Road. On the smaller reserve (No. 63A), located 24 kilometres south, is the community of Ten Houses. In addition, there are a few smaller communities such as Doghole Bay, Eric Lake, and Ace Lake, as well as a few others. A complete history of the Mishkeegogamang First Nation, from the fur-trade era until the early 1970s, can be found in Charles Bishop's ethnohistorical study *The Northern Ojibwa and the Fur Trade* (1974).

Mishkosiminiziibiing Anishinaabeg. See Big Grassy

Misi-zhaaga'iganiing. See McDowell Lake

Missanabie Cree

www.missanabiecreefn.com

Located near the community of Missanabie off Highway 101, between Chapleau and Wawa in northern Ontario. Population estimated at 273 people (INAC does not list a current population). This First Nation has been involved in a long-standing dispute over their traditional territory. In 1905, when Treaty No. 9 was signed in northern Ontario, the Crown did not set aside reserve lands for the 98 members of the Cree people at Missanabie. In 1951, the Missanabie Cree were formally recognized by the Department of Indian Affairs and Northern Development (DIAND) as an Indian band. A civil action was commenced by the Missanabie Cree in 1995 in the Ontario Superior Court, claiming that Canada and Ontario breached Treaty No. 9 by failing to provide the Cree with the land that they were entitled to receive under the Treaty. Eventually, in 2011, the Missanabie Cree and the Government of Ontario signed an agreement to provide the Nation with 15 square miles of land as an initial allotment of a total of 70 square miles, which they were entitled to under Treaty No. 9.

Mississauga

www.mississaugi.com

Located directly west of Blind River, along Highway 17, on the north shore of Lake Huron, at the Mississagi River 8 Reserve, which is 103 kilometres south of Sault Ste. Marie. In 2014, there was a total registered population of 1,271, of which 396 persons reside on-reserve. A signatory of the Robinson-Huron Treaty of 1850 and a member of the Union of Ontario Indians. The community is also a member of the Mamaweswen, the North Shore Tribal Council that represents seven First Nations in the Sault Ste. Marie–Thessalon region. Owns and operates a year-round tourism business called the Chiblow Lake Lodge and provides an elders housing complex. Publishes "The Smoke Signal," which is the First Nation's official news publication.

Mississaugas of New Credit

www.newcreditfirstnation.com

Located near Brantford and Hagersville in south-central Ontario. Consists of one reserve (New Credit 40A) situated 16 kilometres southeast of Brantford. In 2014, New Credit had a total registered population of 2,298 people, of which the on-reserve population was 970 residents. In the late 1600s, a branch of the Mississaugas began a southeastern migration from Georgian Bay into the region north of Lake Ontario. This southern group further split into two groups. One group moved towards the Trent River along Lake Ontario, and the second group travelled west towards Toronto and Lake Erie. It is this second group who are the direct ancestors of the present Mississaugas of the New Credit First Nation. In 1787, the Mississaugas of New Credit surrendered lands in the Toronto area referred to as The Toronto Purchase. This agreement was revisited in 1805 in order to clarify the area purchased. As the European population of southern Ontario grew in the 1800s, it became more difficult for the Mississaugas to continue their traditional hunting and fishing lifestyle, so in 1847 they decided to accept an offer from the Six Nations to establish a settlement on the tract of land held by the Six Nations. The Toronto Purchase remained in dispute for over 200 years, until 2010, when a settlement of the land was reached between the Mississaugas and the Government of Canada.

Mississaugas of Scugog Island

www.scugogfirstnation.com

A First Nation located at Lake Scugog in the Durham Region of south-central Ontario. This community consists of two reserves, one located 42 kilometres southwest of Peterborough, and the other on the islands in Pigeon, Buckhorn, and Stony Lakes. In 2014, the total registered population was 228, of which 178 reside off-reserve. The Mississaugas moved into southern Ontario from their former homeland north of Lake Huron around the year 1700. This move followed the dispersal of the Wendat (Huron) people around 1650. By 1830, the Mississaugas began to move away from Scugog Lake because of the rising waters caused by a dam constructed at Lindsay, which flooded their wild rice beds. In 1844, Chief Crane arranged for the purchase of an 800-acre parcel of land on Scugog Island. In 1996, the Mississaugas began an economic development project called the Great Blue Heron Charity Casino, which has provided much-needed local employment. This caused the population to nearly double during the decade from 2001 to 2011, with the population increasing from 51 to 93 people. The Mississaugas also hold an internationally attended powwow, which is held each summer and grows annually. The community is a member of the Ogemawahj Tribal Council, which represents six First Nations in the Port Perry–Rama region.

Mitaanjigamiing (Stanjikoming)

www.mitaanjigamiing.ca

This is an Ojibwa First Nation located approximately 16 kilometres north of Fort Frances, along the shores of Stanjikoming Bay of Rainy Lake in northwestern Ontario. In 2009, the original name of Stanjikoming Bay First Nation was officially changed to Mitaanjigamiing First Nation. The total registered population in 2014 was 152 persons, of whom 104 live on-reserve. It consists of two reserves, of which the more populated is Rainy Lake 18C, and the other, Agency 1, is shared by three other First Nations. The primary tribal organization is the Grand Council Treaty #3, and it is also a member of the Pwi-Di-Goo-Zing Ne-Yaa-Zhing Advisory Services, a regional tribal council that represents seven First Nations in the Fort Frances–Emo–Mine Centre region of northern Ontario. Elementary and secondary school students are bused 45 minutes daily to Fort Frances, while the Mitaanjigamiing First Nation is a satellite location for the Seven Generations Education Institute Secondary School. The shoreline of Rainy Lake was altered in 1909 to a considerable degree by the construction of a dam at Fort Frances for a paper mill operation. Prior to this construction, people came from all over Manitoba, Red Lake, and Net Lake to this secluded place. The Stanjikoming Bay was filled with wild rice (*manomin*), muskrats, and a variety of water fowl. With the construction of the dam in 1909, the lake water levels rose and flooded the wild rice beds. Flooding once again became a community problem in June 2014, when the CBC News reported that the community had declared a state of emergency (*CBC News* 2014b). The story indicated that the Mitaanjigamiing First Nation was the fifth community in the northwest under a state of emergency because of flooding, caused by rising waters in the Rainy Lake and Lake of the Woods watershed. A request for 20,000 sand bags and shovels was answered by the Ministry of Natural Resources in an attempt to prevent further erosion damage to waterfront properties and roadways along the beachfront.

Mnjikaning. See Chippewas of Rama

Mohawks of Akwesasne

www.akwesasne.ca

The territory of the Mohawks of Akwesasne comprises various islands in the St. Lawrence River and portions of both the north and south shores of the river. It is located not far from Cornwall, Ontario, and the southern part of Akwesasne territory lies in the United States, which consequently is under the jurisdiction of the US federal government and New York state. These various borders are not recognized by the Mohawks of the Akwesasne community. The major problem for the Akwesasne people is that they need to transverse the boundaries in an unimpeded manner in order to travel from one part of their community to another. In 2014, the total registered population was 12,102, with 9,554 persons living on-reserve. The Akwesasne people are represented by the Mohawk Council of Akwesasne, which is a community government represented by four chiefs who are elected from each of the three districts within Akwesasne; *Kawehno:ke* (Cornwall Island), *Kana:takon* (St. Regis, Quebec), and *Tsi:Snaihne* (Snye, or Chenail, Quebec). In 2009, there was a major border crossing dispute over the arming of border services officers with Beretta side arms at the Cornwall Port of Entry, a policy that the Akwesasne claimed would only serve to escalate ongoing tensions in the area and cause further violence.

Mohawks of the Bay of Quinte

www.mbq-tmt.org

Tyendinaga Mohawk Territory is a 18,000-acre Mohawk reserve on the Bay of Quinte in southeastern Ontario, east of Belleville and to the west of Deseronto. The reserve comprised a total registered population of 9,291 persons in 2014, the third-largest band in Ontario, of whom 2,182 live on-reserve. The community derives its name from the Mohawk leader Joseph Brant's traditional name, meaning "two pieces of firewood beside each other." After the American Revolution, the Mohawks, who were allies of the British, were forced out of their traditional homelands in the Mohawk Valley of New York state. The British Crown offered them unsettled land in Upper Canada as compensation for their allegiance. John Deseronto selected the Bay of Quinte because it was allegedly the birthplace of Tekenawait, one of the founders of the original

Haudenosaunee Confederacy in the 12th century. Today, the Mohawk of the Bay of Quinte are currently involved in a land claim dispute with the Canadian government over a stretch of land known as the Culbertson Tract. The Mohawk allege that land originally deeded to them in what is known as the "Simcoe Deed" had been illegally purchased in the 19th century. As of 2011, Band Chief Don Maracle indicated the community's intention to file a lawsuit relating to this claim.

Moose Cree (Moose Factory Band)

www.moosecree.com

The Moose Cree's traditional territory is on the west side of James Bay. The nation has two reserves on a tract of land about 15 kilometres upstream on the Moose River on the southern tip of James Bay, about 240 kilometres north of Cochrane. The Cree had early exposure to European people with the establishment of a Hudson's Bay Company fur-trading post at Moose Factory in 1763. In 1905, the Moose Cree became a signatory to Treaty No. 9. The total registered population comprises 3,950 people, of whom 1,700 people live on-reserve. This is an isolated community accessible via water taxi during three seasons from the town of Moosonee on the mainland. Moosonee has no road access and can only be reached by plane or train. This First Nation is attempting to diversify its economy, which presently relies on tourism, the bush economy, and seasonal construction, by negotiating an agreement with Detour Gold. It has also completed construction of an Aboriginal eco-tourist project known as Washow Lodge. The community is a member of the Mushkegowuk Tribal Council, which represents six First Nations in the Cochrane–Moose Factory region.

Moose Deer Point

www.moosedeerpoint.com

This First Nation is situated within the Township of Georgian Bay, about 30 kilometres south of Parry Sound. It consists of one reserve located 51 kilometres west of Bracebridge, on the east shore of Georgian Bay. The people are descendants of the Potawatomi of the American Midwest, who were allies of the British Government. In the late 1830s, they accepted an invitation from the British to settle in southern Ontario, eventually joining the Beausoleil Band on Beausoleil Island. Later, a combination of both peoples decided to move north and established a settlement at Moose Point, which was surveyed for a reserve in 1917. The total registered membership in 2014 was 472 people, of whom 144 members reside within the First Nation boundaries. In 1969, Jean Chretien, then federal Indian Affairs minister, opened the Moose Deer Point Marina, which, according to their website, was the first marina in Canada owned and operated solely by First Nations people.

Moose Factory Band. See Moose Cree

Moraviantown. See Delaware Nation at Moraviantown

Munsee-Delaware (Munsee of the Thames)

www.munsee.ca

A Lenape-speaking First Nation located 24 kilometres west of St. Thomas, on the north shore of the Thames River in southwest Ontario. The community consists of one reserve with a registered population in 2014 of 612 people, of whom 148 live on-reserve. The Munsees were the northernmost of an affiliated group of Aboriginal villages that came to be known as the Lenni Lenape, or Delawares. Their traditional homeland was composed of settlements along the tributary streams that flowed into the Delaware and Hudson Rivers between the states of Pennsylvania, Delaware, and New York. After the 1500s, with the large influx of European settlers becoming established along the Eastern Seaboard, the Delaware were forced out of their homeland and began a 200-year period of wandering. By the 1830s, there were about 150 Munsee living in the area of the Thames River, which was the source of today's population.

Muskrat Dam Lake

www.firstnation.ca/muskrat-dam-first-nation

There is one reserve located in the Kenora District at Muskrat Dam Lake, which officially gained reserve status in 1976, before which this was a satellite community of Big Trout Lake. In 2014, the total registered population was 432 people, of whom 234 live on-reserve. The community is only accessible by air through the Muskrat Dam Airport and a winter road from Red Lake and Pickle Lake. In 2014, a business partnership was signed between Muskrat Dam Lake and Sachigo Lake First Nations and North Star Air in order to provide more reliable air service to these two First Nations. The Muskrat Dam First Nation is part of the 1929–30 adhesion to the James Bay Treaty of 1905. The community is policed by the Nishnawbe Aski Police Service and is part of the Independent First Nations Alliance of the Nishnawbe Aski Nation.

Naicatchewenin (Northwest Bay)

www.naicatcheweninfirstnation.ca

This First Nation consists of three reserves in the Rainy Lake area, which is approximately 420 kilometres west of Thunder Bay and 60 kilometres northwest of Fort Francis. One of these reserves, Agency 1 Indian Reserve, is shared with three other First Nations. Also known as the Anishinaabeg of Nagaajiwanaang; in the Ojibwa language *Nagaajiwanaang* means "at the place where the current is obstructed." This community is a signatory to Treaty No. 3 of 1873, commonly referred to as the North-West Angle Treaty. It is also a member of the Pwi-Di-Goo-Zing Ne-Yaa-Zhing Advisory Services, a regional chiefs council. The Seven Generations Educational Institute (SGEI) is an Aboriginal-owned and controlled post-secondary institution co-founded by the ten bands in the Rainy Lake tribal area in 1985. Each of the ten bands appointed one member to a board of directors, which functions with the leadership of the executive director. In 2014, the total registered population of the Naicatchewwnin First Nation was 447 persons, of whom 294 people live on-reserve.

Naiscoutaing. See Shawanaga

Namaygoosisagagun (Collins)

www.namaygoosisagagun.ca

Situated approximately 30 kilometres west of Lake Nipigon and the town of Armstrong on the Canadian National Railway (CNR) line in northwestern Ontario. The community is considered an unincorporated area or a non-status Ojibwa First Nation, because it does not have official status as a reserve under the jurisdiction of the Department of Indian Affairs. *Namaygoosisagagun* in the Anishenaabe language means "Trout Lake," which is the Aboriginal name for Collins Lake. About 140 people are registered as community members, although only about 30 people actually live in Collins. The community was originally formed by trappers and their families from Eabametoong (Fort Hope) First Nation on the Albany River, and the Whitesand First Nation on the north shore of Lake Nipigon, who began to trade their furs at the Collins store, which was built in 1920. A school was constructed by Indian Affairs in 1960, but a dispute developed over whether non-status children could attend along with children of Indian status. Eventually, in the 1970s, a new school was constructed under the auspices of the Ontario Ministry of Education. The community is situated in the Robinson-Superior Treaty area and affiliated with the Union of Ontario Indians. For a study of Collins' attempts to promote local economic development and build a tourist lodge at Whitewater Lake, see Edward Hedican, *The Ogoki River Guides: Emergent Leadership among the Northern Ojibwa* (1986).

Naotkamegwanning (Whitefish Bay)

    www.naotkamegwanning.net

    The community is located in northwestern Ontario, 96 kilometres southeast of Kenora and 15 kilometres from Sioux Narrows along the eastern shore of the Lake of the Woods. It consists of four reserves with a total registered population in 2014 of 1,236, of which 755 people live on-reserve. The name *Naotkamegwanning* in the Anishenaabe language means "of the Whitefish Point." The First Nation is a member of the Bimose Tribal Council, a regional tribal council that is a member of the Grand Council Treaty #3. The community has year-round road access and also has an ice road in the winter. Anishenaabe cultural practices and beliefs remain strong in this community, as 48 percent of the population is able to speak their Ojibwa language. The Whitefish Bay Singers, who have released more than ten recordings, are leaders in preserving their traditional culture through their shared songs.

Nawash. See Chippewas of Nawash

Negaw-zaaga'igani Nitam-Anishinaabe. See Sandy Lake

Neguaguon Lake. See Lac La Croix

Neskantaga (Lansdowne House)

    www.neskantaga.com

    This is a remote Oji-Cree First Nation situated along the shores of Attawapiskat Lake in the district of Kenora. It is a signatory to Treaty No. 9, originally as part of the Fort Hope (Eabametoong) band. The community consists of two reserves, one of which, the Summer Beaver Indian Settlement, is shared with the Nibinamik First Nation. The other reserve, the Lansdowne House Indian Settlement, is linked to the rest of Ontario by air service at the Lansdowne House Airport and by winter roads to points south, via the Northern Ontario Resource Trail. As of 2014, the total registered population was 435 people, of whom 338 live on-reserve. The First Nation's council is a member of the Matawa First Nations Management, which is a local chiefs council consisting of ten First Nations in the Long Lac, Webequie, and Ogoki Post area. It is also a member of the Nishnawbe Aski Nation, a tribal political organization representing most of the First Nations in northern Ontario. The Neskantaga First Nation is also actively involved in the Ring of Fire mining development proposals. Chief Peter Moonias, for example, is quoted in a front-page article in the 14 July 2012 issue of *The Globe and Mail* entitled "Natural Resources to Define First Nations Leader's Next Term."

New Credit. See Mississaugas of New Credit

New Post. See Taykwa Tagamou
Nibinamik (Summer Beaver)

www.nibinamik.ca

Nibinamik, which literally means "summer beaver" in the Anishenaabe language, is a remote First Nation in northern Ontario, located about 500 kilometres north of Thunder Bay. It is connected to the rest of the province by its airport and a winter/ice road that leads to the Northern Ontario Resource Trail. In 2014, the total registered population was 440 people, of whom 368 live on-reserve. It is a member of the Matawa First Nations Management, a regional chiefs council, and the Nishnawbe Aski Nation, a tribal political organization representing the majority of First Nations in northern Ontario. The community was also policed by the Nishnawbe Aski Police Service until its detachment was condemned and closed down. The *Nibinamik* First Nation is located on the Summer Beaver Settlement, which it shares with members of the *Neskantaga* (Lansdowne House) First Nation. The reason for this double occupancy of Summer Beaver is that a group of Anglican people, related by kinship, decided to leave Lansdowne House, a Catholic settlement, in 1975. The community had become divided along religious lines and violence had begun to occur between the two denominational groups. *Nibinamik* was not recognized as a separate First Nation until recently, but is now included on the federal government's list of First Nations for Ontario.

Nicickousemenecaning. See Nigigoonsiminikaaning
Nigigoonsiminikaaning (Nicickousemenecaning)

www.nigigoonsiminikaaning.ca

The name of this First Nation means "place abundant with Little-Otter berries" in the Anishenaabe language. It consists of four reserves around the shores of Rainy Lake, which are located about 40 kilometres east of Fort Frances or about 300 kilometres west of Thunder Bay. In 2014, the total registered population was 357 persons, of whom 156 live on-reserve. It is a member of the Pwi-Di-Goo-Zing Ne-Yaa-Zhing Advisory Services, which is a regional tribal council representing seven First Nations in the Fort Frances–Emo–Mine Centre area, which in turn is a member of the Grand Council Treaty #3, a tribal political organization. The community is also a supporter of the Seven Generations Education Institute (SGEI), which is an Aboriginal-owned and controlled post-secondary institution co-founded by the ten bands in the Rainy Lake tribal area in 1985. In addition, the First Nation also has made arrangements with the University of Minnesota in Minneapolis to set up seasonal language camps at the mouth of the Ottertail River. Highlights of the activities at the language camp include trapping camps, wild rice harvesting, fasting, and Ojibwa ceremonies.

Nipissing

www.nfn.ca

Located between the city of North Bay and the municipality of West Nipissing in northeastern Ontario. The community consists of one reserve whose members speak a grouping of Algonquian languages, which includes Odawa, Ojibwa, and Algonquin. This heritage is likely the result of the Nipissings living at a geographical crossroads between two watersheds, since Lake Nipissing drains via the French River into Georgian Bay and via the Mattawa River into the Ottawa River. During the fur trade, the French portaged through the watershed divide to reach the Great Lakes by canoe from settlements around Montreal on the St. Lawrence River. The Nipissing are a signatory to the Robinson-Huron Treaty of 1850. As of 2014, the total Nipissing registered population was 2,594, people, of whom 969 live on-reserve. In January 2014, the Nipissing adopted what is believed to be the first constitution for a First Nation in Ontario. It is supposed to replace the Indian Act, which regulates the governance of First Nations in Canada, but this has not yet been tested in court. The community is a member of the Waabnoong Bemjiwang Association of First Nations, a regional tribal council that represents six First Nations in the Parry Sound–Capreol region.

Nizaatikoong. See Lac des Mille Lacs

North Caribou Lake (Weagamow Lake)

www.firstnation.ca/north-caribou-weagamowround-lake

This is an Ojib-Cree First Nation located in the Kenora District of northern Ontario, consisting of one reserve on the north shore of Weagamow Lake. This is a transcription of the Ojib-Cree word *Wiyaagamaa*, or "Round Lake" which is situated approximately 320 kilometres north of Sioux Lookout. In 2014, the total registered population was 1,096, of which 851 live on-reserve. The community is a member of the Windigo First Nations Council, a regional chiefs council, which represents five First Nations in the Weagamow Lake, Bearskin Lake, and Slate Falls region. It is also a signatory to the 1929–30 adhesion to Treaty No. 9 and is a member of the Nishnawbe Aski Nation, a tribal political organization. The settlement is accessible year-round by air through the Round Lake Airport, Weagamow Air Base, or seasonally by a winter/ice road that branches off the Northern Resource Trail heading north of Pickle Lake. An ethnographic study of the North Caribou Lake First Nation was conducted by Edward S. Rogers, a Royal Ontario Museum anthropologist, from July 1958 to July 1959, which was published as *The Round Lake Ojibwa* (1962).

North Spirit Lake

www.firstnation.ca/north-spirit-lake

This is a small Oji-Cree First Nation in northern Ontario located approximately 170 kilometres northeast of Red Lake, on the southwest shore of North Spirit Lake. It consists of one reserve, which is accessible only by air year-round, with services provided by Wasaya Airlines, and seasonally by a winter/ice road heading north from Red Lake, which is connected to Sandy Lake First Nation and Deer Lake First Nation. In 2014, it had a total registered population of 494 people, of whom 438 live on-reserve. Local services include the Tikinagan Child and Family Services and the Nishnawbe Aski Police Services. This First Nation is also part of the Keewaytinook Okimakanak Council of Northern Chiefs, which represents six First Nations in the Red Lake to Fort Severn region. The community is a signatory to Treaty No. 5, which was originally signed in 1875 with the Saulteaux and Swampy Cree First Nations of the Berens River and Norway House area of northern Manitoba, but an adhesion was made in 1908 to include First Nations in northern Ontario, which included the North Spirit Lake First Nation.

Northwest Angle No. 33

www.firstnation.ca/northwest-angle-no-33

This First Nation consists of two geographically separate land areas known as Northwest Angle No. 33A and Northwest Angle No. 33B. The Northwest Angle No. 33A community is located on the shores of Dog Paw Lake, about 60 kilometres southeast of Kenora in northwestern Ontario. The Northwest Angle No. 33B community is situated on the north shore of Angle Inlet on an island in the Lake of the Woods, 6 kilometres east of the Manitoba border and 160 kilometres southwest of Kenora. In 2014, the total registered population was 523, of which 245 reside on-reserve. The First Nation is represented by the Anishinaabeg Kabapikotawangag Resource Council, a regional tribal council that serves six other First Nations in the Kenora–Sioux Falls region. It is also a member of the Grand Council Treaty #3.

Northwest Angle No. 37

www.firstnation.ca/northwest-angle-no-37

This First Nation is geographically dispersed as it consists of 12 reserves in the Lake of the Woods and Shoal Lake regions near the Manitoba border and Kenora in northwestern Ontario, several of which are shared with the people of other First Nations. Whitefish Bay 34A is the most populous site, situated about 54 kilometres southeast of Kenora. There are also two other main communities: Regina Bay, which is considered the main reserve, is located on Lake of the Woods, approximately 95 kilometres southeast of Kenora off Highway 71; and the Windigo Island community near the Manitoba-Minnesota borders, about 10 kilometres north of Angle Inlet, Minnesota. In 2014, the total registered population was 400 people, of whom 182 reside on-reserve. Air service is provided through the Sioux Narrows Airport located 5 kilometres southeast of Sioux Narrows. The community is represented by the Anishinaabeg of Kabapikotawangag Resource Council.

Northwest Bay. See Naicatchewenin

Obashkaandagaang (Washagamis Bay)

www.firstnation.ca/washagamis-bay-obashkaandagaang

Consists of two reserves; the most populated is Rat Portage 38A, located on the northern portion of the Lake of the Woods, and the other on the Aulineau Peninsula in Lake of the Woods, about 45 kilometres south of Kenora, off Highway 17E. The total registered population in 2014 was 329 people, of whom about 174 live on-reserve. Member of the Bimose Tribal Council and the Grand Council Treaty #3.

Obishikokaang. See Lac Seul

Ochiichagwe'babigo'ining (Dalles)

www.ochiichag.ca

This is an Anishenaabe or Saulteaux First Nation located in the Kenora District of northwestern Ontario, near Sioux Narrows of Lake of the Woods. It consists of two reserves: the Dalles Indian Reserve 38C, which serves as the main reserve, is located about 45 kilometres south of Kenora; and Agency Indian Reserve 30, located on the Aulineau Peninisula of Lake of the Woods, is 10 kilometres northwest of Kenora, which is also shared by 12 other First Nations. In 2014, the total registered population was 442, of which 175 live on-reserve. It is a member of the Bimose Tribal Council, which represents ten First Nations in the Kenora–Dryden area of northwestern Ontario, and the Grand Council Treaty #3. This First Nation has recently settled two grievances against Hydro One and Ontario Power Generation. The grievance against Hydro One started when the company arbitrarily cut down trees and misappropriated land, without making an effort to consult the First Nation, to install steel electricity pylons across from the reserve. Hydro One acknowledged liability (without an apology) by settling the claim for an undisclosed amount. The grievance against Ontario Power Generation resulted from the flooding of over a thousand acres of reserve land when the Whitedog Dam was built, resulting in the loss of cultural activities such as hunting and wild rice harvesting. Ontario Power Generation officially apologized for the harm to the community during a visit by Jake Epp, chairman of the board.

Ogoki Post. See Marten Falls

Ojibways of Batchewana

www.batchewana.ca

This is an Anishenaabe First Nation on the northeastern corner of Lake Superior and the St. Mary's River, adjacent to the city of Sault Ste. Marie, consisting of four reserves. The most populated site is Rankin Location 15D, which, along with Whitefish Island, is situated close to Sault Ste. Marie. The other two reserves are Goulas Bay 15A, 22 kilometres northwest of Sault Ste. Marie, and Obadjiwan, on the southeast corner of Lake Superior. In 2014, the registered population was 2,767, of which 789 live on-reserve. Facilities operated by the First Nation include a cultural centre, health centre, family crisis shelter, elders complex, day care, and arena complex. Economic development enterprises include renewable energy initiatives, such as wind and solar power generation. The Batchewana First Nation is a member of Mamaweswen, the North Shore Tribal Council that represents seven First Nations in the Sault Ste. Marie–Thessalon region.

Ojibways of Garden River. See Garden River

Ojibways of Onigaming (Sabaskong)

www.firstnation.ca/onigaming

An Anishenaabe community in northwestern Ontario situated approximately 113 kilometres north of Fort Frances, off Highway 71, near Nestor Falls. The traditional name of this settlement is *Kakagewaatisoonigaming*, or "Raven's Nest Portage." This community was formerly known as *Sabaskong*, a corruption of the Ojibway name *Shebiiskaang*, which refers to the "old reserve" located near Turtle Narrows on Lake of the Woods. This community is still known locally as *Sab*. The First Nation consists of six reserves in the Lake of the Woods–Sioux Narrows region. The most populated site is Sabaskong Bay 35D, situated on the eastern shore of Lake of the Woods, and it serves as the main reserve. In 2014, the total registered population was 775 persons, of whom 477 live on-reserve. The First Nation is a member of the Anishinaabeg of

Kabapikotawangag Resource Council, a tribal council that represents six First Nations in the Kenora–Sioux Narrows area, and the Grand Council Treaty #3. It is also a supporter of the Seven Generations Education Institute (SGEI), which is an Aboriginal-owned and controlled post-secondary institution co-founded in 1985 by the ten bands in the Rainy Lake tribal area.

Ojibways of Sucker Creek. See Aundeck Omni Kaning

Ojibways of the Pic River (Begetekong Anishinabek)

www.picriver.com

An Anishenaabe First Nation located on the north shore of Lake Superior, consisting of one reserve at the mouth of the Pic River. The reserve is situated off the TransCanada Highway, approximately 352 kilometres northeast of Thunder Bay. It is accessible by Highway 627, adjacent to Pukaskwa National Park. The traditional territory encompasses over 2 million hectares with the combined exclusive and shared territory, although the reserve today comprises only 332 hectares. Pic River First Nation has asserted Aboriginal title and has filed a comprehensive land claim in the Ontario Superior Court for Aboriginal title over its traditional territory. Pic River was not a signatory to the Robinson-Superior Treaty of 1850; however, its members did petition, starting in 1879, for a reserve, and the request was subsequently granted in 1914. In 2014, the total registered population was 1,137, of which 528 live on-reserve. The Pic River First Nation built the Twin Falls Generating Station, a 5.0-megawatt station located on the Kagiano River, and the Umbata Falls Hydro project, a 23-megawatt station located at White River. The power stations have generated more than $1 million in profits. In turn, this income has been used to help finance a variety of community projects, such as a women's crisis centre, a recreation centre, and cable television and high-speed Internet services for the members of the band.

Onigaming. See Ojibways of Onigaming

Oneida of the Thames

www.oneida.on.ca

Commonly referred to as the "Oneida Settlement," this First Nation is located about a 30-minute drive from London. The Nation consists of one reserve with a population of approximately 5,209 band members, of whom 2,030 live on-reserve. The Oneidas (*Onyata'a:ka*) are a Haudenosaunee people whose traditional territory once covered a large section of the eastern part of North America. They migrated into southern Ontario in the 1840s and were associated with two Christian denominations, Methodist and Anglican. By 1877, some of the people began to join the Baptists as well. The Oneida insist that their community be called a "settlement," rather than a "reserve," because they originally purchased their relocation lands in Ontario, as distinct from community lands set aside for First Nations people by the federal government. However, the Oneida Settlement lands are treated as reserve lands in some ways, because the inhabitants are exempt from the taxation that applies to lands outside of INAC's jurisdiction. However, because the Oneida purchased their lands outright, the government does not follow all sections of the Indian Act with regards to the Oneida Settlement, such as the provisions in the Act for the election of self-government. On a larger political scale, the Oneida are members of the Association of Iroquois and Allied Tribes, which is a tribal political organization representing eight Haudenosaunee and Anishenaabe First Nations governments in Ontario.

Osnaburgh. See Mishkeegogamang

Parry Island. See Wasauksing

Pawgwasheeng. See Pays Plat

Pays Plat (Pawgwasheeng)

> www.ppfn.ca

> A small Anishenaabe reserve located on Highway 17 near Rossport, on the north shore of Lake Superior, about 183 kilometres east of Thunder Bay. Membership, according to the Pays Plat First Nation website, is just over 200 people, with about 70 living on-reserve. Also known as *Pawgwasheeng*, or "where the water is shallow" in the Anishenaabe language, Pays Plat was named by French fur traders, meaning "flat land." In 1777, a British fur trader named John Long wintered at Pays Plat and was given the name *Amik* ("beaver"). An account of Long's visit can be found in his journal, *Voyages and Travels of an Indian Interpreter and Trader* (1791). John Long describes his meeting with Chief Quewish as follows: "On the 4th of July we arrived at Pays Plat, on the north side of the Lake [Superior], where we unpacked our goods, and made the bales smaller, having, by the Indians account, one hundred and eighty carrying places to the part where I intended to winter. ... They gave me fish, dried meat, and skins, which I returned with trifling presents. The Chief, whose name was Matche Quewish, held a council, and finding I understood their language, proposed to adopt me as a brother warrior" (Long 1791: 45). The community is within the boundaries of the Robinson-Superior Treaty of 1850, which was followed in 1883 by the construction of the Canadian Pacific Railway (CPR) line along the north shore of Lake Superior.

Peawanuck. See Weenusk

Pic Mobert

www.picmobert.ca

Consists of two small reserves located 53 kilometres east of Marathon on the north shore of Lake Superior. The total registered population in 2014 was 956 people, of whom 348 live on-reserve. The band council is a member of the Nokiiwin Tribal Council, a regional chiefs council, and the Union of Ontario Indians. Community policing is provided by the Anishinabek Police Services. Pic Mobert First Nation is a signatory to the Robinson-Superior Treaty of 1850.

Pic River. See Ojibways of the Pic River

Pikangikum

www.firstnation.ca/pikangikum

This is an Anishenaabe (Ojibwa) First Nation situated on the eastern shore of Pikangikum Lake on the Berens River, part of the Hudson Bay drainage system, located approximately 100 kilometres north of the town of Red Lake. In 2014, the total registered population was 2,689, of which 2,593 live on-reserve. Pikangikum is one of the largest First Nation communities in northern Ontario and has the highest on-reserve population in the Sioux Lookout District. It also has an estimated 75 percent of the population under 25 years of age, with one-third of Pikangikum being less than 9 years of age. The population continues to grow at more than 3 percent annually, with the highest birthrate per capita in the Sioux Lookout zone. As could be expected, this large population of younger persons has had a significant impact on infrastructure programs and services at the community level. The local school was constructed 13 years ago and suffers a severe shortage of classroom space. Community-based programs are generally under-resourced, thus compromising the community's ability to provide programming that will meet its needs. As a result, the community often faces various health and social challenges. It was reported, for example, that Pikangikum suffers from one of the highest suicide rates in the world and showed a pattern of inhalant abuse by young women (Elliott 2000). Another notable characteristic is that the community has a 97-percent retention rate of the Ojibwa language, which is the first language of most students entering school. The community is a signatory to Treaty No. 5 and a member of Nishnawbe Aski Nation, a provincial territorial organization, as well as the Independent First Nations Alliance, which represents five First Nations in northwestern Ontario. An ethnographic study of Pikangikum was conducted in the 1950s by R.W. Dunning, *Social and Economic Change among the Northern Ojibwa* (1959).

Poplar Hill

www.poplarhill.firstnation.ca

A small Anishenaabe (Ojibwa) community located in northwestern Ontario, approximately 120 kilometres north of Red Lake, near the Ontario-Manitoba border. There is no year-round road access so the community can only be reached by air transportation (provided by Wasaya Airways) and winter road. In 2014, the total registered population was 595, with 16 people living off-reserve. This First Nation is within the boundaries of the territory described by the Winnipeg Treaty of 1875, more commonly known as Treaty No. 5. Poplar Hill received full band and reserve status in 1978 when it separated from the Pikangikum Band. The community, however, continues to maintain strong ties with the people of Pikangikum and the Little Grand Rapids Band in Manitoba. Social services are provided by Tikinagan Child and Family Services in Sioux Lookout, a 24-hour nursing station that provides daily clinics, and the Nishnawbe Aski Police Service.

Rainy River (Manitou Rapids)

www.firstnation.ca/rainy-river

This is a Saulteaux (Ojibwa) First Nation located 5 kilometres west of Emo and approximately 48 kilometres west of Fort Frances, on the northern banks of the Rainy River in northwestern Ontario. It is also known locally as *Manidoo bawitigong* or Manitou Rapids, after the name of its reserve, Manitou Rapids 11. The total registered population is 880, of which 375 persons live on-reserve. The First Nation is an amalgamation of seven historical Rainy River Saulteaux bands. Six of them either sold or transferred their reserves in 1914–15 and then began amalgamating into a single band. The Canadian federal government made the amalgamation official in the 1960s. With the "Rainy River First Nations Land Settlement Agreement," some of the former reserves and other lands within the First Nation's customary use area lands were made available for the benefit of the First Nation. Community members belong to the Grand Council Treaty #3 organization and Pwi-Di-Goo-Zing Ne-Yaa-Zhing Advisory Services, which represents seven First Nations in the Fort Frances–Emo–Mine Centre region. Community services are provided, in part, by Weech-it-te-win Family Services. Today, much effort has been made to reclaim some of the lands sold to settlers in the early 1900s. In 1995, a tripartite agreement between the federal, provincial,

and Rainy River First Nations governments repurchased some of the Long
Sault land and established the Long Sault Mounds Historic Park.

Rat Portage. See Anishinabe of Wauzhushk Onigum

Red Rock (Lake Helen)

www.rrib.ca

This Anishenaabe (Ojibwa) First Nation is located on the most northerly point of Lake Superior, close to the junction of TransCanada Highways
11 and 17, about 2 kilometres east of the town of Nipigon and 100 kilometres east of Thunder Bay. The traditional Ojibwa name for the First Nation is
Opwaaganasiniing, meaning "pipestone." In 2014, the total registered population was 1,177, of which 291 persons were living on-reserve. The Red Rock
First Nation consists of two sections, Paramacheene Reserve 53 and Lake
Helen Reserve 53A, which comprise a total area of approximately 950 acres.
Members use the Paramacheene area regularly for fishing, berry picking, hunting, gathering medicinal plants, and to participate in traditional ceremonies,
while the Lake Helen Reserve is the main residential site of the population.
The community is considered an unaffiliated First Nation, although it is a
member of the Union of Ontario Indians. The Red Rock people live within
the boundaries of the Robinson-Superior Treaty of 1850. In 1885, the Crown
surveyed 640 acres of land along the Nipigon River for the purpose of establishing a reserve land base. In 1886, the band received an additional 480 acres
for their land base, at which time there were 166 band members, and in 1914 it
became an Indian Reserve under the Indian Act.

Rocky Bay. See Biinjitiwabik Zaaging Anishinabek

Sabaskong. See Ojibways of Onigaming

Sachigo Lake

www.firstnation.ca/sachigo-lake

This is an Oji-Cree First Nation located on the north shore of Sachigo Lake,
approximately 425 kilometres north of Sioux Lookout and 150 kilometres west
of Big Trout Lake. As of 2014, the total registered population was 884 persons,
of whom 522 live on-reserve. It consists of three reserves, of which the Sachigo
Lake Indian Reserve 1 is the most populous. As a signatory to Treaty No. 9,
Sachigo First Nation is a member of the Windigo First Nations Council, which
represents five First Nations in the Weagamow Lake–Bearskin Lake–Slate Falls
area. The primary tribal organization for the Sachigo population is the Nishnawbe
Aski Nation. It is served by the Nishnawbe Aski Police Service, an Aboriginal
police service. The community is accessible only by air through the Sachigo Lake

Airport, located 2.8 kilometres north of the settlement, or by a winter/ice road branching off the Northern Ontario Resource Trail, heading south via Muskrat Dam Lake First Nation and north from Pickle Lake. Community services include the Tikinagan Child and Family Services, with a head office in Sioux Lookout. Community initiatives include the Sachigo Lake First Nation arena, in which over $1.1 million has been invested in upgrades and rehabilitation. A new elementary school offering Kindergarten through Grade 8 accommodates approximately 103 students, for which INAC provided $9.45 million in construction costs. The school was a winner of the Architectural Excellence for Design Awards, presented by the Ontario Association of Architects.

Sagamok Anishenawbek

www.sagamok.ca

In the Anishenaabe language, *sagamok* means "two points joining." The community consists of one reserve located on the north shore of Lake Huron, about 120 kilometres west of Sudbury. The total registered population in 2014 was 2,789 people, of whom 1,217 live off-reserve. They are signatory to the Robinson-Huron Treaty of 1850. Sagamok's culture and language is made up of the Ojibwa, Odawa, and Potawatomi tribes, which historically were known as the Council of Three Fires. The community is also the first to practise language immersion in Ontario, teaching solely in *Anishenabemowin* from Kindergarten to Grade 3.

Sand Point. See Bingwi Neyaashi Anishinaabek

Sandy Lake (Negaw-zaaga'igani Nitam-Anisinaabe)

www.sandylake.firstnation.ca

Sandy Lake is a fly-in First Nation community located in the boreal forest of northwestern Ontario, situated approximately 450 kilometres northeast of Winnipeg and 600 kilometres northwest of Thunder Bay. In 2014, the total registered population was 2,970, of which 2,587 persons live on-reserve. During the winter months, the community is accessible by ice roads extending from Red Lake, located 227 kilometres to the northeast. The winter roads are drivable for a period of six weeks, during which the Sandy Lake community ships essential materials and equipment for the entire year that would not be economically possible to ship by plane. Although Sandy Lake First Nation has an elected chief and eight councillors, it also has an elders' council of five elected elders, who actively participate and attend council meetings to witness and advise on decisions and resolutions in all matters dealt with by the elected council. The community is not considered to be affiliated with any tribal council; however, it does maintain an association with the Nishnawbe Aski

Nation, a provincial territorial organization representing a majority of northern Ontario First Nations, and is a signatory to Treaty No. 5.

Saugeen. See Chippewas of Saugeen

Scugog Island. See Mississaugas of Scugog Island

Seine River (Ashkibwaanikaang)

www.seineriverfirstnation.ca

This is an Ojibwa First Nation located on Wild Potato Lake, approximately 300 kilometres west of Thunder Bay in northwestern Ontario. It consists of three reserves, the most populated of which is Seine River 23A (called *Ashkibwaanikaang* in Ojibwa) situated on the north bank of the Seine River, about 110 kilometres southeast of Dryden. In 2014, the total registered population was 750 persons, of whom 350 reside on-reserve. The community is a member of the Grand Council Treaty #3, and the Pwi-Di-Goo-Zing Ne-Yaa-Zhing Advisory Services, which is a tribal council representing seven First Nations in the Fort Frances–Emo–Mine Centre region. It is also one of the ten bands in the Rainy Lake tribal area supporting the Seven Generations Education Institute (SGEI), which is an Aboriginal-owned and controlled post-secondary institution founded in 1985. In 2012, a multi-year project was begun, called the Seine River Lake Sturgeon Spawning Project, which incorporates the identification of environmental and Aboriginal traditional knowledge to define the spawning requirements of lake sturgeon on the Seine River downstream of the Sturgeon Falls Dam. The goal of this project is to provide an effective tool to improve the spawning success for lake sturgeon, and to facilitate the recovery and sustainability of lake sturgeon across Canada. In addition, the Seine River First Nation has entered into a partnership with Lakehead University to determine baseline levels of mercury and other heavy metals in the sediment, water, fish, and plants of the Seine River.

Serpent River (Chi Genebek Ziibing Anishinabek)

www.serpentriverfn.ca

This is an Ojibwa, Odawa, and Potawatomi community located on the north shore of Lake Huron, approximately 140 kilometres west of Sudbury and 30 kilometres south of Elliot Lake. Its members are a signatory to the Robinson-Huron Treaty of 1850 and belong to the Union of Ontario Indians. The total population consists of about 1,200 people, of whom 360 presently reside in the community. Since the reserve incorporates about 50 kilometres of shoreline, and in an effort to create greater employment opportunities, the SRFN Development Corporation is planning a cottage lot-leasing program. The community is a member of Mamaweswen, the North Shore Tribal Council, which represents seven First Nations in the Sault Ste. Marie–Thessalon region.

Shawanaga (Naiscoutaing)

www.shawanagafirstnation.ca

The community consists of three reserves located about 30 kilometres northwest of Parry Sound and 150 kilometres southeast of Sudbury. It has a year-round access road from Highway 69 with a First Nation-owned gas bar and convenience store located at the entrance to the community. The total registered population is 549, of which the on-reserve population is 175 people. This First Nation is a signatory to the Robinson-Huron Treaty of 1850. The treaty was initiated when the government sold mining locations with ties to the government in the 1840s. In 1848, a delegation of chiefs went to Montreal to petition the Governor General about this activity, after which a royal commission decided that the land in dispute belonged to the Indigenous inhabitants, and a treaty would be required to sell any more land to settlers. Today, the First Nation has several community services, such as the Shawanaga First Nation Healing Centre, which provides health, healing, and wellness programs to its members.

Sheguiandah

www.sheguiandahfirstnation.ca

Consists of one reserve located about 12 kilometres south of Little Current and 128 kilometres northeast of Sudbury, on the north end of Manitoulin Island in Lake Huron. In 2014, the total registered population was 381 people, of whom 178 reside on-reserve. Manitoulin Island is the largest freshwater lake island in the world. The Odawa name for the island is *Manidoowaaling*, which means "cave of the spirit," in reference to an underwater cave where it is believed a powerful spirit dwells. The Manitoulin Treaty of 1862 was made with the Odawa, Ojibwa, and other First Nations inhabiting Manitoulin Island. In 1952, archaeologist Thomas E. Lee discovered a significant prehistoric site dating to the Paleo-Indian period of about 10,000 years ago at Sheguindah. A year later, in 1953, public interest in the Sheguindah site led to the Ontario government passing legislation to protect its archaeological sites in the province.

Sheshegwaning

www.sheshegwaning.org

Located on the northern shore of Manitoulin Island approximately 112 kilometres west of Little Current, which is accessible by a year-round hardtop road. As of 2013, the total population was 419, of which 111 people live on-reserve.

Its members are a signatory to the Manitoulin Island Treaty and a part of the Union of Ontario Indians. The Sheshegwaning Health Centre provides health promotion and prevention services and operates in conjunction with a network of other First Nation mental health and addiction workers. Economic development consists of several initiatives, including tourism and marketing, environmental management systems, and Nishin crafts. Nishin Lodge allows individuals to enjoy a remote wilderness atmosphere in the heart of a sugar maple forest. The community is a member of the United Chiefs and Councils of Mnidoo Mnising, a tribal organization that represents six First Nations in the Little Current–Sheguiandah area.

Shoal Lake. See Iskatewizaagegan

Six Nations of the Grand River

www.sixnations.ca

This is the most populous First Nation community in Canada, consisting in 2013 of 25,385 band members, of whom 12,175 live on-reserve. The Six Nations reserve is situated about eight kilometres southeast of Brantford. The present reserve represents approximately 5 percent of the original land granted by the 1784 Haldimand Treaty. It is the only territory in North America that has the six Haudenosaunee First Nations living together, namely, the Mohawk, Cayuga, Onondaga, Oneida, Seneca, and Tuscarora. There are also some Delaware living in the territory. The population consists of the following bands, with total population and number of on-reserve residents indicated below.

Nation	Band Name	Total	On-Reserve
Iroquois	Bay of Quinte Mohawk	740	326
	Tuscarora	2,130	973
	Oneida	1,999	758
	Onondaga Clear Sky	778	429
	Bearfoot Onondaga	601	238
	Upper Cayuga	3,503	1,431
	Lower Cayuga	3,538	2,213
	Konadaha Seneca	533	200
	Niharondasa Seneca	368	161
	Lower Mohawk	4,016	2,054
	Walker Mohawk	485	298
	Upper Mohawk	6,018	2,857
Algonquin	Delaware	649	236
Totals		**25,385**	**12,174**

Many Haudenosaunee people allied with the British during the American Revolutionary War. These represented the Six Nations of the Haudenosaunee, or Iroquois Confederacy. After the war, the British offered to resettle the Aboriginal Loyalists in Upper Canada (Ontario) as compensation for properties lost in the United States, and to develop more towns and agricultural communities west of Quebec. Leaders of the Mohawk people, principally John Deseronto and Joseph Brant, met with the British officer Frederick Haldimand, who granted the Mohawks a tract of land near the Bay of Quinte and on the northeast shore of Lake Ontario in 1784. Brant decided that he would prefer to settle on the Grand River, while Deseronto settled at what is now called the Tyendinaga Mohawk Territory.

By 1793, a dispute developed between Joseph Brant and Lieutenant-Governor John Simcoe, with the latter claiming that the original land deed did not allow the Six Nations to sell their property to anyone except to each other or to the British monarch. Brant claimed that the original Haldimand Tract extended to the source of the Grand River, territory to which the Six Nations maintained they were entitled. Joseph Brant and the other chiefs then rejected the deed in 1795 and began to sell large blocks of land in the northern section of the Upper Grand River. However, by 1801 the developers to whom the land had been sold began to fall behind in their payments, which required more land to be sold to make up for the missing payments. Today, the Six Nations reserve covers some 46,000 acres, whereas the original Haldimand Tract comprised about 950,000 acres.

Slate Falls (Bamaji Lake)

www.firstnation.ca/slate-falls-bamaji-lake

This is an Anishenaabe (Ojibwa) First Nation located approximately 122 kilometres north of Sioux Lookout, on the shore of Bamaji Lake in northwestern Ontario. It is accessible by float plane or wheeled aircraft as there is a community airstrip, or by an all-weather road to Sioux Lookout. In 2014, the total registered population was 270 people, of whom 198 reside on-reserve. Slate Falls Nation was one of six new First Nations established under the Six Anishnawbe Aski Bands Agreement between the Government of Ontario and the six Northwestern Ontario bands. Slate Falls First Nation was officially recognized on 15 April 1985, under the Indian Act. People have been living in the area of Slate Falls for more than two centuries. Members of the Osnaburgh House Indian Band established main camps there for managing surrounding traplines and hunting grounds in the 1700s, after which a community began to develop in the region. It is a member of the Windigo First Nations Council, which represents five First Nations in the Weagamow Lake–Bearskin Lake–Slate Falls region. The community is also a signatory to Treaty No. 9, whose boundaries extend across most of northern Ontario.

Stanjikoming. See Mitaanjigamiing

Sucker Creek. See Ojibways of Sucker Creek

Summer Beaver. See Nibinamik

Taykwa Tagamou (New Post)

www.taykwatagamounation.com

This is a Cree First Nation that consists of two reserves. One is located 14 kilometres west of the Abitibi Canyon Hydro Generation Station, between Cochrane and Moosonee. This reserve is set aside for hunting, trapping, and other activities, and is not the principal settlement location. A new reserve was created in 1984 to provide a settlement location for the Taykwa Tagamou First Nation, situated approximately 20 kilometres west of Cochrane. In 2014, the total registered population was 516, of which 139 live on-reserve. For many years, this community was known as the New Post First Nation because of its association with the Hudson's Bay Company post located on the Abitibi River. In 1905, the community became a signatory to Treaty No. 9, also known as the James Bay Treaty. Today, it is affiliated with the Mushkegowuk Tribal Council, which represents six Cree First Nations from Cochrane to Moose Factory.

Temagami (Bear Island)

www.temagamifirstnation.ca

The community is located on Bear Island in the heart of Lake Temagami. The people refer to themselves as the *Teme-Augama Anishnabai,* or "Deep Water by the Shore People." In 2014, the total registered population was 816, of which 261 reside on-reserve. In 1943, Bear Island was purchased by the Department of Indian Affairs from the Province of Ontario for the sum of $3,000, in order to be designated as a permanent reserve. However, official reserve status was not granted until 1971. Later, in 1988, a dispute occurred with the Ontario Ministry of Natural Resources when the expansion of the Red Squirrel logging road was approved through Temagami territory, which precipitated a series of road-blocks in 1988–89. The Ontario government created the Wendaban Stewardship Authority in 1991 to manage four townships near the logging road, but a final decision on the agreement has yet to be determined. See Matt Bray and Ashley Thomson, *Temagami: A Debate on Wilderness* (1990) for further details on the Teme-Augama First Nation's struggles to preserve their wilderness resources.

Thames. See Chippewas of the Thames
Thessalon

www.firstnation.ca/thessalon

One reserve located on the north shore of Lake Huron, about 103 kilometres southeast of Sault Ste. Marie. The total registered population in 2014 was
740, of which 106 live on-reserve. Those living off-reserve mostly reside in the
nearby town of Thessalon. The people are a signatory to the Robinson-Huron
Treaty of 1850. They are affiliated with Mamaweswen, the North Shore Tribal
Council and the Union of Ontario Indians.

Tyendinaga Mohawk Territory. See Mohawks of the Bay of Quinte
Waabigoniiw Saaga'iganiiw Anishinaabeg. See Wabigoon Lake Ojibway Nation
Wabaseemoong Independent Nations (Whitedog)

www.firstnation.ca/wabaseemoong-whitedog

The full name of this First Nation is the Wabaseemoong (literally "Whitedog")
Independent Nations of One Man Lake, Swan Lake and Whitedog. It is an
Ojibwa First Nation located 120 kilometres northwest of Kenora and 13 kilo-
metres east of the Ontario-Manitoba border. The total registered population
in 2014 was 1,905, of which 943 persons live on-reserve. The First Nation consists of four reserves of which the Wabaseemoong Indian Reserve (formerly the
Islington Indian Reserve 29) serves as the main reserve, while another, Agency
Indian Reserve 30 on the Aulneau Peninsula in the Lake of the Woods, is
shared with 12 other First Nations. The community is a member of the Bimose
Tribal Council, which represents ten First Nations in the Kenora–Dryden region, as well as the Grand Council Treaty #3.

Hydroelectric developments in the 1950s flooded much of the First
Nation's traditional territory. At that time the Wabaseemoong First Nation
was composed of three separate communities of One Man Lake, Swan Lake,
and Whitedog. After the flooding, the three communities were amalgamated into one unified band called the Islington Band of Saulteaux, whose
name was changed to the present one on 20 March 1992. In 2011, the
Wabaseemoong Independent Nations signed a settlement agreement with
Ontario Power Generation (OPG), which ended court action and resulted
in the formation of a trust for the proceeds of the settlement administered
by TD Canada Trust. Attending a celebration to commemorate the official signing were Ontario's Minister of Aboriginal Affairs Chris Bentley
and OPG's Chairman Jake Epp, as well as members of the Wabaseemoong
Independent Nations.

Wabauskang

www.firstnation.ca/wabauskang

This is an Anishenaabe (Ojibwa) First Nation consisting of one reserve about 67 kilometres northwest of Dryden. The reserve is also approximately 30 kilometres south of Ear Falls, off Highway 105, and 70 kilometres north of Vermilion Bay along the east shore of Wabauskang Lake. It is serviced by air through Ear Falls Airport, located 13 kilometres northwest of Ear Falls. In 2014, the total registered population was 322, of which 137 persons live on-reserve. The community is a member of the Bimose Tribal Council, which represents ten First Nations in the Kenora–Dryden region, and the Grand Council Treaty #3. The community operates a wood products company called Makoose Wood Innovations, privately owned by Wabauskang members. In important regional news regarding mining development in the area, the *Kenora Daily Miner and News* reported on 11 March 2014 that the Wabauskang First Nation had decided to use its hearing with the Supreme Court of Canada to challenge the Province of Ontario's ability to delegate the carrying out of Aboriginal consultation to mining companies, rather than having the Ministry of Mining and Northern Development deal with First Nations themselves. Wabauskang was granted a hearing at the Supreme Court in October to settle its long-standing fight with Rubicon Minerals over a proposed mining project inside the First Nation's territory *(Kenora Daily Miner 2014).*

Wabigoon Lake Ojibway Nation (Waabigoniiw Saaga'iganiiw Anishinaabeg)

www.wabigoonlakeon.ca

This Anishenaabe or Ojibway First Nation consists of one reserve situated approximately 19 kilometres southeast of Dryden in northwestern Ontario. In 2014, the total registered population was 702, of which 194 persons live on-reserve. The community is a member of the Bimose Tribal Council, a regional chiefs council that represents ten First Nations in the Kenora–Dryden region, and is a signatory to Treaty No. 3 of 1873. The Wabigoon Lake Reserve was first laid out in 1884 and later confirmed by the Ontario government in 1915. Members of the Wabigoon Band living on the western portion of the reserve later moved away and formed the Eagle Lake First Nation. Those living on the eastern portion of the reserve officially changed their name to Wabigoon Lake Ojibway on 7 August 1987. The Wabigoon First Nation has been involved with wild rice harvesting for many generations. When a dam was constructed at Dryden in 1896, extensive areas of *manomin* (wild rice) fields were flooded, causing its virtual extinction in some areas. However, the Wabigoon people transplanted the wild rice plants to other, more favourable areas, which are now protected by the Government of Ontario. Today, these *manomin* fields support the only Native wild rice processing plant in Canada, a facility built by Wabigoon people in 1988.

Wahgoshig (Abitibi)

www.wahgoshigfirstnation.com

One reserve on the south shore of Lake Abitibi, with a total registered population in 2014 of 319 persons, 147 of which are living on-reserve, located near Matheson. The reserve is situated on the portion of Lake Abitibi that divides northeastern Ontario from northwestern Quebec, and is accessible from Highway 101. The area west of the reserve, adjacent to Blueberry Lake, is a perfect habitat for moose, bears, grouse, and other game. Historically, the Lake Abitibi Aboriginal peoples gathered near the site of an important Hudson's Bay Company trading post, which was located at a point called Abitibi Matciteweiak on the Quebec side of the lake. During this time, the people were composed of one band, but later divided into two communities, Wahgoshig (Ontario) and Pikogan (Quebec). The reason for the division is that when the James Bay Treaty was signed in Quebec in June 1906, the treaty commissioners revealed that they were only authorized to negotiate with those persons whose hunting territories lay within Ontario. Those who hunted in Quebec were brought in under Treaty No. 9 and were considered part of the Abitibi Reserve. The Abitibi-Ontario Band changed its name to Wahgoshig in 1986, and a new reserve was established in Ontario, whereas previously they had lived on the Quebec side of Lake Abitibi.

Wahnapitae

www.wahnapitaefirstnation.com

This is an Ojibwa First Nation consisting of one reserve, which is an enclave located entirely within the city boundaries of Greater Sudbury, although it is not legally or politically part of the city. The reserve had a residential population of 102 people in the 2011 Census, while another 200 people currently live off-reserve. The traditional name of the community is *wahnapitaeping*, which means "that place where the water is shaped like a molar." The people are signatory to the Robinson-Huron Treaty of 1850, which was signed by Chief Tahgaiwenene during the treaty negotiations that took place at Sault Ste. Marie. The reserve was not actually properly surveyed until 1884. This situation caused confusion over where the reserve was actually located, since, according to the 1850 treaty, it was indicated that the reserve was to be situated at Wanabitibing, a place about 40 miles inland, near Lake Nipissing. The survey was made apparently without consultation with the Wahnapitae people, who wanted their reserve to be located in another area. The community is a member of the Waabnoong Bemjiwang Association of First Nations, which represents six First Nations in the Parry Sound–Capreol region.

Wahta Mohawks (Gibson Reserve)

www.wahtamohawks.ca

The Wahta community was founded when a group of the Mohawk people moved from Kanesatake, Quebec, to an area in Gibson Township in 1881. Conflicts over land and religion were the reason for the move. The Catholic missionaries (Sulpician), Mohawks and other Haudenosaunee, Algonquins, and Nipissings had occupied land at Oka, Quebec, since the early 1700s, after a grant was made by the French Crown. Conflict over land and timber rights erupted between the Sulpicians and the Aboriginal peoples of Kanesatake soon after the British had defeated the French and took control of New France in 1760. In 1877, the Department of Indian Affairs consulted with the leaders of Oka and found willingness on the part of Chief Onesakenrat and others to leave and form a new settlement in Ontario. In 1881, 44 families were willing to go to the lands found in Gibson Township today known as the Wahta Mohawk Territory. Today, the Wahta Mohawk community consists of two reserves in the District Municipality of Muskoka; one is adjacent to the village of Port Carling on the banks of the Indian River, and the other is located 14 kilometres east of Georgian Bay, near the town of Bala. In 2014, the total registered population for both reserves was 776 people, of whom 160 live on-reserve. The territory is home to the Iroquois Cranberry Growers, which is Ontario's largest cranberry farm, owned and operated by the people of Wahta.

Walpole Island. See Bkejwanong Territory

Wapekeka (Angling Lake)

www.wapekeka.ca

This is an Oji-Cree First Nation in the Kenora District, formerly known as Angling Lake First Nation, located approximately 450 kilometres northeast of Sioux Lookout and 26 kilometres northwest of Big Trout Lake. It consists of two reserves on the shore of Otter Lake. In 2014, the total registered population was 434, of which 425 persons live on-reserve. The community is relatively isolated; however, it does have year-round air service provided by Bearskin and Wasaya Airlines, which make regularly scheduled flights into the community at least three times per day. In terms of communication services, Wapekeka is served by the Wawaytay Radio System, 1 local FM radio system, a cable television system that transmits 16 channels to local homes, and TV Ontario, which has a satellite in the community. It is a member of the Shibogama First Nations Council, which represents five First Nations in the area north of Sioux Lookout in the Kasabonika–Wunnumin Lakes region. The community was policed by the Nishnawbe Aski Police Service until 2012. As of 2013, the Ontario Provincial Police (OPP) has been policing the territory. The two Wapekeka reserves are within the boundaries of the territory described by the 1929–30 adhesion to Treaty No. 9 (the James Bay Treaty) of 1905. In 1947, the beginning of the Angling Lake community was formed as a winter satellite community for families from Big Trout Lake whose traplines were located in the area. Beginning in 1960, permanent communities apart from Big Trout Lake were established. These communities were Kingfisher Lake, Wunnumin Lake, Bearskin Lake, Kasabonika Lake, and Muskrat Dam, Sachigo Lake, and Wapekeka. Wapekeka received official band status and two reserves in 1979. On 28 August 1981, the Angling Lake Band officially changed its name to Wapekeka First Nation. Wapekeka is proud of its experienced and qualified local firefighters, who are recertified every year by the Ministry of Natural Resources.

Wasauksing (Parry Island)

www.wasauksing.ca

This First Nation consists of one reserve located near Parry Sound, composed of 1,073 band members, with about 379 living on-reserve. The population is composed of Ojibwa, Odawa, and Potawatomi First Nations. Their reserve constitutes the Parry Island in Georgian Bay, with 126 kilometres of lakeshore, making it one of the larger islands in the Great Lakes. The Wasauksing people now occupy the entire island, although the ghost town of Depot Harbour on the island was historically a non-Aboriginal settlement. Noted as the home of Francis Pegahmagabow, the most highly decorated Aboriginal soldier in Canadian military history.

Washagamis Bay. See Obashkaandagaang

Washaho Cree Nation. See Fort Severn

Wauzhushk Onigum. See Anishinabe of Wauzhushk Onigum

Wawakapewin

www.firstnation.ca/wawakapewin-long-dog

This is an Oji-Cree First Nation situated in northwestern Ontario at Long Dog Lake along the southeast shoreline of the Ashewieg River, a tributary of the Winisk River, approximately 580 kilometres north of Thunder Bay. It consists of one reserve 20 kilometres southwest of Kasabonika Lake. As of 2014, the total registered population was 73, of which 49 persons live on-reserve. The community is only accessible by air via float planes, as this is one of the last settlements in the north without an airstrip, or by a winter/ice road for two months of the year, maintained by the Ashewieg Winter Roads Corp., which is linked to other roads to the south through Pickle Lake. The people of the Wawakapewin First Nation are members of the Shibogama First Nations Council, which represents five First Nations in the Kasabonika–Wunnumin Lakes region. It is a signatory to Treaty No. 9 of 1905. The signing of the adhesion to Treaty No. 9 at Big Trout Lake in 1929–30 identified the Wawakapewuk as part of the Big Trout Lake Band. In 1964, at least two new communities were formed from those communities associated with the reserve at Big Trout Lake, and in 1976, other communities were established with Wawakeka, Kasabonika, Bearskin Lake, Muskrat Dam, and Kingfisher Lake First Nations establishing themselves as separate bands and eventually gaining reserve status. The Wawakapewuk people still maintain direct family and kinship ties with the members of these surrounding communities. Wawakapewin received band status in 1985 and reserve status in 1998.

Weagamow Lake. See North Caribou Lake

Webequie

www.webequie.ca

Webequie (pronounced *Way-bih-quay*) is an Anishenaabe word meaning "shaking head from side to side." The name is derived from a hunter who observed a merganser, Webequie's symbolic bird, trying to locate a breeze on which to take flight by shaking its head to determine the direction of the wind. The community is located on the northern peninsula of Eastwood Island on Winisk Lake, and 540 kilometres north of Thunder Bay or 450 kilometres north of Sioux Lookout. Webequie is a fly-in community with no summer road access. A winter/ice road connects Webequie to the Northern Ontario Resource Trail. Webequie First Nation is a member of the Matawa First Nations Management, which represents ten First Nations in the region including Long Lac, Webequie, and Ogoki Post in northern Ontario, as well as a member of the Nishnabwe Aski Nation. In 2014, the total registered population was 877, of which 772 persons reside on-reserve. Webequie First Nation only recently gained reserve status, because the treaty commissioners for Treaty No. 9 in 1905 erroneously designated Webequie people as belonging

to the community of Eabametoong (Fort Hope) First Nation, situated approximately 80 kilometres to the southeast of Webequie. It was not until 1985 that
the government recognized Webequie as a distinct band, and separate reserve
status was granted in 2001.

Weenusk (Peawanuck)

www.firstnation.ca/weenusk-peawanuck

Weenusk, or *Winasko Ininiwak*, is a Cree First Nation consisting of one reserve on the west bank of the Winisk River at the mouth of the Asheweig
River, near the southeastern shore of Hudson Bay, making it the second-most
northerly First Nation in Ontario. In 2014, the total registered population was
576, of which 281 persons live on-reserve. In 1986, people of the Weenusk
First Nation were forced to move 30 kilometres southwest to Peawanuck, or "a
place where flint is found," when spring floods swept away much of the original
settlement. Weenusk First Nation is considered an independent member of the
Nishnabwe Aski First Nation, but has now joined the Mushkegowuk Council,
a regional tribal council.

From 1955–65, the Canadian government built 14 radar bases along the
Hudson Bay coast. During this time the people of Weenusk were employed
by the Canadian military. Years later, *Wawatay News* (2010) reported that the
Ontario government was planning to spend $55 million over a 6-year period to
clean up 16 Mid-Canada Line sites that are contaminated with toxic materials, such as mercury, PCBs, and asbestos, and littered with debris and derelict
buildings. Weenusk signed a 3-year, $8 million agreement with Ontario to
provide and operate the base camp, while Ontario signed a 1-year, $3-million
agreement with Winisk 500 Corporation, a band-owned business, to do general clean-up work at Site 500, the largest abandoned radar site in northern
Canada. Work on the large sites was completed in 2016, with clean-up efforts
continuing at five smaller sites (CBC 2016).

West Bay. See M'Chigeeng

Whitedog. See Wabaseemoong

Whitefish Bay. See Naotkamegwanning

Whitefish Lake. See Atikameksheng Anishnawbek

Whitefish River

www.whitefishriver.ca

This is an Ojibwa First Nation community located on the mainland at the
access point to Manitoulin Island on Lake Huron shores, approximately 15 kilometres northeast of Little Current and 110 kilometres southeast of Sudbury

on Highway 6. In 2014, the total registered population was 1,270 persons, of whom 420 live on-reserve. It consists of one reserve whose members belong to the United Chiefs and Councils of Mnidoo Mnising, a tribal council representing six First Nations in the Little Current–Sheguiandah region, and the Union of Ontario Indians. They are also a signatory to the Robinson-Huron Treaty of 1850. Within the territory of the Whitefish First Nation is a significant geographical feature called Dreamer's Rock, which is a tall quartzite outcrop that provided an ideal site for solitary fasting. Native youth from the surrounding area were sent to the summit, where they fasted and, through dreams, received powers from the guardian spirit. The spirit would also advise them of their calling. The dreamer would interpret his dreams with the help of elders and the medicine man. Today, as the Whitefish River First Nation website (n.d.) indicates, "We are an active and progressive community that encourages, supports and promotes local development, education, community wellness and economic development as key to our success." To this end, the community has established a company called Helios Development, which specializes in renewable energy project management and construction.

Whitesand

www.whitesandfirstnation.com

This is an Anishenaabe First Nation located northwest of the north shore of Lake Nipigon, near the town of Armstrong. In 2014, the total registered population was 1,208, of which 371 persons live on-reserve. Originally, this community was situated along the northwest shore of Lake Nipigon near the Whitesand River; however, community members were forced to move in 1942 because of the high water levels caused by flooding. The dispersed community resettled in various small communities along the Canadian National Railway (CNR) line that traverses the north shore of Lake Nipigon. After much discussion among Whitesand band members, a new location for their reserve was selected, immediately north of Armstrong, in the 1980s. This First Nation is part of the Independent First Nations Alliance, which represents five First Nations in northwestern Ontario. The reserve is located within the boundaries of the Robinson-Superior Treaty (1850) and is part of the Nishnawbe Aski Nation. The Whitesand First Nation is policed by the OPP (Ontario Provincial Police) after an agreement between the two parties.

Whitewater Lake

www.firstnation.ca/whitewater-lake

This First Nation community of Anishenaabe-speaking people is presently awaiting federal government approval of band status and therefore does not appear on the official records of Indigenous and Northern Affairs Canada. The reserve has an estimated population of 150 people and is located in the centre of Wabakimi Provincial Park, about 70 kilometres north of the town of Armstrong and 250 kilometres north of Thunder Bay. It joined the Windigo Tribal Council in 2000 and is a member of the Nishnawbe Aski Nation, as well as a signatory to Treaty No. 9. The community has no road access and is only accessible by float plane and boat in summer, and snow machine in winter.

Wikwemikong Unceded (Manitoulin Unceded Indian Reserve)

www.wikwemikong.ca

Wikwemikong, which means "Bay of Beavers," is an unceded Indian reserve in Canada, such that it has not "relinquished title to its land to the government by treaty or otherwise." The reserve is located on the northeastern section of Manitoulin Island and is occupied by Ojibwa, Odawa, and Potawatomi peoples under what is referred to as the Council of Three Fires. The band membership is an amalgamation of three bands: Wikwemikong, South Bay, and Point Grondine (located on the mainland near Killarney). Population statistics for 2009 indicate that the total band membership was 7,278, of which approximately 3,030 reside on-reserve. The reason that the Wikwemikong lands remain unceded today pertains to the Manitoulin Treaty of 1862, made with the Ottawa, Chippewa (Ojibwa), and other Aboriginal peoples occupying the Manitoulin Islands. There was some initial confusion over the number and size of the reserves stipulated in this treaty, but eventually all the tribes agreed to sign the treaty on the promise of sufficient reserves and annuities, except for the Wikwemikong people, who retained ownership of the eastern peninsula of the island. Wikwemikong as it exists today was created in 1968, when the two unceded bands and the Point Grondine band amalgamated as the Wikwemikong band. In 1975, the Wikwemikong Unceded Indian Reserve reasserted sovereignty over the islands off the east end of Manitoulin.

Wunnumin Lake

www.wunnumin.ca

This is an Oji-Cree First Nation located approximately 360 kilometres northeast of Sioux Lookout in northwestern Ontario. In 2014, the total registered population was 667, of which 564 people live-on reserve. Wunnimin Lake is accessible only by air transportation during the summer months; however, a winter/ice road is available in the colder months. It is policed by the Nishnawbe Aski Police Service, an Aboriginal-based community service.

In the Oji-Cree language, Wunnumin Lake is called *Wanaman-zaaga'igan*, meaning "Vermillion Lake" in reference to the vermillion-coloured clay about the lake. Residents of Wunnumin Lake originated from Big Beaver House. After a large forest fire, the community of Big Beaver House relocated to two separate communities, one of which was Wunnumin Lake, established in 1964. Reserve status was granted to the Wunnumin community in 1976. The community is a signatory to the 1929–30 adhesion to Treaty No. 9 of 1905.

Zhiibaahaasing (Cockburn Island)

www.firstnation.ca/zhiibaahaasing-cockburn-island

This is an Odawa and Ojibwa community consisting of two reserves on the west end of Manitoulin Island. The first reserve, on Manitoulin Island, has a total registered population of 162, of which 66 live on-reserve, while the other, located on Cockburn Island, has no permanent population. There has been a significant amount of controversy surrounding a stockpile of more than 1 million tires within the Zhiibaahaasing First Nation. Cockburn Island Tire Recycling plans to process the tires, but due to an equipment malfunction, the facility is not currently operating. Many area residents are concerned about health and environmental consequences should there be a fire. In September 2006, Aboriginal Affairs and Northern Development agreed to provide funding for the removal of the tires. Zhiibaahaasing First Nation is affiliated with the United Chiefs and Councils of Mnidoo Mnising (Manitoulin Island), which represents six First Nations in the Little Current–Sheguiandah area, as well as with the Union of Ontario Indians.

APPENDIX B

INTERNET RESOURCES

Aboriginal News, Communications, and Internet Services

The Kuhkenah Network (K-Net)
www.knet.ca
Kuhkenah is an Oji-Cree term for "everyone, everywhere." K-Net provides information and communications technology, telecommunication infrastructure, and application support in First Nations communities across a vast, remote region of northwestern Ontario. It supports the development of online applications that combine video, voice, and data services requiring broadband and high-speed connectivity solutions. K-Net also operates a service desk for First Nations schools who are receiving Internet access through School-Net.

Turtle Island Native Network (TINN)
www.turtleisland.org
TINN is an independent, Aboriginal-owned and operated news and information network. Its "communities" section includes a fairly complete list of First Nations political organizations in Ontario. It also contains a list of the Ontario Federation of Indian Friendship Centres (OFIFC), and various weblinks to many other First Nation services, training programs, and social organizations, such as the Professional Aboriginal Women's Society of Toronto, Aboriginal Legal Services of Toronto, Grand River Training and Employment, and the Ontario Aboriginal Sport Circle, to name just a few.

Turtle Island News
www.theturtleislandnews.com
Turtle Island News, started in 1994, is Canada's only national Native weekly

newspaper, published every week at the Grand River Territory of the Six Nations in southern Ontario. It is a politically independent newspaper that is wholly owned and operated by Aboriginal people. It is the concept of publisher Lynda Powless, who has almost 30 years of experience working in mainstream media from the CBC to national newspapers. Circulation presently stands at about 20,000 weekly with a growing national and international readership.

Wawatay Native Communications Society (WNCS)
www.wawataynews.ca

WNCS serves the communication needs of First Nations peoples and communities of the Nishnawbe Aski Nation. It does this through the distribution of a bi-weekly newspaper, daily radio programming, television production services, and a multimedia website that seeks to preserve and enhance Indigenous languages and cultures of Aboriginal peoples in northern Ontario. The membership of the society includes 49 First Nation communities within the territory of James Bay Treaty No. 9 and portions of Treaty No. 5.

Windspeaker
www.ammsa.com/publications/windspeaker

Windspeaker, launched in 1983 and known as Canada's national Aboriginal news source, is a magazine owned and operated by the Aboriginal Multi-Media Society (AMMSA). *Windspeaker Magazine* is published 12 times each year. Present national circulation has reached more than 24,000 with a readership in excess of 140,000.

Aboriginal Organizations of Ontario

Note: The following organizations provide only a partial list of various advisory agencies, tribal councils, and other political, economic, and social associations. Readers are advised to consult the various websites of First Nations and the INAC First Nations of Ontario profiles for further information.

Association of Iroquois and Allied Indians (AIAI)
www.aiai.on.ca

The AIAI is one of the oldest Aboriginal organizations in Ontario, established in 1969. It advocates for the political interests of eight member First Nations in Ontario, representing about 20,000 Aboriginal people. As a political territorial organization, it is relatively unique in Canada because its membership is an association of several different member-nations: the Oneida of the Thames near London, the Wahta Mohawk near Parry Sound, the Hiawatha Mohawk near Peterborough, the Mohawks of the Bay of Quinte near Belleville, the Delaware near Chatham, the Batchewana Ojibways near Sault Ste. Marie, and the Caldwell First Nation near Leamington. Each of these nations has different languages, cultural practices, and territories, which span much of the province. However, at AIAI, they form an alliance on political lines to protect their collective Aboriginal and treaty rights.

Centre for Indigenous Theatre (CIT)

www.indigenoustheatre.com

CIT was founded in 1974 by the late James Butler, with the goal of providing a viable Aboriginal theatre school whereby Aboriginal actors, playwrights, and directors would have a forum for exploration and exchange and that the results of this exchange would have a measurable impact on the Aboriginal theatre community. Today, CIT offers a three-year full-time program, as well as summer programs in Peterborough, Ontario, and Lethbridge, Alberta, which embrace the spirit, energy, and inspiration derived from the culture, values, and traditions of Indigenous people. The purpose of the program is to develop contemporary performance skills from a distinctively Indigenous cultural foundation.

Chiefs of Ontario (COO)

www.chiefs-of-ontario.org

The Chiefs of Ontario is a political forum and secretariat for collective decision-making, action, and advocacy for the various First Nations communities located in Ontario. It recognizes the self-determination efforts of the Anishinaabek, Mushkegowuk, Onkwehon:we, and Lenape peoples in protecting and exercising their inherent and treaty rights. COO originated in 1975 as a federation of the four major Ontario First Nations, whose purpose was to provide a unified voice on provincial issues and a single Ontario representative to the Assembly of First Nations.

Independent First Nations Alliance (IFNA)

www.ifna.ca

IFNA is a non-profit regional chiefs council representing Ojibwa and Oji-Cree First Nations in northern Ontario. The council provides advisory services and program delivery to its five member-nations (Kitchenuhmaykoosib Inninuwug, Lac Seul, Muskrat Dam, Pikangekum, and Whitesand). Incorporated in 1989, IFNA is made up of a representative chief from each of the five member-communities. It provides the technical advisory and community development support programs to meet the needs and aspirations of its First Nations on a collective basis, while each member First Nation maintains its autonomy. In turn, IFNA is a member of Nishnawbe Aski Nation, a tribal political organization representing the majority of Treaty No. 5, Treaty No. 9, and the Robinson-Superior Treaty First Nations in northern Ontario.

Mamaweswen, North Shore Tribal Council (MNSTC)

www.mamaweswen.ca

The Tribal Council Program (TCP) was introduced in 1984 and is one component of First Nation Indian Government Support Funding Programs. MNSTC represents seven First Nations (Batchewana, Garden River, Thessalon, Mississauga, Serpent River, Sagamok Anishnawbek, and Atikameksheng Anishinawbek) located along the north shore of Lake Huron, within the Robinson-Huron Treaty area. It provides technical advisory services to communities in the areas of health services, education services, administration, financial management, economic development, employment, and training services.

Matawa First Nations Management (MFNM)

www.matawa.on.ca

MFNM is a tribal council formed in 1988 to provide technical advisory services for Matawa First Nation communities situated north and northeast of Thunder Bay. The name *Matawa* was chosen by the chiefs because, in the Ojibwa and Cree languages, it is used to refer to "the meeting of rivers." Matawa's approach is to integrate modern social and economic development practices with traditional culture and heritage.

MoCreebec Council of the Cree Nation (MCCN)

www.mocreebec.com

MCCN was first established in 1980 at Moose Factory in northern Ontario on James Bay. It offers a variety of programs and services designed to serve the MoCreebec community in fields such as health, housing, employment, education, and communication. *Mission Statement*: Recognizing the supremacy and will of the Creator, the people who have chosen the name Mocreebec renew the social contract of sharing, kindness, strength, and honesty which was the basis for the first meeting of the Aboriginal and European peoples.

Mohawk Nation Council of Chiefs (MNCC)
www.mohawknation.org
The MNCC is the designated representative of the Sovereign Mohawk Nation. The chiefs are sanctioned by the Haudenosaunee Confederacy and are participants in Grand Council sessions affecting the Mohawk Nation and other members of the Confederacy. Other Confederacy Nations include the Oneida, Onondaga, Cayuga, Seneca, and Tuscarora, whose members have built a government with principles based on peace and the participation of its citizens. It is sometimes referred to as a participatory democracy. The Mohawk and other Haudenosaunee Nations consider their government to be a gift from the Creator.

Mushkegowuk Council (MC)
www.mushkegowuk.com
The Mushkegowuk Council represents the interests of the Cree First Nations of northern Ontario, which include the communities of Attiwapiskat, Chapleau Cree, Fort Albany, Kashechewan, Missanabie Cree, Taykwa Tagamou (New Post), and Weenusk. It is intended to respond to and carry out the collective will of all Mushkegowuk members and is committed to providing responsible and accountable political leadership. The Council's goal is to provide quality equitable and accessible support and advisory services to respond to and meet the social, economic, cultural, educational, spiritual, and political needs of Cree First Nations.

Nishnawbe Aski Nation (NAN)
www.nan.on.ca
NAN evolved out of Grand Council Treaty #9, which was established in 1973 as the regional organization representing the political, social, and economic interests of 49 First Nations in northern Ontario who are signatories

to Treaty No. 9 and Treaty No. 5. In 1982, the name changed to Nishnawbe Aski Nation. The main objective of NAN is to represent the social and economic aspirations of NAN peoples at all levels of government in Canada and Ontario, until such time as real, effective action is taken to remedy the problems and challenges experienced by the peoples of Nishnawbe Aski, and to permit the forces of self-determination to establish spiritual, cultural, social, and economic independence.

Nishnawbe Aski Police Service (NAPS)

www.naps.ca

NAPS provides policing services to 35 First Nations in the Nishnawbe Aski Nation territory. First Nations officers are spread across an area equal to two-thirds of the province of Ontario, from the Manitoba border, along the James Bay coast east to the Quebec border. The mission of the Nishnawbe Aski Police Service is to provide a unique, effective, efficient, and culturally sensitive and appropriate service to all people of the Nishnawbe area that will assertively promote harmonious and healthy communities.

Nokiiwin Tribal Council (NTC)

www.nokiiwin.com

Nokiiwin provides advisory services, such as those related to community planning, mining activities, economic development, and governance, for the five First Nations in the region extending from the north shore of Lake Superior to Lake Nipigon, comprising a total population of about 3,500 individuals. The head office is located on the Fort William First Nation.

Ogemawahj Tribal Council (OTC)

www.ogemawahj.on.ca

The OTC traces its origins to the alliance of the Chippewa, Mississauga, and Potawatomi First Nations with the formation of the Council of Three Fires Confederacy, founded in 1690. Since then, they have often worked together by pooling their resources for the use and benefit of all. Three hundred years later, the OTC, founded in 1990, carries on this tradition of cooperation. It was created to provide professional and technical services to its six member–First Nations (Alderville, Beausoleil, Georgina Island, Moose Deer Point, Rama, and Scugog Island).

Ontario Coalition of Aboriginal People (OCAP)

www.o-cap.ca

OCAP is an advocacy organization that represents the rights and interests of off-reserve Aboriginal peoples (Métis, status, and non-status Indians) living in urban, rural, and remote areas throughout the province of Ontario. It is an affiliate member of the Congress of Aboriginal Peoples (CAP). According to its website, OCAP's primary goal is to create and implement a plan to restart many of the programs denied Aboriginal peoples in Ontario, and secondly, to create and manage a consultation process to inform the diverse community across Ontario about what is occurring and how to access programs and services, while gaining feedback on issues and barriers. These goals also include organizing the Aboriginal communities in Ontario.

Ontario Native Women's Association (ONWA)

www.onwa.ca

ONWA is a not-for-profit organization that was established in 1971 to empower and support Aboriginal women and their families throughout the province of Ontario. ONWA's guiding principle is that all Aboriginal ancestry will be treated with dignity, respect, and equality, and benefits and services will be extended to all, no matter where one lives and regardless of tribal heritage. Its head office is located at the Fort William First Nation, near Thunder Bay.

Shibogama First Nations Council (SFNC)

www.shibogama.on.ca

The SFNC was founded in 1984 in the Kasabonika Lake Band Office. The current membership of the SFNC comprises the Kasabonika Lake, Kingfisher Lake, Wunnumin, Wapekeka, and Wawakapewin First Nations of northwestern Ontario. Its primary objective is to initiate, support, and manage projects and programs that improve the social, cultural, economic, educational, recreational, or spiritual life of members of the Shibogama First Nations. The SFNC is also further associated with the Nishnawbe Aski Nation, the Chiefs of Ontario, and the Assembly of First Nations.

Union of Ontario Indians (UOI)

www.anishinabek.ca

The Anishinabek Nation incorporated the Union of Ontario Indians (UOI) as its secretariat in 1949. The UOI is a political advocate for 39 member–First Nations across Ontario. The Union of Ontario Indians is the oldest political organization in Ontario and can trace its roots to the Confederacy of Three Fires, which existed long before European contact. The 39 First Nations have an approximate combined population of 55,000 citizens, or one-third of the province of Ontario's Aboriginal population. The UOI has its headquarters located on Nipissing First Nation, just outside of North Bay, and has satellite offices in Thunder Bay, Curve Lake First Nation, and Munsee-Delaware First Nation.

Wabun Tribal Council (WTC)
www.wabun.on.ca

The WTC serves the six First Nations of Beaverhouse, Brunswick House, Chapleau Ojibwa, Flying Post, Matachewan, and Mattagami, which are situated in relatively close proximity to the WTC headquarters in Timmins, in northern Ontario. WTC was incorporated in 1989 and was formed under INAC's devolution policy to coordinate and deliver services to First Nations communities at the local level. *Wabun*, in both the Cree and Ojibwa languages, means "sunrise," signifying a new day, a new start, or a fresh beginning.

Windigo First Nations Council (WFNC)
www.windigo.on.ca

The WFNC serves the remote northwestern communities of Bearskin Lake, Sachigo Lake, Caribou Lake, Koocheching, Cat Lake, Slate Falls, and Whitewater Lake. Its origins can be traced to 1977, when four chiefs met to discuss their common interests and plan collaborative ventures. One of these ventures was the development of a system of winter roads in order to reduce the cost of air transportation. Thus, the Windigo Lake Transportation Company was born in an attempt to develop more cost-effective means of transporting building materials, store goods, and fuel over land. Today, the WFNC works to deliver a variety of programs and services in the areas of health, education, resource development, and financial advisory services.

National Aboriginal Organizations

Assembly of First Nations (AFN)

www.afn.ca

The Assembly of First Nations (AFN) is a national organization representing First Nation citizens in Canada, which includes more than 900,000 people living in 634 First Nations communities and in cities and towns across the country. The AFN national executive is made up of the National Chief, ten Regional Chiefs, and the chairs of the Elders, Woman's, and Youth councils. Regional chiefs are elected every three years by chiefs in their regions, who are elected by the citizens and members of their respective communities. The National Chief is also elected every three years. The AFN is designated to present the views of the various First Nations (Aboriginal peoples with status under the Indian Act) through their leaders in such areas as Aboriginal and treaty rights, economic development, education, and justice issues.

Indigenous Physicians Association of Canada (IPAC)

www.ipac-amic.org

The aim of IPAC is to collaborate with physicians in training and practice, other health professionals, communities, agencies, and governments to ultimately improve Indigenous health. Past successes have included the development of medical school admissions toolkits to increase the number of Indigenous health professionals in training; mentoring activities to support Indigenous medical students, residents, and physicians; and the creation of a curriculum to improve competence in Indigenous health for all health professionals. IPAC provides knowledge for communities, national Aboriginal organizations, and healthcare providers; advocates for Indigenous peoples' health; and is a support mechanism for Indigenous physicians and students.

National Association of Friendship Centres (NAFC)

www.nafc.ca

The National Association of Friendship Centres is dedicated to the improvement of the quality of life of Aboriginal peoples in urban environments by supporting activities that encourage access to, and participation in, Canadian society. The NAFC is a network of 117 friendship centres and seven provincial/territorial associations nationwide.

Native Women's Association of Canada (NWAC)

www.nwac.ca

The NWAC is a national association affiliated with provincial and territorial associations representing Aboriginal women across Canada. It speaks out about issues affecting Aboriginal women and their families.

Academic Associations and Societies

Canadian Anthropology Society (CASCA)

www.cas-sca.ca

CASCA was originally founded in 1974 as the Canadian Ethnology Society (CESCE). Today, CASCA has over 500 members from across Canada and around the world. Its aims are to ensure continuing financial support for anthropological research, and to commit to excellence in Canadian anthropology graduate programs and in the teaching of undergraduate anthropology. Throughout the history of Canadian anthropology, much of the research has been based on First Nations communities.

Canadian Association for the Study of Indigenous Education (CASIE)

www.casieaceea.org

CASIE promotes the study and dialogue of professors, students, researchers, and practitioners in the field of Aboriginal/Indigenous education. The purpose of this Aboriginal association is to provide a forum for discussion of Indigenous education studies in a Canadian context, and to foster and encourage commitment to research priorities of Indigenous peoples and their communities, as well as respectful research processes within Canadian life-wide and life-long educational spheres.

Canadian Indigenous/Native Studies Association (CINSA)

www.ccednet-rcdec.ca

CINSA is a community of scholars committed to fostering the development of Aboriginal Studies as a discipline informed by, and respectful of, Indigenous intellectual traditions, and to creating a place of respect and dignity for Aboriginal peoples within Canada and the world. Among its objectives are the dissemination of research and the facilitation of communication among members through such means as conferences.

Native American and Indigenous Studies Association (NAISA)
www.naisa.org
NAISA began through meetings held by the University of Oklahoma in
2007 and became incorporated in 2009. It is an international and interdisciplinary professional organization for scholars and community members
interested in all aspects of Indigenous Studies.

Ontario Archaeological Society (OAS)
www.ontarioarchaeology.on.ca
The Ontario Archaeological Society began in 1958 as the joint project of
a group of enthusiastic amateurs. Publication of original and authoritative
archaeological works has always been a major aim of the society. The first
issue of *Ontario Archaeology* appeared in 1958. The society also publishes a
bi-monthly newsletter, *Arch Notes*, as well as the occasional publication series
Monographs in Ontario Archaeology. The OAS also has nine regional chapters,
each of which has its own website and newsletter.

Government Departments and Agencies

Indigenous and Northern Affairs Canada (INAC)
www.aandc.gc.ca
The prime minister of Canada changed the name of Aboriginal Affairs and
Northern Development Canada (AANDC) to Indigenous and Northern
Affairs Canada (INAC) in November 2015. INAC is one of the federal government departments responsible for meeting Canada's obligations to First
Nations, Inuit, and Métis, and for fulfilling the federal government's constitutional responsibilities in the North. INAC is one of 34 federal departments
and agencies involved in Aboriginal and northern programs and services.

Ontario Ministry of Indigenous Relations and Reconciliation
www.ontario.ca/page/ministry-indigenous-relations-and-reconciliation
The Ontario Ministry of Indigenous Relations and Reconciliation (renamed
from Ontario Ministry of Aboriginal Affairs in June 2016) was established
in 2007 as a stand-alone ministry that replaced the Ontario Secretariat of
Aboriginal Affairs. The Ministry's mandate is to promote collaboration and coordination across ministries on Aboriginal policy and programs in the province.

Journals and Publications

American Indian Quarterly (AIQ)
www.nebraskapress.unl.edu/product/American-Indian-Quarterly,673174.aspx
AIQ is a peer-reviewed interdisciplinary journal that provides a forum for diverse voices and perspectives spanning a variety of academic disciplines, focusing on the First Nations of North America. It publishes works that contribute to the development of American Indian Studies as a field and to the sovereignty and continuance of North American Indian Nations and cultures.

Canadian Journal of Native Studies (CJNS)
www.brandonu.ca/native-studies/cjns
The CJNS is the official publication of the Canadian Indian/Native Studies Association. The journal publishes research in the field of Native Studies and, although the majority of articles deal with Indigenous peoples in Canada, it also publishes articles dealing with Indigenous peoples worldwide. It comes out on a bi-annual basis and publishes original scholarly activity, which is refereed by peer review.

International Indigenous Policy Journal (IIPJ)
www.iipj.org
The IIPJ is a peer-reviewed journal led by an advisory board made up of distinguished people from Australia, Canada, the US, and the Russian Federation. Among the journal's goals are to promote evidence-based policy-making and to encourage equality-based research on partnerships with Indigenous peoples. The journal is sponsored by Western University in Ontario and Indigenous and Northern Affairs Canada (INAC).

Native Studies Review (NSR)
www.publications.usask.ca/nativestudiesreview
The *Native Studies Review* began publication in 1984 as a refereed bi-annual journal by the Native Studies Department of the University of Saskatchewan. The journal's mandate is to feature original scholarly research on Aboriginal perspectives and issues in contemporary and historical contexts. As a multi-disciplinary periodical, it publishes articles dealing primarily with a Canadian focus, but welcomes submissions with an international focus.

Ontario Archaeologist

www.ontarioarchaeology.on.ca

This is a peer-reviewed journal of the Ontario Archaeological Society, which often publishes articles on the past First Nations of Ontario. Regional chapters also have their own newsletters, which publish archeological investigations of local or regional interest.

Museums, Archives, and Cultural Centres

Canadian Museum of Civilization

www.civilization.ca

The history of the Canadian Museum of Civilization begins in 1856 with the establishment by the Geological Survey of Canada. Today, the museum (located in Gatineau, Quebec, directly opposite Parliament Hill) is divided into Research and Collections Branches. Research is conducted in the fields of archaeology, ethnology (particularly focused on the First Nations of northern North America), folklore, and Canadian history.

Hudson's Bay Company Archives

www.gov.mb.ca/chc/archives/hbca

The Hudson's Bay Company was founded in 1670 by a Royal Charter and given access to a vast territory in Canada's north, called Rupert's Land. The HBC archives are a treasure trove of documents and related material pertaining to the fur trade and later development of a retail empire. It is especially informative concerning the First Nations of Canada's northern provinces and territories, as fur traders documented the social, economic, and political aspects of Native life for over 300 years. A microfilm service is available, as well as opportunities for family history research, which can be accessed through your local library.

Royal Ontario Museum (ROM)

www.rom.on.ca

The Royal Ontario Museum's diverse collections of world cultures and natural history make it one of the largest museums in North America. The ROM is also the largest field-research institution in Canada, with research and conservation activities that span the globe. It also participates in an active publication program, as well as providing an online image collection of ROM artifacts and specimens. The material collections and research publications are particularly informative about the First Nations of Ontario.

Whetung Ojibwa Centre

www.whetung.com

The Centre is located on the Curve Lake First Nation Reserve, near Peterborough. It evolved out of a fishing lodge opened by the Whetung family in the early 1900s and continues today as a family-run business. The Centre features the works of such well-known Ojibwa artists such as Benjamin Chee Chee, Norval Morrisseau, and Daphne Odjig. It also has an extensive crafts shop with sculptures, carvings, masks, and quill boxes.

Wikwemikong Heritage Organization

www.wikwemikongheritage.org

The Heritage Organization is located on the Wikwemikong Unceded Indian Reserve on Manitoulin Island in northern Ontario. The Organization aims to uphold the uniqueness of Anishenaabe ways of utilizing a holistic approach as initiated by the Ojibwa, Odawa, and Potawatomi First Nations. It is a non-profit organization committed to the preservation and enhancement of Anishenaabeg culture through education and participatory cultural opportunities with both Native and non-Native people. The Organization also includes an extensive reference library, which contains resources dealing specifically with Anishenaabe history, culture, and language.

Woodland Cultural Centre

www.woodland-centre.on.ca

The Woodland Cultural Centre is located in Brantford, Ontario, and was established in 1972 under the direction of the Iroquois and Allied Indians upon the closure of the Mohawk Institute Residential School. It is a non-profit organization that preserves and promotes the culture and heritage of the First Nations of the Eastern Woodland area. The Centre originally began with a focus on collecting research and artifacts to develop its library and museum collections. The Centre's programming began to change in the 1990s, emphasizing the needs and diversity of First Nations artists with an expanded art collection and an annual juried art exhibition called *First Nations Art.*

Research and References

Aboriginal Culture
www.ontariotravel.net/en/play/aboriginal-experiences/aboriginal-culture
This website is sponsored by the Ontario government through Travel Ontario.
It is designed to direct interested parties to various Aboriginal experiences,
such as powwows and outdoor activities, and resource centres on Aboriginal
culture such as heritage organizations, guided tours, eco-travel, Indigenous
art collections, and traditional foods.

Ipperwash Inquiry (2007)
www.ipperwashinquiry.ca
The Ipperwash Inquiry was established by the Government of Ontario under
the Public Inquiries Act. Its mandate was to inquire and report on events
surrounding the death of Dudley George, who was shot during a 1995 protest by First Nations representatives at Ipperwash Provincial Park and later
died. The Inquiry was also mandated to make recommendations that would
avoid violence in similar circumstances in the future. The Report, containing
findings and recommendations, was made public on 31 May 2007.

Treaty Commission of Ontario
www.chiefs-of-ontario.org/treaty-commission
The Report of the Ipperwash Inquiry recommended that provincial and
First Nation governments should establish a permanent, independent, and
impartial agency called the Treaty Commission of Ontario (TCO) to facilitate and oversee the settling of land and treaty claims in Ontario. In light
of this, the Chiefs Assembly passed Resolution 08/65—Creation of Chiefs
Advisory and Technical Committees in the Area of the Treaty Commission
and Reconciliation Fund, directing the Political Confederacy to create the
Chiefs Advisory Committee (CAC), whose mandate would be to complete
work necessary for the establishment of a Treaty Commission of Ontario.

Truth and Reconciliation Commission of Canada (TRC)
www.trc.ca
The Indian Residential Schools Truth and Reconciliation Commission
(TRC) was officially established on 2 June 2008. The TRC is part of the
court-approved Indian Residential Schools Settlement Agreement negotiated

between legal counsel for former students, church members, government representatives, the Assembly of First Nations, and other Aboriginal organizations. All of the documents and research gathered by the TRC throughout its mandate will be accessible in a new national research centre.

GLOSSARY

Aboriginal: The indigenous or original inhabitants of a particular territory; in Canada, includes the Indian, Inuit, and Métis peoples, according to the Constitution Act of 1982 (Section 35).

Aboriginal nation: A sizable body of Aboriginal people with a shared sense of national identity that constitutes the prominent population in a certain territory or collection of territories, according to the Royal Commission on Aboriginal Peoples (RCAP) of 1996.

Algonquian (or Algonkian): The largest Aboriginal language family in Canada; includes such First Nation languages as Cree, Blackfoot, Ojibwa, and Mi'kmaq.

altithermal period: The hottest and driest climatic period in North America during the last 20,000 years, extending from about 4,500 to 7,000 BP; roughly corresponds with the Lake Nipissing stage.

Anishenaabe: The Ojibwas' term for themselves; usually translated as meaning "original people."

annealing: A method of hardening metal by alternative heat and cooling applications.

anthropology: The scientific study of humankind from social, linguistic, biological, and archaeological perspectives.

archaeology: The scientific study of extant and extinct cultures through the examination of material artifacts and other remains.

Assembly of First Nations: The national-level political organization representing Aboriginal persons with legal status under the Indian Act, comprising over 630 communities across Canada (see www.afn.ca).

band: Under the Indian Act, Section 2(1), simply means a body of Indians (First Nations people with status) for whom the Canadian government has set aside lands for their common benefit. In anthropology, the term means a territorial-based social group, usually of relatively small scale, whose members live by hunting and gathering.

Before Present (BP): Generally has replaced the previous designation of AD (*anno Domini*, "in the year of our Lord") and BC ("before Christ"). However, a newer designation for dates is also used, with BCE (Before the Common Era) and CE (Common Era), such that BCE represents dates based on calibrated radiocarbon dates. See Anthony (2007: 467–70) for a detailed explanation.

bilateral descent: The system of kinship structure in which an individual belongs equally to the kindred of both parents.

Bill C-31 (1985): An amendment to Canada's Indian Act that allowed for the reinstatement of Indian status under application for Aboriginal persons who had previously lost their status; under this Act, neither women nor men would lose their legal status as a result of marriage to non-status persons.

Canadian Shield: A large area of exposed Precambrian igneous rock that forms the ancient geological core of North America.

chiefdom: A type of socio-political organization characterized by a centralized political structure, a redistributive economy, and a large sedentary population; intermediate between tribal and state-level societies.

Chippewa-Stanley stage: A period from about 5,000 to 8,000 BP, with low water levels in the Upper Great Lakes region.

clan: A unilineal kin group in which members regard themselves as descended from a common ancestor, usually legendary or mythological; previously called a "sib" in anthropological literature.

colonialism: A policy whereby a nation seeks to establish long-term social, political, and economic domination over another people, usually by the installation of an administrative structure using members of the dominant society to facilitate control.

Congress of Aboriginal Peoples: A national-level Aboriginal organization representing non-status and Métis people founded in 1994; formerly known as the Native Council of Canada, established in 1971.

co-residential group: A local Aboriginal settlement usually situated on the shores of a lake in the centre of the trapping territory of its members.

cross-cousins: Cousins whose related parents are siblings of unlike sex. Offspring of a person's mother's brother or father's sister.

culture area: A geographical territory within which the cultures tend to be similar in some significant aspects, such as subsistence strategies or social organization.

cultures: The integrated sum total of learned behaviour traits characteristic of the members of various societies.

Dene: A term used in Athapaskan languages of northwestern Canada, meaning "the people."

Eastern Woodlands: A large culture area situated in eastern North America comprising the Great Lakes to the Atlantic coastal range, once consisting of dense hardwood forests and relatively mild temperatures; principally occupied before European contact by Haudenosaunee horticultural societies.

ethnocentric: Evaluating other people or their culture on the basis of a belief in the superiority of one's own way of life or cultural standards.

ethnography: A method of research devoted to the descriptive recording of cultures based on certain information-gathering techniques, such as participant observation, carried out through fieldwork.

ethnology: A research approach devoted to the analysis, systematic interpretation, and comparison of cultural material with the intention of producing meaningful generalizations about human behaviour.

exogamy: Marriage outside of a specific social group of which a person is a member, as required by custom or law; contrasts with endogamy, which is marriage within a specific group.

fieldwork: A technique of ethnography used to gather information on human behaviour; usually involves living for an extended period of time in a human population and conducting research by participating and observing people in different cultures.

First Nation: Refers to Aboriginal people with status under the Indian Act; has begun to replace the terms **Indian** and **band**.

First Nation community: A term that refers to a geographical area set aside for Aboriginal people with status under the Indian Act; it is becoming the preferred term, replacing **reserve**.

horticulture: Cultivation of crops using simple hand tools, such as a hoe or digging stick, usually without fertilization or irrigation.

Indian: According to Canada's Indian Act Section 2(1), means a person who, pursuant to this Act is registered as an Indian or is entitled to be registered as an Indian.

Indigenous and Northern Affairs Canada (INAC): Formerly known as Aboriginal Affairs and Northern Development (AANDC). Name was changed by Prime Minister Trudeau in November 2015. A federal government department responsible for meeting Canada's obligations to First Nations, Inuit, and Métis and for fulfilling the federal government's constitutional responsibilities towards Aboriginal peoples. INAC is one of 34 federal departments and agencies involved in Aboriginal and northern programs and services.

in situ: A Latin term meaning "found in place."

Ipperwash Inquiry (2007): An investigation initiated by the Ontario government in 2003 under the Public Inquiries Act, with a mandate to report on events surrounding the death of Dudley George of the Stony Point First Nation while engaging in a 1995 protest at Ipperwash Provincial Park. The Honourable Sidney B. Linden was appointed commissioner with hearings in Forest, Ontario, and a report was released by Ontario's Attorney General Michael Bryant on 31 May 2007 (see www.ipperwashinquiry.ca).

Iroquois kinship terminology: A system of kinship reckoning in which various relatives are "classified" together. For example, in the Iroquois system, members of one's nuclear family are classified with more distant kinfolk, such that an Iroquois child refers to his mother's sister with the same term that is used to refer to one's mother. Similarly, the term for "father" is also extended to include one's father's brother. In addition, children of one's mother's sister and father's brother are also correspondingly referred to as one's "brothers" and "sisters."

kinship system: The customary complex of statuses and roles governing the behaviour of relatives.

kinship terminology: The set of names applied to the various statuses in a kinship system; the linguistic labels used in the classification of kin in particular categories that are used to designate certain genealogical connections between individuals.

Lake Nipissing stage: A postglacial stage from about 3,500 to 5,000 BP, during which water levels in the Upper Great Lakes rose some 200 metres above present sea level.

Lake Ojibwa-Barlow: A large glacial lake in northern Ontario that formerly occupied an area between the height-of-land north of Lake Superior and the Hudson Bay ice sheet.

Laurentide: An ice sheet that covered most of northern North America, emanating out of Hudson Bay.

lineage: A unilineal descent group that traces descent from a common ancestor, who lived not more than five or six generations back in time.

lingua franca: A mixture of different languages; any language serving as a medium between different peoples.

mastodons: Extinct elephants that browsed on leaves, grasses, and shrubs in forested regions.

matrilateral: Descent principle that is determined through one's mother's brother; kin on one's mother's side of a family; see **patrilateral**.

matrilineal descent: A principle of descent that is reckoned through one's mother's kin or the female line; serves to define group membership and inheritance rights.

matrilocal residence: Pertaining to the practice whereby a married couple settles in or in close proximity to the domicile of the wife's family.

Métis Nation Council: A national-level political and cultural organization founded in 1983 with the goal of promoting Métis self-government.

Midewiwin: A religious organization among several Algonquian peoples, also known as the Grand Medicine Society.

moraines: Accumulations of stones, earth, and sand that was carried and then deposited by glacial activity.

National Association of Friendship Centres: An organization dedicated to the improvement of the quality of life of Aboriginal peoples in urban environments (www.nafc.ca).

Native: A term widely used in previous decades as a cover term for all Aboriginal persons, but is not as popular today, although *Native American* is a cover term still commonly used in the United States.

non-status Indians: Aboriginal persons who are not recognized as having legal status under Canada's Indian Act.

nuclear family: A social group comprising married parents and their children, usually living in the same residence.

Old Copper Culture: A culture specializing in the manufacture of copper tools, weapons, and personal ornaments whose members lived in the Upper Great Lakes region from about 3,500 to 7,000 BP.

Ontario Ministry of Indigenous Relations and Reconciliation: The Ontario Ministry of Indigenous Relations and Reconciliation (renamed from Ontario Ministry of Aboriginal Affairs in June 2016) was established in 2007 as a stand-alone ministry to replace the former Ontario Secretariat of Aboriginal Affairs. Its mandate is to promote collaboration and coordination across ministries on Aboriginal policy and programs, representing the approximately 300,000 First Nations, Métis, and Inuit Ontarians (see www.ontario.ca/page/ministry-indigenous-relations-and-reconciliation).

ossuary: A large pit in which bones of deceased individuals are buried together, often having been removed from temporary grave sites.

parallel cousins: Cousins whose related parents are of like sex. The offspring of a person's mother's sister or father's brother.

participant observation: A research technique that involves living with the people of a particular culture or community over an extended period of time, such that researchers attempt to immerse themselves in the day-to-day activities of the group under study.

patrilateral: Relatives on a person's father's side of a family or descent group; see also **matrilateral**.

patrilineal descent: Pertaining to unilineal descent traced through the father or male line, such that group membership and inheritance rights are established and defined; see also **matrilineal descent**.

patrilocal residence: Pertaining to the post-marital residence pattern whereby a married couple settles in or near the domicile of the husband's family; see also **matrilocal residence**.

pictographs: Paintings, usually made with a compound of red ochre used as a pigment, on the granite rocks of the Precambrian Shield.

polygynous family: A social unit consisting of a man married to two or more women simultaneously and their children; each woman and her children may occupy a separate household from other such units.

potlatch: A First Nations institution of ceremonial feasting and gift-giving found on Canada's Northwest Pacific Coast; a type of redistributive economic and political system commonly associated with chiefdoms and central authority structures.

projectile points: Bifacial constructed stone tools, usually hafted to the end of a spear or arrow.

quartzite: A rock used for making stone tools, because it chips and flakes like flint.

radiocarbon dating: A method of dating organic material by measuring the amount of radiocarbon (carbon 14) in the sample, thereby determining how long ago a specimen died. A method reasonably accurate for dating material from the last 50,000 years.

registered Indians: Aboriginal persons with legal status under Canada's Indian Act.

reserve: In the context of the Indian Act, a geographical area specifically set aside for the habitation of status Indians and administered by the federal government through the Department of Indigenous Affairs and its minister; land set aside by the Crown for the use and benefit of an Indian band.

ripple or parallel flaking: The removal of horizontal flakes from a projectile point, appearing as a ripple effect.

settlement patterns: The manner in which social groups organize their geographic living spaces.

shaman: A religious specialist who has received his or her power directly from supernatural sources or powers.

slash-and-burn: A form of shifting cultivation in which there is recurrent clearing and burning of forest cover with planting in the burned fields; see **horticulture**.

stratigraphy: Refers to the layers of soil in an archaeological site; lower soil layers, and the objects within these layers, are considered older than those layers deposited above.

Subarctic: A large culture area south of the Arctic region, ranging from the Atlantic coast to the Rocky Mountains, consisting of a vast coniferous forest, relatively cold temperatures, and thousands of lakes and rivers; a region occupied principally by eastern Algonquian and western Dene hunters and gatherers.

subsistence economies: Production and exchange of food items meant for local consumption; also includes tools, knowledge, and practices through which such food is secured.

swidden: See **slash-and-burn**.

taconite: A grade of iron ore found in the Lake Superior region that tends to flake like flint and is therefore considered a useful material for the manufacture of stone tools and weapons.

Treaty Indians: First Nations persons, or the descendant of such people, who signed a treaty or other similar agreement with the British Crown or the later Canadian government. Usually, such a person is entitled to annuities, residential areas, preferred hunting rights, or other benefits as stipulated in certain treaties.

tribes: Social groups speaking a distinct language or dialect and possessing a distinct culture that sets them off from other tribes. They are not necessarily organized politically, nor do they have a centralized decision-making body; associated with horticulture or pastoralism as a subsistence strategy.

unilineal: Pertaining to descent through one parent only.

Woodland period: An archaeological designation for a time period generally beginning about 3,000 BP characterized primarily by the manufacture and use of pottery, but also could include the practice of complex burials such as mound building, the adoption of horticulture, and sedentary settlement patterns.

REFERENCES

Abel, K. 2006. *Changing Places: History, Community and Identity in Northeastern Ontario.* Montreal: McGill-Queen's University Press.

Alfred, T. 2014. "Idle No More and Indigenous Nationhood." In Kino-nda-niimi Collective, ed., *The Winter We Danced*, pp. 347–48. Winnipeg: ARP Books.

Alfred, T., and J. Corntassell. 2011. "Being Indigenous: Resurgences against Contemporary Colonialism." In M.J. Cannon and L. Sunseri, eds., *Racism, Colonialism, and Indigeneity in Canada*, pp. 139–44. Don Mills: Oxford University Press.

Anthony, D.W. 2007. *The Horse, the Wheel, and Language: How Bronze-Age Riders from the Eurasian Steppes Shaped the Modern World.* Princeton, NJ: Princeton University Press.

APTN National News. 2012. "Brazeau: Attawapiskat Chief's Hunger Strike Doesn't Set 'Good Example for Young Aboriginal Youth.'" 12 December.

Asch, M. 2014. *On Being Here to Stay: Treaties and Aboriginal Rights in Canada.* Toronto: University of Toronto Press.

Attawapiskat First Nation. 2012. "Consolidated Financial Statements." Retrieved March 19, 2017 from www.attawapiskat.org/wp-content/uploads/2012-Consolidated-Financial-Statements.pdf.

Barrett, S.R. 2002. *Culture Meets Power.* Westport, CT: Praeger.

Battiste, M., and S. Youngblood Henderson. 2011. "Eurocentrism and the European Ethnographic Tradition." In M.J. Cannon and L. Sunseri, eds., *Racism, Colonialism, and Indigeneity in Canada*, pp. 11–19. Don Mills: Oxford University Press.

Belanger, Y.D. 2010. *Ways of Knowing: An Introduction to Native Studies in Canada.* Toronto: Nelson Education.

Biggar, H.P. 1924. *The Voyages of Jacques Cartier.* Ottawa: Publications of the Public Archives of Canada, No. 11.

Bishop, C.A. 1974. *The Northern Ojibwa and the Fur Trade.* Toronto: Holt, Rinehart and Winston.

———. 1981. "Territorial Groups before 1821: Cree and Ojibwa." In W.C. Sturtevant, ed., *Handbook of North American Indians*, Vol. 6, pp. 158–60. Washington, DC: Smithsonian Institution.

Boas, F. 1897. *The Social Organization and the Secret Societies of the Kwakiutl Indians.* Report of the U.S. National Museum, 1895. Washington, DC: Smithsonian Institution.

Borrows, J. 1997. "Wampum at Niagara: The Royal Proclamation, Canadian Legal History, and Self Government." In M. Asch, ed., *Aboriginal and Treaty Rights in Canada: Essays on Law, Equality and Respect for Difference*, pp. 155–72. Vancouver: University of British Columbia Press.

Boyd, M., and C. Surette. 2010. "Northernmost Precontact Maize in North America." *American Antiquity* 75 (1): 117–33.

Bray, M., and E. Epp. 1984. *A Vast and Magnificent Land: An Illustrated History of Northern Ontario.* Thunder Bay: Lakehead University.

Bray, M., and A. Thomson, eds. 1990. *Temagami: A Debate on Wilderness.* Toronto: Dundurn Press.

Brown, J.S.H. 1980. *Strangers in Blood: Fur Trade Company Families in Indian Country.* Vancouver: University of British Columbia Press.

Brown, J.S.H., and R. Brightman. 1988. *"The Orders of the Dreamed": George Nelson on Cree and Northern Ojibwa Religion and Myth, 1823.* Winnipeg: University of Manitoba Press.

Cairns, A.C. 2000. *Citizens Plus: Aboriginal*

Peoples and the Canadian State. Vancouver: University of British Columbia Press.

Calverley, D. 2006. "The Impact of the Hudson's Bay Company on the Creation of Treaty Number Nine." *Ontario History* 98 (1): 30–51.

Canada. 1891 [1979]. *Indian Treaties and Surrenders.* Ottawa: Queen's Printer.

Cannon, M.J., and L. Sunseri, eds. 2011. *Racism, Colonialism, and Indigeneity in Canada.* Oxford: Oxford University Press.

CBC News. 2013a. "Idle No More Protests Held across Canada." 11 January.

———. 2013b. "Idle No More Targets Canadian Travel Routes." 5 January.

———. 2013c. "Ring of Fire Mining May not Benefit First Nations as Hoped, Internal Memo from Aboriginal Affairs Paints Troubling Picture." 29 June.

———. 2014a. "Lynn Gehl Challenges Indian Status Denial in Ontario Court." 20 October.

———. 2014b. "Mitaanjigamiing First Nation Declares State of Emergency." 19 June.

———. 2016. "Clean-up of Cold War Radar Bases in Northeastern Ontario Complete." 30 May. Retrieved 19 March 2017 from www.cbc.ca/news/canada/sudbury/northern-ontario-radar-bases-cleanup-1.3606905.

Centre for Indigenous Governance, Ryerson University. n.d. Centre for Indigenous Government. Retrieved 29 November 2014 from www.ryerson.ca/cig.

Chilton, E.S. 2005. "Farming and Social Complexity in the Northeast." In T.R. Pauketat and D.D. Loren, eds., *North American Archaeology*, pp. 138–60. Malden, MA: Blackwell Publishing.

Christie, G. 2007. "Police-Government Relations in the Context of State-Aboriginal Relations." In M.E. Beare and T. Murray, eds., *Police and Government Relations: Who's Calling the Shots?* pp. 147–82. Toronto: University of Toronto Press.

Chute, J.E. 1998. "Shingwaukonse: A Nineteenth-Century Innovative Ojibwa Leader." *Ethnohistory* 45 (1): 65–101.

Coates, K. 2015. *#IdleNoMore: And the Remaking of Canada.* Regina: University of Regina Press.

Constitution Act, 1982 (RSC). 1982. Ottawa: Queen's Printer.

Copway, G. 1847. *The Life, History, and Travels of Kah-ge-ga-gah-kowh (George Copway), a Young Indian Chief of the Ojibwa Nation.* Philadelphia: James Harmstead.

Coser, L. 1964. *The Functions of Social Conflict.* New York: The Free Press.

Coulthard, G.S. 2014. *Red Skins, White Masks: Rejecting the Colonial Politics of Recognition.* Minneapolis: University of Minnesota Press.

CTV News. 2013. "Idle No More Co-Founder Supports Spence, not Blockades." 13 January.

Darnell, R. 2000. "Recent Contributions to Algonquian Linguistics." *Northeast Anthropology* 59: 65–71.

Dawson, K.C.A. 1983. *Prehistory of Northern Ontario.* Thunder Bay: Historical Museum Society.

Devens, C. 1992. *Countering Colonization: Native American Women and Great Lakes Missions, 1630–1900.* Berkeley: University of California Press.

Devries, L. 2011. *Conflict in Caledonia: Aboriginal Land Rights and the Rule of Law.* Vancouver: University of British Columbia Press.

Dewdney, S. 1975. *The Sacred Scrolls of the Southern Ojibway.* Toronto: University of Toronto Press.

Dewdney, S., and K.E. Kidd. 1962. *Indian Rock Paintings of the Great Lakes.* Toronto: University of Toronto Press.

Dickason, O.P., and W. Newbigging. 2010. *A Concise History of Canada's First Nations.* 2nd ed. Don Mills, ON: Oxford University Press.

Driben, P., and R.S. Trudeau. 1983. *When Freedom Is Lost: The Dark Side of the Relationship between Government and the Fort Hope Band.* Toronto: University of Toronto Press.

———. 1986. *Aroland Is Our Home.* New York: AMS Press.

Dunk, T.W. 2007. *It's a Working Man's Town: Male Working-Class Culture.* 2nd ed. Montreal: McGill-Queen's University Press.

Dunning, R.W. 1959. *Social and Economic Change among the Northern Ojibwa.* Toronto: University of Toronto Press.

Eid, L. 1979. "The Ojibwa-Iroquois War: The War the Five Nations Did Not Win." *Ethnohistory* 26 (4): 297–324.

Elliott, Louise. 2000. "Ontario Native Suicide Rate One of Highest in World, Expert Says." Canadian Press, 27 November. Retrieved 19 March 2017 from www.hartford-hwp.com/archives/41/353.html.

Ellis, C.D., ed. 1995. *âtalôhkâna nêsta tipâcimôwina: Cree Legends and Narratives.* Winnipeg: University of Manitoba Press.

Feit, H.A. 2005. "Hunting and the Quest for Power: The James Bay Cree and Whitemen in the Twentieth Century." In R.B. Morrison and C.R. Wilson, eds., *Native Peoples: The Canadian Experience*, pp. 181–223. Toronto: McClelland and Stewart.

Fenton, W.N., and E. Tooker. 1978. "Mohawk." In W.C. Sturtevant, ed., *Handbook of North American Indians*, Vol. 15, pp. 466–80. Washington, DC: Smithsonian Institution.

Fiddler, Chief T., and J.S. Stevens. 1985. *Killing the Shamen.* Moonbeam, ON: Penumbra Press.

Fisher, A.D. 1973. "The Cree of Canada: Some Ecological and Evolutionary Considerations." In B. Cox, ed., *Cultural Ecology*, pp. 126–39. Toronto: McClelland and Stewart.

Frideres, J.S., and R. Gadacz. 2008. *Aboriginal Peoples in Canada.* 8th ed. Toronto: Prentice-Hall.

Garrad, C., and C.E. Heidenreich. 1978. "Khionontateronon (Petun)." In W.C. Sturtevant, ed., *Handbook of North American Indians*, Vol. 15, pp. 394–97. Washington, DC: Smithsonian Institution.

Garrick, R. 2010. "Marten Falls, Webequie Set up Blockade in Ring of Fire." *Wawatay News*, 4 February.

Gillman, H. 1873. "Ancient Works at Isle Royale, Michigan." *Appletons Journal of Literature, Science and Art* 10: 123–258.

Ginoogaming First Nation. 2014. "Matawa Chiefs Sign Ring of Fire Framework." 26 March. Retrieved 10 November 2014 from www.ginoogamingfn.ca/.

Globe and Mail. 2012. "Natural Resources to Define First Nations Leader's Next Term." 14 July.

———. 2013a. "Idle No More Protests beyond Control of Chiefs." 1 January.

———. 2013b. "Bob Rae Jumps into Ring of Fire." 24 June.

Goddard, I. 1978. "Eastern Algonquian Languages." In W.C. Sturtevant, ed., *Handbook of North American Indians*, Vol. 15, pp. 70–77. Washington, DC: Smithsonian Institution.

Gordon, J., and the Founders of Idle No More. 2014. "The Idle No More Manifesto." In Kino-nda-niimi Collective, ed., *The Winter We Danced*, pp. 71–72. Winnipeg: ARP Books.

Graham, E. 1975. *Medicine Man to Missionary: Missionaries as Agents of Change among the Indians of Southern Ontario, 1784–1867.* Toronto: Peter Martin Associates.

Grand Council Treaty #3. n.d. *The Paypom Treaty.* Retrieved from www.gct3.ca/about/history/paypom-treaty.

Grant, J.W. 1984. *Moon of Wintertime: Missionaries and the Indians of Canada in Encounter since 1534.* Toronto: University of Toronto Press.

Griffin, J.B. 1961. *Lake Superior Copper and the Indians: Miscellaneous Studies of Great Lakes Prehistory.* Ann Arbor: University of Michigan, Museum of Anthropology, Papers 17.

Griffiths, R., ed. 2004. *Our Story: Aboriginal Voices on Canada's Past.* Toronto: Doubleday.

Hallowell, A.I. 1934. "Some Empirical Aspects of Northern Saulteaux Religion." *American Anthropologist* 36: 389–404.

———. 1936. "The Passing of the Midewiwin in the Lake Winnipeg Region." *American Anthropologist* 38 (1): 32–51.

———. 1942. *The Role of Conjuring in Saulteaux Society.* Philadelphia: University of Pennsylvania Press.

Hamilton, S. 2013. "A World Apart? Ontario's

Canadian Shield." In M.K. Munson and S.M. Jamieson, eds., *Before Ontario: The Archaeology of a Province*, pp. 77–95. Montreal: McGill-Queen's University Press.

Harper, S. 2008. *Text of Prime Minister Harper's Apology*. 11 June. Retrieved from www.ainc-inac.gc.ca.

Hawthorn, H.B., ed. 1966/67. *A Survey of the Contemporary Indians of Canada*. Ottawa: Queen's Printer.

Hedican, E.J. 1986. *The Ogoki River Guides: Emergent Leadership among the Northern Ojibwa*. Waterloo, ON: Wilfrid Laurier University Press.

———. 1990a. "Algonquian Kinship Terminology: Some Problems of Interpretation." *Man in the Northeast* 40 (Fall): 1–15.

———. 1990b. "On the Rail-Line in Northwestern Ontario: Non-Reserve Housing and Community Change." *Canadian Journal of Native Studies* 19 (1): 15–32.

———. 2001. *Up in Nipigon Country: Anthropology as a Personal Experience*. Halifax: Fernwood Books.

———. 2008a. *Applied Anthropology in Canada: Understanding Aboriginal Issues*. 2nd ed. Toronto: University of Toronto Press.

———. 2008b. "The Ipperwash Inquiry and the Tragic Death of Dudley George." *Canadian Journal of Native Studies*. 28 (1): 159–73.

———. 2012a. "Policing Aboriginal Protests and Confrontations: Some Policy Recommendations." *The International Indigenous Policy Journal* 3 (2): 1–17.

———. 2012b. *Social Anthropology: Canadian Perspectives on Culture and Society*. Toronto: Canadian Scholars' Press.

———. 2013. *Ipperwash: The Tragic Failure of Canada's Aboriginal Policy*. Toronto: University of Toronto Press.

Hedican, E.J., and J. McGlade. 1982. "The Old Copper Problem." *Anthropological Journal of Canada* 20 (1): 16–21.

———. 1993. "A Taxometric Analysis of Old Copper Projectile Points." *Man in the Northeast* 45: 21–38.

Heidenreich, C. 1971. *Huronia: A History and Geography of the Huron Indians, 1600–1650*. Toronto: McClelland and Stewart.

Henderson, J., and P. Wakeham, eds. 2013. *Reconciling Canada: Critical Perspectives on the Culture of Redress*. Toronto: University of Toronto Press.

Hertzberg, H.W. 1966. *The Great Tree and the Longhouse: The Culture of the Iroquois*. New York: Macmillan.

Hickerson, H. 1962a. *The Southwestern Chippewa: An Ethnohistorical Study*. Menasha, WI: Memoirs of the American Anthropological Society 92.

———. 1962b. "Notes on the Post-Contact Origin of the Midewiwin." *Ethnohistory* 9: 404–23.

Highway, T. 2004. "Hearts and Flowers." In R. Griffiths, ed., *Our Story: Aboriginal Voices on Canada's Past*, pp. 177–99. Toronto: Doubleday.

Hodgins, B.W., and J. Benedickson. 1989. *The Temagami Experience: Recreation, Resources, and Aboriginal Rights in the Northern Ontario Wilderness*. Toronto: University of Toronto Press.

Hoffman, W.J. 1891. "The Midewiwin, or 'Grand Medicine Society' of the Ojibwa." In *7th Annual Report of the Bureau of American Ethnology for the Years 1885–1886*, pp. 149–300. Washington, DC: Bureau of American Ethnology.

Holmes, W.H. 1901. "Aboriginal Copper Mines of Isle Royale, Lake Superior." *American Anthropologist* 3: 684–96.

Honigmann, J.J. 1953. "Social Organization of the Attawapiskat Cree Indians." *Anthropos* 48 (5–6): 809–16.

———. 1981. "West Main Cree." In W.C. Sturtevant, ed., *Handbook of North American Indians*, Vol. 6, pp. 217–30. Washington, DC: Smithsonian Institution.

Hunt, G.T. 1940. *The Wars of the Iroquois: A Study in Intertribal Trade Relations*. Madison: University of Wisconsin Press.

Hurley, W.M and I.T. Kenyon. 1970. *Algonquin Park Archaeology*. Toronto: Department of Anthropology, University of Toronto, Research Report No. 3.

Indian Act (RSC). 1985. Retrieved 21 December 2014 from www.laws-lois.justice.gc.ca/eng/act/i-5.

Indian Claims Commission. 1975. *Indian Claims in Canada*. Ottawa: Indian Claims Commission.

Innis, H.A. 1970. *The Fur Trade in Canada*. Toronto: University of Toronto Press.

Jenning, J.D. 1989. *Prehistory of North America*, 3rd ed. Mayfield, CA: Mountain View.

Johnston, B. 1999. "How Do We Learn Language? What Do We Learn?" In L.J. Murray and K. Rice, eds., *Talking on the Page: Editing Aboriginal Oral Texts*, pp. 43–51. Toronto: University of Toronto Press.

Johnston, C.M. 1964. *The Valley of the Six Nations*. Toronto: University of Toronto Press.

Jorgensen, J.G. 1972. *The Sun Dance Religion: Power for the Powerless*. Chicago: University of Chicago Press.

Jury, W.W. 1965. "Copper Artifacts from Western Ontario." *The Wisconsin Archaeologist* 46 (4): 223–46.

———. 1973. "Copper Cache at Penetanguishene, Ontario, Canada." *The Wisconsin Archaeologist* 54 (2): 84–106.

Kelsay, I.T. 1984. *Joseph Brant, 1743–1807: A Man of Two Worlds*. Syracuse, NY: Syracuse University Press.

Kennedy, C.C. 1967. *A Preliminary Report on the Morrison's Island Site, Pontiac County, Quebec*. Ottawa: National Museum of Canada, Bulletin 206.

Kenora Daily Miner and News. 2014. "Wabauskang to Attack Ontario's Ability to Delegate Aspects of Aboriginal Consultation to Industry at Supreme Court." 11 March. Retrieved 22 November 2014 from www.kenoradailyminerandnews.com/2014/03/11/wabauskang-to-attack-ontarios-ability-to-delegate-aspects-of-aboriginal-consultation-to-industry-at-supreme-court.

Kuehn, S.R. 1998. "New Evidence for Late Paleoindian-Early Archaic Subsistence Behavior in the Western Great Lakes." *American Antiquity* 63 (3): 457–76.

Labelle, K.M. 2013. *Dispersed but not Destroyed: A History of the Seventeenth-Century Wendat People*. Vancouver: University of British Columbia Press.

Landes, R. 1968. *Ojibwa Religion and the Midewiwin*. Madison: University of Wisconsin Press.

Lawrence, B. 2013. *Fractured Homeland: Federal Recognition and Algonquin Identity in Ontario*. Vancouver: University of British Columbia Press.

Lawrence, B., and E. Dua. 2011. "Decolonizing Antiracism." In M.J. Cannon and L. Sunseri, eds., *Racism, Colonialism, and Indigeneity in Canada*, pp. 19–27. Don Mills, ON: Oxford University Press.

Lee, T.E. 1954. "The First Sheguindah Expedition, Manitoulin Island, Ontario." *American Antiquity* 20: 101–11.

———. 1956. "The Position and Meaning of a Radiocarbon Sample from the Sheguiandah Site, Ontario." *American Antiquity* 22: 79.

———. 1957. "The Antiquity of the Sheguiandah Site." *Canadian Field Naturalist* 71 (3): 117–37.

Levine, M.A. 2007. "Determining the Provenance of Native Copper Artifacts from Northeastern North America: Evidence from Instrumental Neutron Activation Analysis." *Journal of Archaeological Science* 34 (4): 572–87.

Linden, S.B. 2007. *Report of the Ipperwash Inquiry*. Toronto: Publications Ontario. Retrieved from www.ipperwashinquiry.ca.

London Free Press. 2009. "Ipperwash Park to Re-Open in 2010." 28 May.

Long, J. 1791 [1974]. *Voyages and Travels of an Indian Interpreter and Trader*. Reprinted by Coles Publishing, Toronto.

Long, J.S. 1989. "'No Basis for Argument'? The Signing of Treaty Nine in Northern Ontario, 1905–1906." *Native Studies Review* 5 (2): 19–54.

———. 2006. "How the Commissioners Explained Treaty Number 9 to the Ojibway and Cree in 1905." *Ontario History* 98 (1): 1–29.

———. 2010. *Treaty No. 9: Making the Agreement to Share the Land in Far Northern Ontario in 1905*. Montreal: McGill-Queen's University Press.

Lounsbury, F.G. 1978. "Iroquoian Languages." In W.C. Sturtevant, ed., *Handbook of North American Indians*, Vol. 15, pp. 334–43. Washington, DC: Smithsonian Institution.

Lovis, W.A. 2008. "Hunter-Gatherer Archaeology and the Upper Great Lakes Archaic." *SAA Archaeological Record* 8 (5): 27–30.

Macklem, P. 1997. "The Impact of Treaty 9 on Natural Resource Development in Northern Ontario." In M. Asch, ed., *Aboriginal and Treaty Rights in Canada*. Vancouver: University of British Columbia Press.

MacNeish, R.S. 1952. "A Possible Early Site in the Thunder Bay District, Ontario." *National Museum of Canada Bulletin* 126: 23–57.

Martin, S.W.J. 2008. "Languages Past and Present: Archaeological Approaches to the Appearance of Northern Iroquoian Speakers in the Lower Great Lakes Region of North America." *American Antiquity* 73 (3): 441–63.

McCarthy, T.L. 2008. "Iroquoian and Iroquoianists: Anthropologists and the Haudenosaunee at Grand River." *Histories of Anthropology Annual* 4: 135–71.

Molto, J.E. 1983. *Biological Relationships of Southern Ontario Woodland Peoples: The Evidence of Discontinuous Cranial Morphology*. Ottawa: National Museum of Man, Archaeological Survey of Canada, Mercury Series 117.

Morissonneau, C. 1978. "Huron of Lorette." In W.C. Sturtevant, ed., *Handbook of North American Indians*, Vol. 15. pp. 389–93. Washington, DC: Smithsonian Institution.

Morris, Hon. A. 1880 [1979]. *The Treaties of Canada with the Indians of Manitoba and the North-West Territories*. Reprinted by Coles. Toronto: Belfords, Clarke.

Morrisseau, N. 1965. *Legends of My People the Great Ojibway*. Toronto: Ryerson Press.

Morrison, J., and O. Greenberg. 1982. "Group Identities in the Boreal Forest: The Origin of the Northern Ojibwa." *Ethnohistory* 29 (2): 75–102.

Morse, B., ed. 1985. *Aboriginal Peoples and the Law: Indian, Metis, and Inuit Rights in Canada*. Ottawa: Carleton University Press.

Muckle, R.J. 2012. *Indigenous Peoples of North America: A Concise Anthropological Overview*. Toronto: University of Toronto Press.

Munson, M.K., and S.M. Jamieson, eds. 2013. *Before Ontario: The Archaeology of a Province*. Montreal: McGill-Queen's University Press.

Murray, L.J., and K. Rice, eds. 1999. *Talking on the Page: Editing Aboriginal Oral Texts*. Toronto: University of Toronto Press.

Nahrgang, K. 2013. "An Aboriginal Perspective." In M.K. Munson and S.M. Jamieson, eds., *Before Ontario: The Archaeology of a Province*, pp. 203–11. Montreal: McGill-Queen's University Press.

National Post. 2013. "Idle No More Founders Distance Themselves from Chiefs." 1 January.

Neylan, S. 2003. *The Heavens Are Changing*. Montreal: McGill-Queen's University Press.

Niezen, R. 1994. "Healing and Conversion: Medicine Evangelism in James Bay Cree Society." *Ethnohistory* 44 (3): 463–91.

———. 2010. *Public Justice and the Anthropology of Law*. Cambridge: Cambridge University Press.

———. 2013. *Truth and Indignation: Canada's Truth and Reconciliation Commission on Indian Residential Schools*. Toronto: University of Toronto Press.

Northern Life. 2010. "Whitefish Lake First Nation Scores Mike Holmes." 23 December.

Ontario Ministry of Indigenous Relations and Reconciliation. 2014. Land Claims. Retrieved 13 December 2014 from www.ontario.ca/aboriginal/land-claims.

Ontario Ministry of Natural Resources. 2013. "Far North Ontario: Community-based Land Use Planning in the Far North of Ontario." Retrieved from www.mnr.gov.on.ca/en/

Business/Far/North.

Otterbein, K.F. 1964. "Why the Iroquois Won: An Analysis of Iroquois Military Tactics." *Ethnohistory* 11 (1): 56–63.

Palmater, P. 2014a. "Indian Status: Why Lynn Gehl's Court Challenge Matters." *CBC News*, 20 October.

———. 2014b. "Why Are We Idle No More?" In Kino-nda-niimi Collective, ed., *The Winter We Danced*, pp. 37–40. Winnipeg: ARP Books.

Patterson, P. 1972. *The Canadian Indian: A History since 1500*. Toronto: Collier-Macmillan.

Paxton, J.W. 2010. "Joseph Brant and His World: 18th Century Mohawk Warrior and Statesman." *Ontario History* 102 (1): 126.

Pentland, D.H., and H.C. Wolfart. 1982. *Bibliography of Algonquian Linguistics*. Winnipeg: University of Manitoba Press.

Petersen, O.M. 1974. *The Land of Moosoneek*. Moosonee, ON: Bryant Press.

Pleger, T.C. 2000. "Old Copper and Red Ochre Social Complexity." *Midcontinental Journal of Archaeology* 25 (2): 169–90.

Poelzer, G., and K.S. Coates. 2015. *From Treaty Peoples to Treaty Nation*. Vancouver: University of British Columbia Press.

Popham, R.E., and J.N. Emerson. 1954. "Manifestations of the Old Copper Industry in Ontario." *Pennsylvania Archaeologist* 1: 3–19.

Preston, R. 2002. *Cree Narrative: Expressing the Personal Meanings of Events*. 2nd ed. Montreal: McGill-Queen's University Press.

Quimby, G.I. 1960. *Indian Life in the Upper Great Lakes, 11,000 B.C. to A.D. 1800*. Chicago: University of Chicago Press.

Ray, A.J. 1974. *Indians in the Fur Trade: Their Role as Hunters, Trappers and Middlemen in the Lands Southwest of Hudson Bay 1660–1870*. Toronto: University of Toronto Press.

Ray, A., and D.B. Freeman. 1978. *"Give Us Good Measure:" An Economic Analysis of Relations between the Indians and the Hudson's Bay Company before 1763*. Toronto: University of Toronto Press.

Reid, C.S., and G. Rajnovich. 1991. "Laurel: A Re-Evaluation of the Spatial, Social and Temporal Paradigms." *Canadian Journal of Archaeology* 15: 193–234.

Rickard, T.A. 1934. "The Use of Native Copper by the Indigenes of North America." *Journal of the Royal Anthropological Institute of Great Britain and Ireland* 64: 265–88.

Rhodes, R., and E. Todd. 1981. "Subarctic Algonquian languages." In J. Helm, ed., *Subarctic*, Vol. 6, pp. 52–56. Washington, DC: Smithsonian Institution.

Rogers, E.S. 1962. *The Round Lake Ojibwa*. Toronto: Royal Ontario Museum, Occasional Paper 5, Art and Archaeology Division.

———. 1963. "Changing Settlement Patterns of the Cree-Ojibwa of Northern Ontario." *Southwestern Journal of Anthropology* 19: 64–88.

———. 1978. "Southeastern Ojibwa." In W.C. Sturtevant, ed., *Handbook of North American Indians*, Vol. 15, pp. 760–71. Washington, DC: Smithsonian Institution.

Rogers, E.S., and D.B. Smith, eds. 1994. *Aboriginal Ontario: Historical Perspectives on the First Nations*. Toronto: Dundurn Press.

Rogers, E.S., and J.G.E. Smith. 1981. "Environment and Culture in the Shield and Mackenzie Borderlands." In W.C. Sturtevant, ed., *Handbook of North American Indians*, Vol. 6, pp. 130–46. Washington, DC: Smithsonian Institution.

Rogers, E.S., and J.G. Taylor. 1981. "Northern Ojibwa." In W.C. Sturtevant, ed., *Handbook of North American Indians*, Vol. 6, pp. 231–43. Washington, DC: Smithsonian Institution.

Rose, F. 2008. "Inter-Community Variation in Diet during the Adoption of a New Staple Crop in the Eastern Woodlands." *American Antiquity* 73 (3): 413–39.

Royal Commission on Aboriginal Peoples. 1996. *Report of the Royal Commission on Aboriginal Peoples*. Ottawa: Canada Communication Group.

Salisbury, R.F. 1986. *A Homeland for the Cree: Regional Development in James Bay, 1971–1981*. Montreal: McGill-Queen's University Press.

Schmalz, P.S. 1991. *The Ojibwa of Southern*

Ontario. Toronto: University of Toronto Press.

Schwarz, M.T. 2013. *Fighting Colonialism with Hegemonic Culture: Native American Appropriation of Indian Stereotypes*. Albany: State University of New York.

Scuderi, L.A. 2002. "The Holocene Environment." In A.R. Orme, ed., *The Physical Geography of North America*, pp. 86–97. Oxford: Oxford University Press.

Shkilnyk, A. 1985. *A Poison Stronger than Love: The Destruction of an Ojibwa Community*. New Haven, CT: Yale University Press.

Sidky, H. 2004. *Perspectives on Culture*. Upper Saddle River, NJ: Pearson Education.

Smith, D.B. 1987. *Sacred Feathers: The Reverend Peter Jones (Kahkewaquonaby) and the Mississauga Indians*. Toronto: University of Toronto Press.

———. 2013. *Mississauga Portraits: Ojibwe Voices from Nineteenth Century Canada*. Toronto: University of Toronto Press.

Smith, J.G.E. 1981. "Western Woods Cree." In W. C. Sturtevant, ed., *Handbook of North American Indians*, Vol. 6, pp. 256–70. Washington, DC: Smithsonian Institution.

Statistics Canada. 2008. *Aboriginal Peoples of Canada, 2006 Census*. Cat. No. 92-593-XCB. Ottawa: Statistics Canada.

Steckley, J.L. 2007. *Words of the Huron*. Waterloo, ON: Wilfrid Laurier University Press.

Steckley, J.I., and B.D. Cummins. 2008. *Full Circle: Canada's First Nations*. 2nd ed. Toronto: Pearson Prentice Hall.

Steinbring, J. 1976. "A Short Note on Materials from the Cummins Quarry Site (DcJi-I) Near Thunder Bay, Ontario." *Ontario Archaeology* 26: 21–30.

Surtees, R.T. 1969. "The Development of an Indian Reserve Policy in Canada." *Ontario History* 61: 87–98.

———. 1982. *Canadian Indian Policy*. Bloomington: Indiana University Press.

Sutton, M.Q. 2011. *A Prehistory of North America*. Upper Saddle River, NJ: Prentice Hall.

Tanner, A. 2005. *Bringing Home Animals: Religious Ideology and Mode of Production of the Mistassini Cree Hunters*. St. John's: Institute of Social and Economic Research, Memorial University of Newfoundland.

Tooker, E. 1963. "The Iroquois Defeat of the Huron: A Review of Causes." *Pennsylvania Archaeologist* 33 (1–2): 115–23.

———. 1964. *An Ethnography of the Huron Indians, 1615–1649*. Bulletin 190. Washington, DC: Smithsonian Institution, Bureau of American Ethnology.

———. 1978. "The League of the Iroquois: Its History, Politics, and Ritual." In W.C. Sturtevant, ed., *Handbook of North American Indians*, Vol. 15, pp. 418–41. Washington, DC: Smithsonian Institution.

Toronto Star. 2007. "Canada Votes against U.N. Aboriginal Declaration." 13 September.

———. 2008. "Seeking Truth about Lost Children." 29 May.

Trigger, B.G. 1969. *The Huron: Farmers of the North*. New York: Holt, Rinehart and Winston.

———. 1985. *Natives and Newcomers: Canada's "Heroic Age" Reconsidered*. Montreal: McGill-Queen's University Press.

———. 1987. *The Children of Aataentsic: A History of the Huron People to 1660*. Montreal: McGill-Queen's University Press.

United Nations. 2007. *United Nations Declaration on the Rights of Indigenous Peoples*. Retrieved 21 December 2014 from www.un.org/esa/socdev/ unpfii/documents/DRIPS_en.pdf.

Wabauskang First Nation. 2014. "Supreme Court Confirms Ontario Must Respect Treaty Rights." Press release, 11 July. Retrieved 22 November 2014 from www.chiefs-of-ontario. org/node/921.

Wallace, A.F.C. 1956. "Revitalization Movements: Some Theoretical Considerations for Their Comparative Study." *American Anthropologist* 58 (2): 264–81.

———. 1969. *The Death and Rebirth of the Seneca*. New York: Alfred A. Knopf.

———. 1978. "Origins of the Longhouse Religion." In W.C. Sturtevant, ed., *Handbook of North American Indians*, Vol. 15, pp. 442–48.

Washington, DC: Smithsonian Institution.

Wawatay News. 2010. "Weenusk Radar Site to Be Cleaned." 16 September.

Weaver, S.M. 1972. *Medicine and Politics Among the Grand River Iroquois*. Ottawa: National Museums of Canada.

———. 1978. "Six Nations of the Grand River, Ontario." In W.C. Sturtevant, ed., *Handbook of North American Indians*, Vol. 15, pp. 525–36. Washington, DC: Smithsonian Institution.

White, M.E. 1978. "Neutral and Wenro." In W.C. Sturtevant, ed., *Handbook of North American Indians*, Vol. 15, pp. 407–11. Washington, DC: Smithsonian Institution.

Wightman, W.R., and N. Wightman. 1997. *The Land Between: Northern Ontario Resource Development, 1800 to 1990s*. Toronto: University of Toronto Press.

Williams, T., and K. Murray. 2007. "Comment on: Police-Government Relations in the Context of State-Aboriginal Relations." In M.E. Beare and T. Murray, eds., *Police and Government Relations: Who's Calling the Shots?* pp. 176–80. Toronto: University of Toronto Press.

Wittry, W.L., and R. Ritzenthaler. 1957. "The Old Copper Complex: An Archaic Manifestation in Wisconsin." *The Wisconsin Archaeologist* 38: 311–29.

Wright, J.V. 1963. *An Archaeological Survey of Along the North Shore of Lake Superior*. Ottawa: National Museums of Canada.

———. 1965. "A Regional Examination of Ojibwa Culture History." *Anthropologica* 7 (2): 189–227.

———. 1967. "Some Aspects of Early and Mid-Seventeenth Century Exchange Networks in the Western Great Lakes." *Michigan Archaeologist* 13: 181–97.

———. 1972. *Ontario Prehistory: An Eleven-thousand-year Archaeological Outline*. Ottawa: National Museums of Canada.

———. 1981. "Prehistory of the Canadian Shield." In W.C. Surtevant, ed., *Handbook of North American Indians*, Vol. 6, pp. 86–96. Washington, DC: Smithsonian Institution.

———. 1995. *A History of the Native People of Canada, Vol. I (10,000–1,000 BC)*. Ottawa: Canadian Museum of Civilization, Archaeological Survey of Canada, Mercury Series Paper 152.

———. 1999. *A History of the Native People of Canada, Vol. II (1,000 BC–AD 500.)*. Ottawa: Canadian Museum of Civilization, Archaeological Survey of Canada, Mercury Series Paper 152.

Zoltai, S.C. 1965. "Glacial Features of the Quetico-Nipigon Area, Ontario." *Canadian Journal of Earth Sciences* 2: 247–69.